M. 5.8.86

COINS AND INVESTMENT

To my parents, my godson Tony Robson, and all those who have encouraged my interest in numismatics

COINS AND INVESTMENT

A Consumer's Guide

J. Pearson Andrew

LONDON

© J. Pearson Andrew 1986
First published 1986

B. A. Seaby Ltd
8 Cavendish Square
London W1M 0AJ

Distributed by
B. T. Batsford Ltd
P.O. Box 4, Braintree, Essex CM7 7QY

All rights reserved. No part of this
publication may be reproduced, stored
in a retrieval system or transmitted
in any form or by any means, electronic,
mechanical, photocopying, recording or
otherwise, without the prior permission
of the publishers.

ISBN 0 900 652 90X

Typeset by Latimer Trend & Company Ltd, Plymouth
Printed in Great Britain
by Billings, Worcester

Contents

1	**The World of Coins**	1
2	**The Coin Market – The Price of a Coin**	10
3	**Buying Coins**	35
4	**Investing in Coins**	44
5	**The Market: Past, Present and Future**	61
6	**Protecting Coins**	75
7	**Selling Coins**	82
8	**Forgery**	87
	Dictionary of Coins and their History	96

Appendices

1	**Major Coin Auctioneers**	149
2	**Dealers**	151
3	**Priced Catalogues and Handbooks**	157
4	**Coin Magazines**	160
5	**Further Reading and Works of Reference**	161

Acknowledgements

I would like to thank the unknown person who 'slipped' my father an Irish half-crown in his change about thirty years ago. This sparked my interest in numismatics.

My thanks are also due to those who encouraged my interest in past coinages during my formative years, but especially to Mr E. M. Bargh.

Barbara Andrew, who introduced me to the pastime of writing, deserves a special mention.

With regard to this book I thank all those who have supplied illustrations, namely Christie's, Glendining & Co., Sotheby's, B. A. Seaby Ltd. and Spink & Son Ltd.

The help given by those who read parts of the book whilst in its draft and manuscript stages is greatly appreciated. My particular thanks go to Miss M. Benison M.A. (Oxon) and Graham Roberts B.A. However, all omissions and errors, as well as opinions expressed, are my own.

Last, but not least, I thank Jackie Shelford, who has had the unenviable task of deciphering my handwriting and translating it to a neatly typed format.

1
The World of Coins

Coin collecting has been described as one of man's oldest hobbies. It is reputed that prior to the birth of Christ, the Ptolemaic kings of Egypt collected Greek coins. In Suetonius's *Life of Augustus*, written in about AD 75, we learn that the Romans not only held their own antique coins in high esteem, but also prized the coins of foreign nations. One of the earliest known collectors in Europe was Pope Boniface VIII (*c.*1235–1303). Members of the House of Hapsburg, one of the principal sovereign dynasties of Europe from the fifteenth to the twentieth century, were also coin collectors. Their interest initially lay in the Roman coinage, probably because the effigies of the Roman emperors on the coins complemented the family gallery of portraits of the various Holy Roman emperors. From contemporary documents we know that the Hapsburgs were in possession of classical coins as early as the thirteenth century and by the time Maximilian I became Emperor in 1493, the coin collection at the Viennese court was famous.

The Renaissance, that period of intellectual revival which swept Europe between the fourteenth and sixteenth centuries, had a two-pronged effect on the world of numismatics. Recognising that classical coins were a superb source of information about the past, scholars and wealthy fashionable families turned their attention to the accumulation of coins and other objects from former days. Records reveal that even in 1465 the Medici coin cabinet contained one hundred gold, and five hundred and three silver coins. Over the ensuing years some two thousand bronze coins were added, as well as pieces in precious metals. Throughout Europe, scholars, grandees and royalty began forming their own collections. Prince Maximilian I (1597–1651) established the Bavarian royal collection; Joachim II (1535–71) started the Berlin coin cabinet and James VI of Scotland (James I of England) introduced his son Prince Henry to the world of numismatics. This cabinet, which was later added to by Charles I, was seized and dispersed by the Puritans after Charles's execution. The collection formed by subsequent British monarchs was acquired by the British Museum, London, early in the nineteenth century.

However, the Renaissance was not merely a revival in learning. Man's creative powers were also stimulated in his quest for a richer, more fulfilling life. It is therefore not surprising that there was a move away from the symbolic, almost abstract, art forms of the Middle Ages to more realistic styles. This movement resulted in a complete reappraisal of coin designs and even to the introduction of a new art form – the medal. In 1438, the Emperor John VIII Palaeologus, the imposing but weak Western ruler of Constantinople, visited the Italian town of Ferrara to attend a Council for the reconciliation of the Eastern and Western Churches. As court painter to Duke Nicolo of Ferrara, Antonio Pisano, known as Pisanello, was no doubt called upon to immortalise the Emperor. Seen against the growing interest in classical coins and medallions, the imposing retinue of the penultimate 'Roman' Emperor impressed Pisanello to such a degree that he captured the event on a medal. The piece was an instant success and the portrait inspired many later artists. It no doubt also encouraged the coin designers and engravers of the day to aspire towards greater things.

Coin collecting has been described as the pastime of scholars. Certainly, as the educational system expanded in the United Kingdom and in other parts of the world, so did the interest in numismatics. During the eighteenth century, the young British nobleman on the Grand Tour of Europe would form, with the guidance of his tutor, his cabinets of classical coins and related material. Upon his return home, these would grace the library of his country house. During this century, and particularly over the past three decades, coin-collecting has become a rapidly expanding hobby with millions of supporters. No longer may numismatics be dubbed the sole prerogative of the learned. Today, individuals from nearly all educational and socio-economic backgrounds derive pleasure either from simply collecting coins or from their accumulation and study. In recent years, coins have also been viewed as an ideal 'alternative investment', but more of this later.

What is the lure of coins from a past age? Armande Benison captures the fascination of historic coins in the poem *Coin Bliss*:

> My hoard is richer than a miser's dream,
> a catalyst I lovingly caress.
> Tracing each bas-relief my fingers seem
> to rouse long-buried grief or happiness
> of monarchs, beggars, soldiers, merchants, priests,
> Since Croesus rode, proud in his curtained litter,
> since Alexander bargained, since those Feasts
> of sybaritic Rome, on to the glitter
> of the Renaissance, on to the British scene –
> Hastings, the Black Death, the Bosworth Field –
> the Tudor Henrys and the Virgin Queen.
> More than the chronicles they have revealed.
> Numismatists, by coin-psychometry
> revive, at will, mankind's lost pageantry.

It is difficult to define precisely the spell that is woven over those who are attracted to the pursuit of collecting old money. The psychiatrist may well convincingly argue that modern man accumulates gold and silver currency and labels himself a numismatist to satisfy his miserly instincts. Whereas the picture of the miser of old pawing over his chest of gold coins would be even more socially unacceptable in this day and age, the systematic accumulation of valuable historic coins is certainly not at variance with social acceptability.

As Armande Bension correctly states in *Coin Bliss*, coins evoke the past as opposed to just being pieces of history. One can imagine a collector looking at his 'tribute penny' of Tiberius and recalling the biblical passage, 'Render unto Caesar the things that are Caesar's', and wondering whether the coin that graces his cabinet was the one to which Christ was referring. As a country's coinage tells its history, a representative collection of past currency does reveal 'mankind's lost pageantry' as well as the less glittering occasions. For example, the coinage of England reflects its early invading powers through its locally-struck Roman, Anglo-Saxon and Norman coinages. The extravagant nature of Henry VIII is revealed by the debasement of his coinage, which was struck from a lower than normal standard of metal. The disruption caused by the Civil War and the poor pecuniary circumstances of Charles I are well illustrated by the preponderance of provincial mints which struck coins, known as 'siege pieces', from the domestic silver kept at the strongholds held by the Royalists. This emergency coinage was struck so that Charles could pay his army. Similar circumstances are reflected in the coinages of other nations.

It is as a series of pictorial historical documents that coins have the largest impact. Their contribution as a contemporary illustration of time past is immediately apparent. In what form, other than numismatic items, could a member of the public so readily obtain portraits, for example, of Alexander the Great, Julius Caesar, Alfred the Great, Elizabeth I, Louis XV or Napoleon, which were made at the time the person was living? The answer, of course, is nowhere. Additionally coins provide a 'photograph in metal' of many famous sculptures and buildings which have long since vanished. Consequently when a damaged sculpture is found, it can be restored using as a guide a contemporary coin portraying the item in its original glory. The ruined statue of Nike, the Winged Victory of Samothrace, now in the Louvre in Paris, was pieced together with the aid of its portrayal on a coin of Demetrius Poliorcetes of Macedon struck in *c.*303 BC. Coins make a further contribution to our understanding of the past that is not quite so obvious. They can provide scholars with a great deal of evidence about the political, economic and social history of the world. Coins found at archaeological sites can help to date settlements and provide evidence of trade patterns between different communities. However, it is not the purpose of this book to detail the use of coins as an investigative medium into time past.

Above all, coins are an art form. As we conduct our daily financial transactions we give no thought to the coins that comprise our small change. The only time that individuals generally give current coinage more than a cursory glance is when a new design or denomination appears in their own country, or when they are abroad and are confronted with a currency with which they are not familiar. It is then that the design, shape and size of a current coin receives detailed examination.

It is therefore not surprising that the majority of people do not immediately regard contemporary coins as an art form. Since the birth of coinage in Asia Minor two and a half thousand years ago, coins have been produced in large quantities, but, whilst a large number are exquisite pieces of workmanship, many more are of little artistic merit. Link this with a decline in standards – which sadly can deteriorate rapidly in a brief period – and what remains is a most uninspired piece of metal for use as a medium of exchange. Political or economic instability – for example when inflation is raging and there is a need to produce coins at a rate in excess of normal output – has in the past resulted in hastily struck items where the social need far outweighed any leaning towards the artistic. After all, the first and foremost role of a coin is to serve as a social commodity, i.e. to provide a nation with a readily acceptable medium of exchange that lifts from its shoulders the time and trouble of bartering in order to obtain all daily needs.

Looking at many of the world's present mass-produced coinages, one may be forgiven for considering that coins are not an art form. Today coins are generally struck in low relief. In other words, the height of the design does not rise above the rim of the piece. The legend around the design may be viewed by some as a further boundary to artistic freedom. However, enter Time's winged chariot and allow yourself to be transported back to the beginning of coinage. The Greeks had few conventions on which to draw when they produced their coins; apart, that is, from other artistic mediums. We know that in prehistoric Minoan and Mycenean Greece, metal and ivory plaques were engraved with artistic designs. Furthermore, the ancient Greeks used seals for both personal communications and business 'documents'. There can be little doubt that the true origin of engraved dies for coins is to be found in the ancient art of engraving seals. The seals simply contained a device or design and that was all. It is therefore not surprising that the early coins followed this style, i.e. that they were not bound by restrictions as to the depth of design or the need for long inscriptions which framed their design.

Many consider that, as a series, the coinage struck in Sicily between 480 and 360 BC has never been surpassed. Words alone cannot describe the beauty of the great classical coin masterpieces struck from dies engraved by such artists as Eukleidas, Kimon, Euainetos and others elsewhere in the ancient world. These metallic miniatures must be seen to be fully appreciated.

It is also necessary to consider the conditions under which these coins, and indeed later specimens, were created in order to appreciate fully the work that went into their production. It should be borne in mind that the world's mints were not mechanised until the sixteenth and seventeenth centuries, so until that time all coins were struck by hand. The technique was somewhat primitive compared to the ultra modern 'coin factories' of today.

The mint worker's (or moneyer's) basic tools were an anvil, a hammer, a pair of tongs and a pair of shears. However, before he could produce the coin, he required a pair of dies. These would be prepared by the engraver cutting the design, in intaglio, into hard metal. This was a task requiring great patience as well as skill. It was also a time-consuming process. Medieval dies were not individually engraved but were made up by using numerous 'punches', each containing part of the final design. During the eighteenth century 'master dies' were used to produce punches, which until that time were still cut by hand. Since the nineteenth century the cutting of the 'master die' itself has been undertaken mechanically. Nowadays, a reducing machine automatically cuts the master die from a nickel-plated copper electrotype reproduction of the artist's original model, which of course is several times larger than the eventual coin.

However, the basic technique employed in striking coins remained little changed from ancient times until the introduction of mechanised mints in the seventeenth century. On receiving the dies from the engraver, the Greek moneyer would set the lower die in his anvil. Upon this a red-hot blank of metal of the required weight, fineness and shape would be placed. Swiftly he would place the upper die, which was mounted on a metal cylinder, also known as a punch, on this blank and give it several heavy blows with a hammer. This force would transfer the intalgio design of the dies to the metal blank and thus create a coin, with its design in relief.

Before the advent of machinery, blanks were obtained by hammering ingots into sheets of the required thickness which would then be cut to size with shears. Needless to say, this primitive method did not result in perfection. Leonardo Da Vinci wrote: 'No coins can be considered good which do not have the rim perfect; and in order to ensure the rim being perfect it is necessary first that the coins be absolutely round.' Leonardo went on to describe a machine that would produce 'perfect' blanks – he also included sketches. Unfortunately such a machine was not constructed during his lifetime.

During the early sixteenth century the great influx of gold and silver from South America began to leave its mark on the European economy. The bullion first found its way to Spain where it was used to pay for the King of Spain's many commitments, particularly in the Netherlands. Consequently, with the increased money supply, there was a sharp rise in prices in Europe. We all know of the political and social consequences of inflation. One particular problem during the sixteenth century was that the money supply was almost entirely in the form of coins (and to some extent bullion). Paper money was not commonplace, so the mints were therefore hard pressed to transform the bullion into coins. As a result some of the workmanship at the mints deteriorated.

The remedy was to use coining machinery. Such devices were perfected at Augsburg in the latter part of the first half of the century. The machinery was demonstrated at the European courts, but unfortunately the moneyers were so opposed to the introduction of machinery, fearing loss of employment, that it was not generally established until a century later.

In 1551, Henry II of France established the Moulin des Étuves under the direction of Guillaume de Marillac. This was founded at the western end of L'Île du Palais. It was equipped with a rolling mill (powered by the waters of the Seine) for producing the sheets of metal, a cutter for obtaining the blanks and a screw-press for striking coins. The result was that the coins were round and evenly struck. However, the established moneyers, still wielding their hammers, strongly protested at the use of machinery. So loud were their protests that the Moulin des Étuves was taken off regular coinage work after 1562. In about 1560, Eloye Mestrelle, either an unhappy or a dischargede employee at the Paris Mint, arrived in London.

Mestrelle was responsible for the introduction of the mill or press into England. It would appear from contemporary documents that his machinery was similar to that used at the Moulin des Étuves. Although the resultant coins were superb, the moneyers protested about machinery resulting in the loss of employment and the project was abandoned. Mestrelle was dismissed, and, falling on hard times, derived his income from counterfeiting coins of the realm. He was discovered and executed for his misdemeanours.

By 1640, French coins were almost entirely struck by machine. Great Britain, however, did not finally abandon the hand striking of her currency until 1662. Broadly speaking, the coinage of the Western World can be divided into three main categories: Ancient, Hammered and Milled. 'Ancients' include the coins of ancient Greece and Rome. Both these civilisations struck coins over a wide geographic area. 'Hammered' refers to coins of the Middle Ages and of later periods until the introduction of mechanised mints. The use of the word 'Milled' does not refer to the grained edge of the coins, but to the method of manufacture. The early mint machinery was powered by a horse-drawn mill and the resultant coins became known as 'mill money'. At a later stage when a milled edge was placed on the coinage, 'mill' and 'milled' became synonymous. These three broad categories greatly simplify the coinage of the Western World, but completely ignore the coinages of other cultures, e.g. Byzantine, Islamic, Indian and Chinese coins.

Before proceeding, it would be interesting to consider the phrase, 'Every coin tells a story'. Mention an interest in coins to those uninitiated into the world of numismatics and they will consider that such a pastime is very limited, being restricted to the accumulation of old or foreign currency. However, the study of coinage opens many other avenues. While exploring the world of coins one may well find oneself accumulating knowledge in the fields of engineering, geography, metallurgy, lettering, heraldry, art, economics, politics, theology, language, costume, architecture and of course history. It is therefore not surprising that educationalists have been known to regard coins as an advantageous key to further knowledge.

The mere accumulation of coins can of course be an end in itself. However, to look to the 'other side of the coin' and discover that every coins does tell a story is far more satisfying. Before closing this chapter, let us look at just three coins from different parts of the globe:

Australia: 1813, New South Wales Holey Dollar or Five Shillings

The history of this coin is interesting and dates back to the time of the Napoleonic Wars. England, hard pressed to provide herself, let alone her colonies, with sufficient coin, eventually sent 40,000 Spanish dollars or pieces of eight to Australia in 1812. Previous attempts to supplement Australia's coinage with this denomination had been fraught with problems; no sooner had the coins been landed than they were used in foreign trade and thus lost to the colony forever.

In his determination that this shipment should not suffer the same fate, Governor Lachlan Macquarie gave orders for the middle of each dollar to be punched out, leaving a ring and a 'dump', i.e. the centre of the original coin. The two resultant pieces were valued at five shillings and fifteen pence respectively, making a total of six shillings and threepence (6s. 3d.). However, since the value of the silver content was only four shillings and ninepence (4s. 9d.), the process gave rise to a welcome profit for the Australian government and also helped ensure that the 'coins' would stay in the country. Anyone attempting to export them would lose nearly 25 per cent of their value in Australia. Such a pecuniary loss was sufficient to keep the pieces where the government wanted them – in the country.

On 19 November 1981, Spink Auctions (Australia) Pty. Ltd. sold an 1813 New South Wales five shillings or holey dollar for AS$50,000. Struck from a Charles III Madrid mint 8 reales of 1802, it is one of the finest holey dollars known, for both the coin and countermark are in extremely fine condition. In the same sale, a New South Wales fifteen pence or dump sold for AS$17,000. Both prices were auction records at the time.

THE WORLD OF COINS

Great Britain: 1887 Sixpence

As the Golden Jubilee of Queen Victoria approached, it was considered that the celebration would be an ideal opportunity to introduce a new design on the coinage. Between 1838 and 1886 all the gold and silver coins issued for circulation, with the exception of the 'Gothic' crowns and florins, bore the Queen's 'Young Head'.

The leading artists of the day were invited to submit designs for the new currency and whilst J. E. Boehm's portrait of the monarch was accepted for the obverses of all the gold and silver coins, the Mint fell back on the past work of its former engravers for the reverses. Boehm, later Sir Joseph, was Sculptor in Ordinary to Her Majesty and a Royal Academician. As a sculptor he will be remembered for his colossal statues of Queen Victoria at Windsor, John Bunyan at Bedford (also in the U.K.) and the Prince of Wales at Bombay. Although they acclaimed his working in stone, the Victorian public were very displeased with his portrait of their Queen on the Jubilee coinage (**12**).

Why, one may ask, did the portrait cause so much offence? The cause of the criticism is quite simple; Victoria is portrayed wearing a very small crown perched on the top of her head over a widow's veil. The latter, which would have been made from black lace, was worn of course out of respect for her late husband, the Prince Consort. It is the small crown that offends. However, it was an item that the queen did wear. If you go along to the Tower of London, it can still be seen amongst the Crown Jewels. It is said that Victoria bought it because she found her full-size crown too heavy. Now comes an interesting point. Place your finger over the crown and view the queen's effigy – it is that of a normal widowed lady in mourning. Was it Victoria who insisted that she be portrayed wearing this headgear and no one dared tell her that it did not suit her? We shall never know.

What we do know is that the authorities made one mighty mistake in their choice of design for the reverse of the sixpence. Very carelessly they chose an identical design for both the sixpence and half sovereign; Boehm's portrait on the obverse and the shield of Great Britain within a Garter on the reverse. The criminal fraternity could not believe their luck and the authorities their lack of foresight. By gilding the sixpence, the swindlers could pass it for twenty times its value, i.e. as a half-sovereign. The Mint set about remedying their error as swiftly as the criminal element of society began gilding the coins. The shield and Garter was replaced with the words SIX PENCE within a wreath.

Interestingly, the 'withdrawn' type' is not worth as much as its replacement; clearly the Mint did not act as swiftly as it may have hoped. Both types of sixpence, even in good condition, retail at modest prices.

United States of America: Susan B. Anthony Dollar

In October 1978, the Senate and the House of Representatives of the United States of America authorised the amendment of the Coinage Act of 1965 to change the size, weight and design of the one dollar coin. In July 1979, the new coin, known as the Susan B. Anthony dollar, received an unenthusiastic reception from the American people.

The piece nevertheless is interesting. Its unique 11-sided inner border and the fact that it was the first USA coin in circulation to bear the actual portrait of an American woman, as opposed to the effigy of a symbolic female, received much publicity. The obverse of the dollar bears the profile of Susan B. Anthony (1820–1906). Susan Anthony was an early crusader for equal rights for women and a pioneer to win for women the right to vote. In President Carter's words, Susan Anthony was chosen to adorn the coin so as to, '... *symbolize for all American women the achievement of their inalienable right to vote ... the continuing struggle for the equality of all Americans.*' In 1920 her life-long work culminated in the ratification of the 19th Amendment to the Constitution, giving nation-wide suffrage to women. However, at the time of the launch of the coin, Susan Anthony's numismatic connection was not widely publicised. She was a direct descendant of Charles Anthony, the brother of Derick Anthony, who was appointed Chief Engraver of London's Mint on 29 September 1551. Derick Anthony continued in office until 12 July 1599 when he was succeeded by his son. As Chief Engraver, Anthony engraved the dies for Mestrelle's experimental 'mill money'. His series of portraits of Queen Elizabeth I on the machine-produced coins are superb.

However, to return to what the Press has dubbed the 'SBA dollar'. The reverse bears the symbolic eagle of the Apollo 11 spacecraft landing on the moon. The Apollo 11 was christened 'The Eagle' and landed at Tranquility Base on 20 July 1969. In tribute to this event the design originally appeared on the Eisenhower dollar coins of 1971–8.

Despite a heavy publicity campaign to persuade the American public to accept the new coin, the SBA dollar proved most unpopular. By the end of 1981, the U.S. Treasury Department officially recognised that the American people just did not like the piece.

2
The Coin Market – The Price of a Coin

There is far more to the world of coins than their place in history. It is important for any individual, whether he is a collector or an investor, to understand as much as possible of the workings of the coin market. A better understanding of the market will help ensure that the correct price is paid for a coin. It is a complex subject and one which has received little detailed attention in past works. However, just as those who are employed in financial markets have an intuitive feel of the mechanics that determine price, so the coin dealer and experienced collector intuitively know their market. As with any subject, the only real lesson is experience. However, it is hoped that this chapter will unravel the tangled web of factors which determine the price of a coin.

Factors which determine the price of coins

The commercial value of any coin depends on four factors:

1. Its exact design, mint mark or date.
2. Its *exact* state of preservation.
3. The demand for it in the market at any given time.
4. The availability of similar coins in the market at the same period of time.

At a small provincial U.K. auction in 1979, an 1827 copper penny sold for a staggering £1,200. Not only had the piece never been placed in circulation, but it was nearly as shiny as on the day it was struck – technically it was described as having *original full mint lustre*. In other words, the coin had been carefully preserved for more than 150 years. By contrast, an identical example of the same rare coin, which had been subject to only slight circulation, was only worth about £80 at the time. This well illustrates that the condition of a coin is of paramount importance in determining its value. However, although a coin's state of preservation should be ultimate in any prospective purchaser's mind, it is not the first determinant of value. To put the matter in its most simplified form, if there is no demand for a particular item, whether it is a coin or a domestic appliance, then it is unsaleable. Therefore, before we look at a coin's state of preservation, we must first turn our attention towards the economic factors.

Demand

The demand in the market is influenced by many factors. Disposable income, or available capital, are two dominant determinants of demand. Therefore, in times of economic depression, available funds may be limited for any form of expenditure, let alone for buying coins. On the other hand, even when funds are available to purchase coins, people may feel that with the economic uncertainty, it would be prudent to retain their assets in a liquid form in case of need. They may be worried about losing their jobs, a downturn in the profits from their businesses or a fall in investment income. At times of high interest rates, the prospect of good yields from money deposited in a bank account or similar, may be too tempting an opportunity to miss, and so coins will seem a less favourable alternative.

There are other factors too that may reduce or completely eliminate an individual's demand for coins. In 1980 the Reagan Administration repealed legislation whereby investment in collectables by various retirement plans resulted in attractive tax advantages for the investor. This move resulted in many Americans who were investing their pension contributions in rare coins and other 'alternatives', to return to conventional securities. Consequently the coin trade lost many 'fringe" clients who were buying purely with an eye to capital appreciation, with tax advantages as an added bonus.

It is not unusual for a period of quiet to follow a flurry of activity in the coin market. Many of those who entered the world of coins may have done so purely to follow fashion. One cannot expect a market to rise constantly, so after a steep upward movement in price, the established dealers and collectors as well as the nouveau investment-orientated entrants step off the roundabout in order to stand back and assess the situation. Demand will fall as a result, but all prospective buyers look to auction realisations to ensure that no bargains are missed. Therefore, the short or medium-term effect is a levelling-off or fall in demand, which results in either a price plateau or a fall in prices.

However, the long-term trend of the demand for quality coins has always been upwards. The demand has increased firstly as a result of existing numismatists buying more material and, more importantly, from newcomers entering the field. The first instance is easier to analyse than the second, but both causes for a general increase in demand do have some common ground. As real disposable incomes rise, which is generally during a period of economic buoyancy, the public at large have more funds to devote to areas other than basic living expenses. The standard collector's 'buying cycle', linked to the fact that the number of numismatists has grown over time, leads to a 'perpetual' increase in demand in the long term.

In his youth, the typical collector will buy modestly within a very limited budget. When he is established on his career path, more funds are available. However, when he settles down to married life and the expenditure of establishing a home and raising a family, his collecting activities will be curtailed until such time as there are less pressing financial demands on his available income. Thus, the aggregate demand of individual collectors increases over time. A sustained increase in aggregate demand is only experienced when new collectors become attracted to the world of coins.

The lure of coins for the new collector was discussed in chapter 1. It was also mentioned that in recent years coins have been viewed as an ideal 'alternative investment'. With the popularisation of antique collecting in the 1960s, it was soon realised that objects, whilst not yielding interest, did increase in value over time and thus yield a capital gain upon disposal. Undoubtedly, one of the steepest general rises in British coin prices took place during 1973 and 1974, when the value of stock market securities was collapsing. At the time rare coins and the like were a far more attractive proposition to the public as a depository for their money than conventional securities. Consequently, there was an influx of non-numismatists into the market and the total demand for material increased. A high percentage of those who were lured towards coins by pure financial motivation, and who were expertly guided, became fascinated by the subject and stayed in the market. Others, riding on a euphoric wave, not realising the major differences in the mechanisms of the Stock Exchange and the art market, were disillusioned, cut their losses when prices dipped, and never returned. Their action caused prices to decline further.

There can also be an increase in demand resulting from a general influx of interest in a particular culture. For example, up until the final quarter of the 1970s, there was little attention paid to the fascinating coinages of the Middle East. This lack of appeal was said to have its roots in the fact that the coins, since they seldom carried the head of a ruler, lacked interest to Western collectors. The situation, it was held, was aggravated by the fact that the Arabic inscriptions were only understood with difficulty in the West. Furthermore, the Arabs themselves were not attracted to their past coinage and consequently the market for Islamic coins was confined to a small band of dedicated scholars and collectors. The consequent small demand from individuals without vast resources resulted in low prices, even for extremely rare items. Prices can be made to escalate by just two individuals with unlimited funds who are equally determined to acquire the same items.

However, the arguments that the historic coinage from this part of the world would never gain a strong following, completely ignored the possibility that there would be an indigenous demand. After all, a region's past coinage is an integral part of its culture. In 1976, Sotheby's commenced specialised sales of Islamic art, its Department of Coins & Medals holding its first sale entirely devoted to Islamic numismatics in 1978. The latter sales attracted increasing attention and when a small library of Islamic and Oriental numismatic books was included in an auction of Islamic coins in April 1980, the prices were described as 'shattering'. Dealers, anxious to ensure that their reference libraries contained all the necessary volumes relating to the subject of Islamic coins, vied with each other to acquire the tomes. As a result, the prices realised were generally three times that of expectation. This was a very clear indication that this fascinating field was being taken seriously.

In March of the following year two dealers, Galerie des Monnaies of Geneva and Spink of London, commenced battle at lot one of a Sotheby's Islamic Coin sale and, with brief pauses to allow others to join in, did not call it a day until the last coin had been placed on the auction block. An Ibrahim or Marwan II dinar of AD 744 (AH 127), a major date rarity in the series of Omayyad Post-Reform dinars, sold for £13,000 against an estimate of £2,500–£3,000. More revealing was the fact that the same coin would have sold for around £250 in 1975. It was clear, with prices for rarities repeatedly realising figures so out of line with general expectations, that neither dealer was merely buying for stock. Whilst both remained silent as to the identity of their client or clients, it was reasonable to assume that the final purchasers were Arabs. In October 1982, a Post Reform Umayyad gold dinar of AH 77 – the most important date in the history of the Islamic coinage – sold for 400,000 Swiss francs at a sale of Islamic coins in Basle, Switzerland. The specimen is of the greatest rarity.

The demand for a particular series can fall in relation to the total demand for coins generally. This is particularly so with Ancient coins, where the emphasis away from teaching classics in schools is said to be the reason for proportionately fewer of the total number of collectors showing an interest in Greek coins. Furthermore, demand for a particular series or type of coin, can increase rapidly and fall again even faster. For example, just prior to decimalisation in the U.K., 1959 halfcrowns, a denomination that was demonetised in 1970, were eagerly sought by the public. Indeed, in 1970 specimens in mint state were changing hands at £25 each. This price was quite unrealistic for a very common modern coin. When rationality returned to the scene, examples could be had for £1 each.

However, demand is but one of the economic determinants of price.

THE COIN MARKET — THE PRICE OF A COIN

Supply

It is the interaction of demand with the supply of a commodity that determines its price in a free market. In economic terms, price tends towards that level which equates supply and demand. The number of historic or modern coins in the world at any particular moment in time is fixed. The amount of genuine ancient Greek drachmas, eighteenth-century German thalers, nineteenth-century American silver dollars, Victorian Australian sovereigns or English Tudor silver coins, for example, cannot be increased. However, the supply of coins into the market can vary over time. Should supply exceed demand, then prices will fall. Such occurrences are not impossible even where choice material is concerned.

Although the total number of coins cannot increase, it will be appreciated that the whereabouts of all coins is not known; vast quantities may lie in the ground, forgotten for centuries. In addition to this, many specimens are in private or national collections and their owners or custodians may not wish, or indeed cannot because of trusts, to dispose of one single coin, least of all their entire collection. Sometimes the owner of a few coins does not appreciate the fact that they are valuable, or that the sentimental value of their 'heirlooms' far outweighs any commercial interest. There is also a strange psychology regarding members of the public and the few stray coins in their possession. When told they are worth little, they say it is not worth their selling. In cases where the coins are valuable, they decide it is worth their retaining the pieces. Thankfully, there are exceptions to this general rule.

The most dramatic way in which the supply of coins can be increased is by hoard material entering the market. The advent of the pastime of 'treasure hunting', encouraged by the sale of metal detectors, has resulted in the discovery of vast quantities of coins. Generally, the finds consist of common pieces in poor condition and consequently they are of no great commercial value. Nevertheless, the discovery of any hoard of coins is of great importance to numismatic scholars. In many cases they are the sole guide as to the coinage in circulation at a given period in the past and thus not only assist the historian in determining trade patterns, but are the main aid to the numismatist for dating and classifying coins. As a result, laws in many parts of the world require all hoard material to be handed to the relevant authorities and only those coins not required for study purposes or for retention in national collections are returned to the finder. Consequently, not all coins discovered buried in the ground, find their way into the market.

For example, when a splendid hoard of medieval gold coins and jewellery was found at Fishpool, Nottinghamshire in 1966, only 85 of the 1,237 pieces were not retained by the British Museum. The 85 returned pieces were subsequently consigned for sale at auction. The resultant hammer prices were not out of line with expectation. However, it will be appreciated that when vast quantities of previously rare coins are found, market prices do dip if the majority become available for purchase. Perhaps the most dramatic example of such an occurrence was the discovery of 8,640 Norman coins at Beauworth, Hampshire, in 1833. All the silver pennies of William I (1066–87) are scarce to rare except for one particular type. Thanks to the Beauworth Hoard containing 6,439 specimens of this denomination struck between 1083 and 1086, the last type in the series is comparatively common. Consequently, specimens generally sell today at about half of the normal price of a scarce example of a William I Penny.

However, not all the coins that find their way into dealers' trays or are placed on the auction block come from hoards. In addition to buying, a collector also parts with coins. As his interests become more specialised, he may dispose of his general collection acquired during his early collecting days. Alternatively, he may decide to sell one or two coins in order to obtain a great rarity. As he becomes more discerning, he may also part with some pieces that do not conform to his new minimum standards of condition. Financial circumstances may, of course, force him to part with his entire collection. So, in addition to demanding coins, the collector also supplies the market.

Few private collections have remained intact to be handed down from one generation to the next. Almost inevitably, either the person who has spent a lifetime forming his cabinet of coins, or his heirs, decides to sell. Thus, the items that have been siphoned from the market over many years return 'en bloc'. The market's reaction to the return of the material is a little like the father welcoming the re-appearance of the prodigal son. The more discerning the collector, the more ecstatic is the numismatic fraternity. The sale acts as a catalyst in the market; in other words, albeit that the supply of available coins has immediately increased, demand rises proportionately more. This situation has become more noticeable in recent years, thus emphasising that quality coins are becoming more difficult to secure. The market has never experienced a state of saturation on the disposal of a quality collection.

Although certain collections appear to be resistant to dispersal, they too can find their way on to the auction block. When Joseph Durkee bequeathed a fine collection of Roman gold coins to The Metropolitan Museum of Art, New York in 1898 and when seven years later J. Pierpont Morgan presented the same institution with the John Ward Collection of Greek coins – which was probably the most famous collection of its kind – neither gentleman would ever have thought that the Museum would sell them at a later date. However, that is precisely what did happen. In 1972 the Durkee bequest was auctioned with other Roman gold coins and the following year the John Ward Collection was placed under the hammer. Public opinion against the sale of these coins was so strong that a third planned dispersal of the Museum's numismatic items was cancelled and the coins were presented to the American Numismatic Association.

Very occasionally a really old collection does appear at auction. The earliest to have been sold in London in recent years was formed by Archbishop Sharp (1645–1714). Dr John Sharp was appointed Archbishop of York in 1691. From a note in his Will we know that he began collecting coins in 1687. Whilst some of the pieces were placed in the cabinet by his descendants, the vast majority of the coins were collected by Sharp himself. Incredibly, the collection remained in the family for over two hundred and fifty years. The coins were sold in two parts; in 1966 Sotheby's auctioned the foreign items and in 1977 Glendining & Co. offered the British and colonial' specimens.

Another remarkable dispersal was of the cabinet of coins and medals of the *Late Collector* sold by Sotheby's in 1974. The legatees who subsequently owned the cabinet, which incidentally had been locked in a garden shed for many years, wished to remain anonymous. Nevertheless, it may be revealed that the executors were more than surprised when the coins and medals realised more than a quarter of a million pounds sterling. The cabinet was mainly formed in the eighteenth century, a few specimens being added in the nineteenth century. It was typical of the kind to be found in many great English country houses.

Great coin rarities have found their way to the auction houses in the most unusual of ways. One lady calling at Sotheby's counter in 1976 was anxious to consign some fairly miscellaneous coins that had been handed down through her family since the middle of the last century. Her need for cash outweighed the sentimental value of the coins. As she was signing the consignment note, the expert who had examined her assorted coins noticed the charm-bracelet she was wearing. Among the objects worn to bring her good luck was a mounted coin, and as it transpired, it was extremely lucky for her, for it was an 1852 Australian Port Phillip Quarter Ounce. This unofficial piece realised £11,000 when it was sold in February 1977, the price being a record at that time for a British Colonial issue. Another interesting case was that of a chest of drawers. It had been consigned to Christie's for sale and whilst making his examination the furniture expert found a coin wedged in one of the drawers. It was a pattern dollar of Queen Liliuocalani of Hawaii, dated 1891. Fifty pieces only had been struck and needless to say the coin realised more than the chest of drawers!

Clearly the discovery of isolated single coins has little effect on the aggregate supply of material to the market. If for any reason individuals decide to hold on to their collections, material becomes scarce and consequently even if demand remains static, prices will rise. In recent years, whilst there has not been a noticeable fall in the supply of numismatic items, demand for quality material has generally outstripped its availability. The situation therefore has resulted in a rising price trend. Although logically this should attract more material on to the market, dealers world-wide all remark that it is becoming increasingly difficult to obtain choice coins.

In the previous section (on Demand), we stated that a flurry of activity in the coin market is often followed by a period of quiet. The short or medium-term effect is a levelling-off or fall in demand which results in either a price plateau or a fall in prices. As price is determined by the interaction of demand and supply, it will be appreciated that the course prices take following a decrease in demand, depends equally on the supply of coins into the market. If both demand and supply fall, prices can remain static. However, if the supply of material increases when demand has decreased, prices will fall. The presence of investors disposing of their coins at a time when demand is easing can result in quite sharp price declines in the short term. The effect of investors in the market is analysed in chapter 4, 'Investing in Coins'. Advice on investment strategy is also given.

Condition

It will be appreciated that some coins are in greater demand than others and certain specimens are in short supply – in other words, they are rare. The layman is not always alone in immediately jumping to the conclusion that it is the date, some variant in the design or generally the fact that few specimens of a particular type were struck, that makes one coin more valuable than another. Admittedly these factors are very important, but it must never be forgotten that a coin's *exact state of preservation* is of prime importance in determining its value.

Coins are, and were, primarily made for use. Admittedly coins, like stamps, can be produced especially for the collector market and consequently the specimens are lovingly preserved by their owners. A pattern, or unofficial design for a coin, is struck as a suggested type for a new coinage and will similarly be carefully kept by its owners. Therefore, such pieces are almost inevitably found in superb condition. However, the coins struck for general circulation have never been handled with respect. Small change is kept in pockets and purses where the individual coins are subjected to all kinds of 'torture'. They are banged against each other and thus suffer scratches, cuts and bruises. If this were not enough, they are thrown across counters, dropped into collecting boxes, fed into slot machines, used as levers to remove lids from tins and hurled into wells and fountains to bring their owners good luck. The damage they can suffer over time is thus enormous. They are nearly always worked to death in lubricating the economic machinery of their country. Admittedly some manage to escape by hiding in crevices or are lucky enough to be hidden by their owners. The majority are not so fortunate and when their design is hardly distinguishable after heavy usage over many years, the issuing authority scoops them from circulation, throws them into a melting pot and uses the metal to strike the next generation of currency. With the advent of fully mechanised coining techniques, not even mints treat coins intended for circulation with respect. As soon as they are born, i.e. struck, they are sent scuttling down chutes, along conveyor belts and plunged into trucks before being scooped into bags and transported to banks where they enjoy a short rest before being subjected to torture at the hands of the public.

Nevertheless, despite this ill-treatment, many old coins have survived. Admittedly the majority look the worse for wear, but, incredibly, a fair proportion have survived, even from the earliest of times, that show little sign of having been in circulation. Needless to say, such pieces are not generally available in abundance! Not only are coins in this condition not so readily obtainable, compared to coins in an average state of preservation, but their supply into the market has decreased over time. This can be basically explained by the fact that whilst their total number has not decreased, the aggregate demand for such items has increased. Man always strives for perfection, and the world of coins is no exception to this basic goal. As described earlier, a collector may sell coins that do not conform to his minimum standards of condition in order to acquire the necessary finance to obtain a great rarity that is seldom offered. Although this may mean that he wishes to obtain an average example of a specimen of which only a handful was struck, it could also mean that he wants to acquire a coin that is neither rare nor common, but which is in an exceptional state of preservation. It will be appreciated that a common coin in near mint condition can be as rare, if not rarer, than a worn specimen of another coin that was only struck in small numbers. In other words, fate has preserved the chosen few. Man, in striving to acquire perfection will use his financial muscle to achieve his goal and consequently, such pieces sell at a considerable premium over a coin in average condition.

Whether one buys a coin for investment or pleasure, it is essential that the correct price is paid. The importance of a coin's condition cannot be over-stressed as it is crucial in determining its value. Even the minutest wear, which is barely noticeable to the eyes of the layman, can radically affect the price one should pay for a specimen. A coin could be worth £1,000 in absolute mint state but not even £1 if badly worn. The importance of condition in determining a coin's worth was neatly illustrated at a recent London auction. Because time will make the prices out-dated, the sale and the identity of the coin will not be revealed, but the general message is clear.

A perfect specimen of a silver coin struck during the nineteenth century was placed on the auction block. The item realised £1,400. The auction house's coin expert commented after the sale: 'The price shows how significant quality can be, as this specimen was in absolute mint state and if it had even the slightest mark, I feel sure it would only have realised half the price.'

Interestingly, an identical coin in the same sale, but exhibiting slight surface marks on close inspection, thus indicating that it had seen little circulation, sold for £540. Another identical piece was also offered. However, the raised surfaces did reveal slight traces of wear, which is compatible with the coin having experienced slight circulation. The piece sold for £280, or one-fifth of the price for the perfect specimen. It is important to recognise that there is no fixed relationship between the value of coins in different conditions. The differentials not only vary between different coins, but also alter over time. The respective reasons for these states of affairs are firstly that some coins in good condition are scarcer than others, and secondly that in the quest for the ultimate in condition, the gap between perfect and 'near perfect' may become too great in the market's eyes, and coins in the latter condition therefore appear to be superb buys and the perfect specimens relatively expensive. When the market forms this opinion, the resultant change in buying patterns will vary the relationship between the price of two identical coins, in addition to the fact that they are in different states of preservation.

Coins are graded in two ways; namely a descriptive and a numerical classification. As the grading of a coin is a subjective matter, readers will not be surprised to hear that opinions can differ as to the grading of a particular piece. Rather like beauty, the state of a coin's preservation is in the eyes of the beholder. Like all skills, the grading of coins can only be acquired over time by handling actual specimens. The descriptive terms used in dealers' lists, sale catalogues and works of reference are:

Proof

Proof coins are struck from specially prepared dies. They may have been made to fulfil the role played by printers' proofs, i.e. as samples, or for presentation to important persons, or for sale to collectors. Generally, the relief is sharper than for normal currency coins. The appearance of such coins can be enhanced by the design being 'frosted' and by the field of the coin having a brilliant mirror-like surface. The frosting effect on the raised surface of the specimen is obtained by treating the corresponding incuse parts of the die with a weak acid solution. Occasionally, proof coins are struck with the surface of the coin having a matt finish, e.g. the U.K. proof coins of 1902.

NB 'Proof' is not a grade of condition.

Prooflike

Early strikings of normal currency coins tend to have the sharpness and brilliance of a Proof coin. The appearance of these pieces is due to newly-engraved dies. Probably 'early striking' would be a better description of such coins.

NB 'Prooflike' is not a grade of condition.

THE COIN MARKET — THE PRICE OF A COIN

Fleur de Coin (FDC)
This grading classification is the ultimate in condition. It only applies to a coin which is in perfect mint state, i.e. the piece is in *absolutely* perfect condition. Even the faintest and smallest of scratches (referred to collectively as 'hairlines') would bar a coin from being awarded the unqualified FDC tag.
NB The term is not used in the United States of America.

Brilliant Uncirculated (BU)
In relation to the period to which coins have been collected, this is a relatively new term. Strictly it should only be applied to 'modern coins', i.e. those struck from the beginning of the nineteenth century. Automated mint production results in every currency coin leaving the mint bearing imperfections, i.e. hairline scratches and edge knocks, caused by contact with other coins. These marks will only be revealed upon close inspection and not by a cursory glance with the naked eye. To qualify for the addition of the word 'Brilliant', an uncirculated coin has to have retained its *full* lustrous colour, i.e. be as 'bright' as on the day it was struck (in technical terms to have full mint lustre). Such items sell at a premium over their 'dull' counterparts. One also sees the degree of lustre qualified, i.e., 'with 70 per cent lustre'. The term BU is particularly useful where bronze, copper or nickel-brass coins are concerned. Attempts to revitalise a toned or tarnished specimen by chemical means can be detected with ease by the experienced. Such coins lack true lustre and are pale and pasty, with a pinkish tinge in the case of bronze coins.

Uncirculated (UNC)
This term is used to describe coins which have never been in circulation, but which have lost their original mint lustre owing to exposure to the atmosphere.

Extremely Fine (EF)
A coin so described should be virtually perfect; in other words it should show little sign of having been in circulation. Upon close inspection (a × 10 magnifying glass will be useful) very slight wear on the high points of the design will be revealed. Additionally, there will be a greater number of hairline scratches than those on an Uncirculated coin.

Very Fine (VF)
Coins graded thus will show definite signs of circulation. Whilst having lost the sharpness of Extremely Fine specimens, the general detail will be very clear. Slight wear will be seen on the raised surfaces of the design.

Fine (F)
Noticeable signs of wear will be seen on the raised parts of the design, indicating that the coin has seen considerable circulation or that the design is weak owing to faulty striking. Although the main features of pieces so graded will be quite bold and clear, the details of the design will have a faded quality.

THE COIN MARKET — THE PRICE OF A COIN

Fair
A coin so described will be worn, but the legend and main features of the design will still be distinguishable. This grading will also be applied to coins that were very weakly struck. The North American equivalent of this grading is Very Good. It is becoming an increasingly popular term in other parts of the world.

Poor
This indicates a very worn piece, of no value as a collector's coin, unless extremely rare. The North American term for this state of preservation is Fair.

Grading may be qualified by the use of such terms as Good Extremely Fine (GEF or EF+); Nearly Very Fine (NVF) and the like, thus indicating that a piece is better than, or nearly in, a certain state of preservation. Further, one may encounter EF/VF, signifying that the obverse is Extremely Fine and the reverse Very Fine. A coin described as VF-EF means that the coin is between Very Fine and Extremely Fine condition owing to uneven wear or faulty striking. Phrases such as 'bold Fine, or 'pleasing EF' are self-explanatory. The dealer or auctioneer in such instances is attempting to express the general appearance and desirability of the coin.

In recent years, dealers and collectors have become far more sophisticated in grading. If a modern auction catalogue or dealer's list is compared to its late nineteenth-century counterpart, it is obvious that the former has a far more professional approach to the state of a coin's preservation.

The United States of America is the largest market for coins in the world. Indeed, it is estimated that sixty-five per cent of the total international turnover in numismatic coins is conducted in the United States. The interest is predominantly in 'modern' coinage, i.e. nineteenth century and later, for unlike European countries, its numismatic history does not span the centuries to the times before Christ. In 1949, Dr William H. Sheldon devised a numerical system of grading which was published in *Early American Cents* and revised in *Penny Whimsy* in 1958 and 1976. In 1977 the American Numismatic Association (A.N.A.) issued *Official A.N.A. Grading Standards for United States Coins* (OAGS) arranged and edited by Ken Bresset and Abe Kosoff. OAGS, which is based on the system originally devised by Dr Sheldon, combines the descriptive method of coin grading with a numerical value scale.

European and Australian dealers have so far not adopted the numerical grading system of OAGS, but this does not mean that in time they will not do so. The following is an extract from the Official A.N.A. Grading System. It is reprinted by courtesy of the American Numismatic Association, P.O. Box 2366, Colorado Springs, CO 80901, U.S.A.:

'Proof–70 (Perfect Proof): A Proof–70 or Perfect Proof is a coin with no hairlines, handling marks, or other defects; in other words, a flawless coin. Such a coin may be brilliant or may have natural toning.

Proof–65 (Choice Proof): Proof–65 or Choice Proof refers to a proof which may show some very fine hairlines, usually from friction-type cleaning, friction-type drying or rubbing after dipping. To the naked eye, a Proof–65 or a Choice Proof will appear to be virtually perfect. However, ×5 magnification will reveal some minute lines. Such hairlines are best seen under strong incandescent light.

Proof–60 (Proof): Proof–60 refers to a proof with some scattered handling marks and hairlines which will be visible to the unaided eye.

Impaired Proofs: Other comments: If a proof has been excessively cleaned, has many marks, scratches, dents or other defects, it is described as an impaired proof. If the coin has seen extensive wear then it will be graded one of the lesser grades – Proof–55, Proof–45, or whatever.

MS–70 (Perfect Uncirculated): Mint State 70 or Perfect Uncirculated is the finest quality available. Such a coin under ×4 magnification will show no bag marks, lines or other evidence of handling or contact with other coins.

MS–65 (Choice Uncirculated): This refers to an above average Uncirculated coin which may be brilliant or toned (and described accordingly) and which has fewer bag marks than usual; scattered occasional bag marks on the surface or perhaps one or two very light rim marks.

MS–60 (Uncirculated): MS–60 or Uncirculated (typical Uncirculated without any other adjectives) refers to a coin which has a moderate number of bag marks on its surface. Also present may be a few minor edge nicks and marks, although not of a serious nature. Unusually deep bag marks, nicks and the like must be described separately. A coin may be either brilliant or toned.

Choice About Uncirculated–55: Abbreviation: AU–55. Only a small trace of wear is visible on the highest points of the coin. As is the case with other grades here, specific information is listed in the following text under the various types, for wear often occurs in different spots on different designs. (*The main text of OAGS describes each US coin type.*)

About Uncirculated–50: Abbreviation: AU–50. With traces of wear on nearly all of the highest areas. At least half of the original mint lustre is present.

Choice Extremely Fine–45: Abbreviation: EF–45. With light overall wear on the coin's highest points. All design details are very sharp. Mint lustre is usually seen only in protected areas of the coin's surface such as between the star points and in the letter spaces.

Extremely Fine–40: Abbreviation: EF–40. With only slight wear but more extensive than the preceding, still with excellent overall sharpness. Traces of mint lustre may still show.

Choice Very Fine–30: Abbreviation: VF–30. With light even wear on the surface; design details on the highest points lightly worn, but with all lettering and major features sharp.

Very Fine–20: Abbreviation: VF–20. As preceding but with moderate wear on highest parts.

Fine–12: Abbreviation: F–12. Moderate to considerable even wear. Entire design is bold. All lettering, including the word LIBERTY (on coins with this feature on the shield or headband), visible, but with some weaknesses.

Very Good–8: Abbreviation: VG–8. Well worn. Most fine details such as hair strands, leaf details, and so on are worn nearly smooth. The word LIBERTY, if on a shield or headband, is only partially visible.

Good–4: Abbreviation: G–4. Heavily worn. Major designs visible, but with faintness in areas. Head of Liberty, wreath, and other major features visible in outline form without centre detail.

About Good–3: Abbreviation: AG–3. Very heavily worn with portions of the lettering, date, and legends being worn smooth. The date barely readable.'

It is essential that coins are accurately graded, for if not they will be incorrectly valued. Table 2.1 (overleaf) illustrates the retail price of three different coins in three different states of preservation. A common fault amongst collectors is to overgrade, and consequently to overvalue, their coins. The same applies to some coin dealers. A combination of a lack of experience in grading coins and purchasing from a dealer who is 'optimistic' in this direction, can spell disaster for the newcomer. It is therefore essential for the novice to purchase from established and experienced dealers of good repute. Possibly tempted by a discount below the prevailing 'catalogue price', the new collector may find that he has brought a Good Very Fine specimen for ten per cent or so below 'the price' for an Extremely Fine example, i.e. he has paid £250 for something worth £150.

In a perfect world, one would only collect coins in absolute mint state. Readers do not need reminding that the world is not Utopia and the acquisition of historic coins in the same condition that they left the mint a few centuries earlier is very much the exception rather than the norm. Although it is not impossible to set and adhere to such a collecting criterion, anyone who attempts this would find his collecting very frustrating. Besides, unless funds were unlimited, the resultant 'collection' would be very small, if indeed it could be viewed as a collection.

THE COIN MARKET — THE PRICE OF A COIN

Table 2.1 Examples of the retail prices of a coin in different states of preservation

Coin	Condition	F £	VF £	EF £	UNC £
A		15	55	200	450
B		15	50	300	1250
C		8	26	75	140
D		1	7	35	55

Note: The data well illustrates that there is no strict relationship between the value of coins in different conditions.

Many collectors strive to obtain the best specimens they can afford within their price range; indeed, the pure numismatist will, in order to fill a gap, be quite willing to accept a coin that has been subjected to the rigours of circulation. Provided one recognises a piece's imperfections and does not pay the price for a perfect or near perfect specimen, no harm is done.

Toning

There are factors other than the degree of wear on the coin's surface that affect a coin's value. Just as one may refer to a musical instrument having a 'rich tone', so a coin which is deepened and enriched in colour by time may be said to be 'toned'. Though one may see an item described as having 70 per cent mint lustre (thus indicating that the item has lost some of its original shine), one may also see the phrase 'rich dark tone' in a dealer's list or auction catalogue.

Whilst numismatists prefer modern copper and bronze coins to have original mint lustre, it will be appreciated that even coins in mint condition may develop a patina if they have been exposed to the atmosphere. Although such coins do not command as high a premium as a specimen with full mint lustre, if the patina is even, they will realise more than examples with 'patchy' toning or partial lustre, or specimens that can just be viewed as 'dull'. The patina found on ancient bronze coins increases the value considerably. Generally the patina is brown or green, or a combination of the two hues. A green patina must not be confused with verdigris which detracts from a coin's value.

The precious metals also tone. Many nineteenth and early twentieth-century silver specimens are found with a light golden tone that give the coins a delightful glow. The patina can also be darker; sometimes even black. I find the dark damson tone with a hint of olive green particularly attractive. This is especially so when the *field* (the flat part of the coin between the inscription or edge and the design) is of a deeper tone than the relief design. Look a little closer and the bust may be speckled with red and gold lights. Gold coins can be found with a light red tone. There is far more to a coin than a design on a metal blank. Whilst toning is a matter of personal taste, a pleasing tone does increase a coin's value. Conversely, a 'patchy' or unpleasant tone can reduce a coin's value. Table 2.2 illustrates how aesthetic toning enhances the price as well as the coin.

Table 2.2 An indication of how toning affects a coin's value

Condition	Comment	Price
Good EF-FDC	Attractively toned	£700
Good EF	Pleasingly toned	£560
EF	Toned	£550
EF	—	£500

Note: The above data was extracted from a leading London dealer's lists over a two month period. The data refers to coins of the same date and type. Consequently the price differential purely relates to condition and toning.

Cleaned coins

The subject of toning leads to another field – cleaned coins. Sadly, many members of the public are under the mistaken impression that the dull coins in their possession have to be cleaned before they attempt to dispose of them. More coins that have been wondrously well preserved since their striking are ruined by injudicious cleaning than by any other means. Above, it was revealed that minimal wear can considerably reduce the value of a coin. Metal polish is an abrasive, and this, linked to the rubbing of the piece with a cloth, wears the surface of a coin in addition to removing the patina. A severely polished coin will lose most if not all of its value. Similarly, coins inexpertly cleaned by liquid chemicals sell at a discount compared to an uncleaned item. Only by handling coins will the reader become able to recognise specimens that have been unacceptably cleaned. This is where a friendly dealer is invaluable. An indication of how cleaning and polishing affects the value of a coin is seen in Table 2.3 overleaf. Further information on cleaning coins is given in chapter 4.

Artificial toning

In time, of course, cleaned specimens will 'tone down'. Before central heating became the standard form of heating for the home, collectors

Table 2.3 How cleaning and polishing detracts from a coin's value

	£
Unpolished or untreated	200
Severely polished	90
Lightly polished	130
Treated with 'Silver Dip' or other proprietary fluid	90

Note: The above data refers to coins of the same date and type in a comparable state of preservation apart from the polishing or cleaning. It will be appreciated that the valuations ultimately depend on the degree of polishing etc.

would leave cleaned items exposed for a long period in a room where a coal fire burned. In time, the oxidisation process resulted in the coin returning to somewhere near its uncleaned appearance. Other methods of 'dulling' coins range from placing them in guttering to exposing them to the elements in industrial or city environments. In the States 'toning fluid' is marketed; however, like the method of inducing toning by the use of a proprietary liquid antiseptic, its use is frowned upon by the true connoisseur. To the expert eye, such treatments will be obvious.

There is no precise rule to aid detection of coins so treated. However, if the toning does not appeal, or does not 'look right', there is the possibility that the coin may have been assisted instead of acquiring its deep tone slowly over the passage of time. Occasionally, one may see, 'dark tone (probably artificial)' in a sale catalogue or dealer's list. A coin which has been cleaned and subjected to induced toning will fetch only 30 or 40 per cent of the price of an untreated specimen, according to the degree of the cleaning and 'toning'. Likewise one would expect an uncleaned but noticeably artificially toned coin to sell at up to 20 per cent of its naturally-toned counterpart.

Edges

Having carefully scrutinised the surface of a coin, do not forget to inspect the edge. Whether coins have been circulated or not, they may have been dropped, thus resulting in edge knocks. When handling a coin, one should guard against the consequences of accidentally dropping the piece by ensuring that a soft carpet and not a hard concrete floor is at one's feet! Needless to say, edge knocks do reduce the value of a coin. Likewise an item that has been mounted and worn as jewellery will similarly be worth less than its unmounted counterpart. Examine the edge of a coin for the tell-tale scratch marks of the mount that may have been placed round the piece's circumference. Beware too of specimens that have had a soldered fixed mount removed. One should beware of attempts to disguise damage to the milled edge by the removal of such a mount and subsequent 'renovation' of the milling.

All items that have been subjected to such treatment are worth less than specimens that have not been mounted. Whilst mentioning coins being used as jewellery, it is appropriate to say something of gilded coins, which have been treated to look more appealing. Such pieces do appear on the market from time to time. Both gold and silver coins were so treated. Table 2.4 illustrates how edge knocks, mounting and gilding can affect the price of a coin.

Table 2.4 Examples of the retail prices of a gold coin with edge knocks or which has been used as jewellery

	£
Coin with no edge knocks and which has not been mounted or gilded, etc.	650
With edge knock	550
Specimen removed from 'loose' ring mount	325
Coin with soldered mount removed	270
As above but coin also gilded	240

Note: The above data refers to coins of the same date and type in a comparable state of preservation apart from the stated defects.

At the time of their circulation, hammered coins were subjected to clipping, i.e. the removal of part of the edge of the piece for personal gain. The clipper, having acquired his piece of metal at the expense of the Treasury, would put the coin back into circulation. Needless to say, a coin that has been attacked in this manner sells at a discount. The reduction in value is dependent upon the extent of the clipping.

Other factors

It should be noted that a sharply struck specimen will command a higher price than a 'normally' struck coin. Conversely, poorly struck specimens will sell at a discount. Hammered and ancient coins, by virtue of their method of manufacture, are not the most uniform of items. Readers will therefore appreciate that those which are well-struck on round even flans sell at a premium over specimens which are normally encountered. Poorly struck pieces or those that are struck 'off centre' on the blank will be less valuable than those which conform to the acceptable norm.

Coins which have been bent, holed or mutilated in some other way are of no commercial value, apart from the price they would realise as bullion, unless the items are extremely rare. It is not unknown for holes in coins to be 'filled in'. However, if not immediately noticeable to the untrained eye, a good magnifying glass will reveal attempts to renovate such mutilated specimens to their original glory. Likewise bent coins, which were often exchanged as keepsakes by lovers in the days of yore, may be subjected to attempts to return them to their original state. 'Attempts' is the correct word, for a bent coin can never successfully be straightened.

Beware of 'improvements' to coins. This term refers to attempts to pass a coin as being in a better state of preservation than it really is. No, the vendor does not resort to a sleight of hand at the conclusion of the deal. In simple terms, a coin, say, in Good Very Fine condition has had part of its design re-engraved. Thus, at a quick glance, the coin's raised surfaces may appear not to be worn. However, upon closer inspection, it will be apparent that the finer details of the design which have been lost through circulation have been re-engraved back on to the piece. Such practices are easily noticeable without the use of a magnifying glass and are quite obvious when such an aid is used. Needless to say, such 'improvements' far from improve a coin's value. Indeed, unless extremely rare, such specimens are of no commercial value.

Conclusion

From the above it will be appreciated that assessing a coin's exact state of preservation is a complex matter. However, by handling coins the reader will soon gain the necessary experience to assess all the plus and minus factors which determine a coin's condition. As his or her knowledge of the price structure in the market increases, so will his ability to translate a coin's attributes or defects into financial terms. Just as a motorist, when contemplating overtaking another moving vehicle, does not have to solve a differential equation before knowing whether his move is feasible, so those in the coin world, through experience, can intuitively assess a coin's value. At the end of this chapter are some guidelines to help readers to acquire the financial 'feel' of the market. However, first the fourth determinant of a coin's value must be discussed.

Design, legend, mintmark or date

Design

As with a postage stamp, a minor variation in the coin's design can radically affect its value. For instance, in 1979, a Very Fine William III British shilling could have been acquired for £32. However, in that year, a Bold Very Fine specimen sold at a London auction for a staggering £13,000. Needless to say, there is a vital difference, other than the price, between the two examples. The £32 refers to a 'normal' 1696 shilling struck at the London mint. On such pieces the monarch's hair is turned outwards above and below the crown of the head. Numismatists refer to this as the 'First Bust'. The king's hair on the 1696 London shilling which realised £13,000 went across the breast. This variation is known as the 'Second Bust'. Specimens of the former are common, whereas the latter is the only known example. Interestingly, this possibly unique shilling was originally spotted by a collector whilst sorting through a box of miscellaneous coins at an antique shop in the picturesque British cathedral city of Salisbury. One shilling and sixpence – 7½p – was paid for the coin.

Sometimes a coin variety is created completely by accident. In 1935 Canada struck its first silver dollar for circulation. As this year coincided with the Silver Jubilee of King George V, it was considered appropriate that the coin should commemorate the event. Consequently, the obverse legend which framed Percy Metcalfe's traditional portrait of the monarch indicated that the king was in the twenty-fifth year of his reign. Incidentally, this was Canada's first commemorative coin.

The reverse bears a modernistic representation of an Indian and a voyageur (a travelling agent for a fur company) paddling a canoe by an islet on which there are two wind-swept trees. This design, which is the work of Emmanuel Hahn, proved extremely popular. Consequently, it appeared on the coinage of George VI and indeed during the present reign.

During the 1950s technical problems plagued the mint. In the process of polishing or repolishing the dies, the four shallow water lines to the right of the canoe tended to disappear. The *Charlton Standard Catalogue of Canadian Coins* has this to say on the subject: 'Collectors have decided arbitrarily that a certain pattern of partial water lines at the right-hand end of the canoe should be collected separately and command a premium over dollars with perfect water lines or other partial lines configurations. The so-called Arnprior configuration consists of 2½ (often frequently called 1½) water lines at the right. Any trace of the bottom water line disqualifies a coin from being an Arnprior. One should also beware of coins that have had part of the water lines fraudulently removed.'

An Extremely Fine 1955 dollar with normal water lines is priced in a recent edition of Charlton at Can$35. A 1955 Arnprior variety in the same condition bears a price tag of Can$250. The specimens with 2½ water lines are called *Arnprior* because in 1955 the mint made up an order of two thousand silver dollars for a firm in Arnprior, Ontario. The term has been applied to any 'Voyageur' dollar with defective water lines.

It will be appreciated that there is a direct link between the supply of a coin and its exact design. For example, in 1866 the United States struck 49,625 'Liberty Seated' dollars. All but two of the surviving specimens bear the reverse motto 'In God We Trust'. Those four additional words on the face of the coin radically affect its value, compared to the price that would be realised by the two coins without the motto.

Legend

The legend can also have a dramatic effect on the value of a coin. This is particularly so with the earlier coinages. For example, the English hammered coinage is rich in varieties as well as types of coins. King Stephen's 'Regular Regal Issues' contains a penny known as the Watford type. The obverse bears a bust of the monarch, holding a sceptre, and the reverse a cross moline with a lis symbol in each of the cross's angles. The obverse legend generally reads STIEFNE (R., RE., or REX) or some variant for King Stephen. In the 1987 edition of Seaby's *Standard Catalogue of British Coins*, such pieces are priced at £250 in Very Fine condition. However, a similar coin bearing the obverse legend PERERIC or PERERICM is known. Such items are catalogued at £1,250 in the same condition. Scholars are uncertain as to the meaning of the PERERIC legend. It is, however, generally accepted that it is a meaningless inscription deliberately used to strike an anonymous coinage either prior to Stephen's claim to the throne or alternatively during his period of captivity during the Civil War.

The early coinages also tend, by virtue of the poor literacy standards of the moneyers, to bear non-uniform legends. Thus, whilst ANG FR HI or ANG FR HIB is the normal abbreviation for England, France and Ireland in the Queen's titles on an Elizabeth I sixpence, ANG FRA HI is also encountered. It is also known for the monarch's name to be blundered; ELZABETH for Elizabeth, etc. One has to assess the financial importance of such differences in the light of demand. If the variation from the norm only generates an academic curiosity, then the commercial value of the coin will only command a small premium in the market, if any.

In recent years the public have tended to concentrate on the acquisition of coins in choice condition as opposed to rare varieties of coins. In time, the emphasis may change.

Mint mark or date

A mint mark is a term borrowed from Roman and Greek numismatics where it was used to indicate the place of mintage. For example:

> HT – Heracleia Thraciae
> K – Carthage
> MD or MED – Mediolanum (Milan)

On early medieval European coins, a mark was generally used to show where the legend began, not where a coin was made. In the pious fashion of the Middle Ages, a cross was preferred. The medieval use of such symbols explains why they are sometimes referred to as 'initial marks'. In England the initial mark became an heraldic symbol as opposed to a cross in 1461. We therefore find the rose and sun of York, the boar's head of Richard III, etc. Other European countries also used heraldic symbols as initial marks.

Since the dating of coins was not usual in medieval times – indeed, the first dated English coin appeared in 1548 – marks had a periodic significance, changing from time to time. When a heraldic mark is used to date a coin it is known as a *privy mark*. While the dating of coins became the accepted norm in Tudor England, the tradition of the privy mark remained until the mid-seventeenth century.

Additionally, these marks were used to signify the mint master responsible for the coinage. Thus, the periodic change of the symbol referred to above may have coincided with a change of official. Alternatively, the symbol itself may have been a mark that was more directly linked to the name of the official. For example, when John Bowes was responsible for striking the coinage of England's 'Boy King', Edward VI, coins emanating from the mint under his control (Durham House) carried a bow to signify Bowes. Other marks were less subtle. William Sharrington, Mint Master at Bristol during the reigns of Henry VIII and Edward VI, until his conviction for treason in 1549, used the initials WS.

The mark could also serve the purpose of a code referring to the actual maker or workshop responsible for the coin's production. As with the ancient coinage, the mint mark came to be used and indeed still is used, to signify where the piece was struck. For example, Australian gold coins may bear an M or S signifying that the piece was struck at either Melbourne or Sydney; Canadian coins bearing an H or C indicate that the piece was struck at either Birmingham (England) by Ralph Heaton & Sons (now The Birmingham Mint Limited) or Ottawa, and likewise a D on an American coin signifies that it was struck at Denver. Mint marks can have a significant effect on a coin's value. Reference should be made to the various standard catalogues for further details.

Every country's coinage has her date rarities. England has its 1933 penny; the United States the 1804 dollar; Australia her 1919 shilling and

THE COIN MARKET — THE PRICE OF A COIN

Canada the 1921 fifty cents. 'Key Date' coins capture the public's imagination. The reason for a particular coin of a certain date being rare is due to either few being minted (the obvious explanation) or to the greater part of those that were struck being melted down and not issued. Details of date rarities can be obtained from the various standard catalogues.

Gaining conversancy with the market

The four major factors which determine the value of a coin have now been discussed. As Goethe wrote: 'All theory, dear friend, is grey, but the golden tree of actual life springs ever green'. Transforming the interaction of supply, demand and condition of a particular coin into commercial terms is an art that can only be acquired by practical experience. Although the theoretical analysis of the determinants of the price of a coin initially appear complex, it is amazing how quickly newcomers to the world of coins can, with guidance, weave their way through the maze of possible pitfalls with an acceptable degree of competence.

Having decided which series of coins appeals, the prospective purchaser can obtain an indication of the value of specific coins by referring to the various standard catalogues and priced handbooks. Details of those in print at the time of the publication of this volume can be found in appendix 3. It will be appreciated that such works have various uses for the collector:

1. They indicate retail values at the time the volume went to press. Prices for modern coins are generally given in at least three states of preservation. Priced handbooks devoted to ancient coins tend to give values for a coin in an 'average grade' only.
2. They are a useful means by which an individual can possibly identify a coin from a known series.
3. They indicate the major type, variety and date rarities, etc.

Standard catalogues and priced handbooks relating to particular coinages of interest are an essential part of a collector's library. However, good as these publications are, it will be appreciated that the retail prices stated, whilst correct at the time of going to press, will alter over time. Thus whilst an excellent starting point in assessing a coin's value, they should be read in the light of changing circumstances.

Unlike prices for commodities and stocks and shares, no daily list of coin prices is published. However, the numismatic press does print 'current prices' for selected series on a regular basis. Titles of coin magazines published at the time of going to press, are given in appendix 4. However, it will be appreciated that only a selection of revised prices can be given in each issue. Furthermore, the periodicals naturally tend to concentrate on the more popular series of their own country's coinage. One should also ascertain the method of compilation of such lists. Claims that the data has been obtained by feeding auction realisations and prices from dealers' lists into a computer should be treated with caution. Whilst the given figure in 'current prices' is an average drawn from a varying number of sources, one can question its accuracy. If the standards of grading are not uniform, then the 'average' price printed in such lists will be distorted. Usually no indication of the age of the in-put data is given. A safeguard against such discrepancies is the independent check of the resultant figures by a professional numismatist or panel of expert dealers. One has more confidence in lists compiled in this manner than by solely utilising a computer. Current prices based on either an individual's or panel's knowledge of the market, *ceteris paribus*, is likewise desirable. It is well worth while subscribing to at least one good coin magazine or newspaper. In addition to the information on prices, they contain features, news, auction results, and, of course, dealers' and auctioneers' advertisements.

However, the prudent collector, even if certain coin periodicals contain price information on the series that is his main interest, will also subscribe to auction catalogues (and the subsequent lists of 'Prices Bid') as well as to dealers' selected listings of their stock currently offered.

The importance of auction realisations in keeping those interested in coins well-informed of the market, is best summarised by the long-established London auctioneers Glendining & Co. The company states in each sale catalogue: '*Lists of Prices Bid* are issued after each Sale, thus giving at a glance a reliable guide to value. The final test of value must always be auction prices rather than the figures given in books of reference, for changing times and fashions soon render the latter obsolete and misleading.' However, do bear in mind that an isolated price is not a trend. Freak prices, which may be either higher or lower than expectations, do occur at an auction. Thus, one has to continually monitor sale results in order to eliminate such distortions.

Annual subscriptions to auction catalogues and lists of 'Prices Bid' are not expensive. However, unless funds are unlimited, it is not viable to subscribe to every auction house's coin catalogues. One has to be selective. If interested in ancient coins, there is little point in subscribing for the catalogues of an auction house generally specialising in U.S. or Australian coins. Specialist catalogues can be ordered as and when they are published. On the other hand, if there are a fair proportion of sales containing coins of interest, there are cost advantages in subscribing to catalogues on an annual basis. A list of the major auction houses worldwide specialising in coin sales is given in appendix 1. Details of forthcoming sales appear in the coin and general press. Details of subscription rates for catalogues are obtainable from each auction house.

The majority of dealers issue lists of coins that are available for purchase. These vary from simple listings produced by means of stencils, to well-presented glossy publications containing articles and pertinent editorial comment. One of the oldest such periodicals is Spink's *Numismatic Circular*. This first appeared in 1893. The forerunner of Seaby's *Coin & Medal Bulletin* was first published in 1926. Both periodicals are published ten times a year and contain selections of coins ranging from the earliest of times right through to the present day. As both companies deal in all of the world's past and present coinages, the material, as well as the prices, is diverse. Items listed frequently range from a few pounds to several thousand. Details of a dealer's regularly published lists or bulletins are generally found in their advertisements in the coin press. It will be appreciated that a small charge is generally made to cover printing costs and postage.

By studying the prices realised at auction and those quoted in dealers' lists, the collector is continually kept up-to-date with market prices and learns how to assess a coin's attributes and defects in financial terms. However, it should be borne in mind that the grading of a coin is a subjective matter and some dealers and auction houses are more optimistic than others in this direction. Conversely, others are overcautious. Whilst it is stressed that there are exceptions to generalisations, the former situation tends to be more likely for fairly newly established concerns, particularly when they are based in the provinces. Only experience and talking to fellow collectors will determine whether one dealer's NEF is another's EF or vice versa.

Illustrated dealers' lists and auction catalogues perform another very useful function. If the photography is good, the collector can compare the written description with the illustration of the coin itself. A useful self-educating game is to look at the photograph first and compare one's own assessment of the coin's state of preservation to the description given in the list or catalogue. Nevertheless, photographs, however good, are no real substitute for handling actual coins. The established professional dealer and experienced collector will always find time to pass on knowledge regarding grading, and indeed all aspects of numismatics, to the novice. In addition to periodic visits to dealers of repute, it is well worthwhile for those interested in numismatics to join a national or local coin club or society. Details of forthcoming meetings are generally found in the coin press. Dealers can often give the address of the secretary of clubs in the area. Another source for information is the local library.

3
Buying coins

'Many have been ruined by buying good pennyworths'
Benjamin Franklin

Having outlined the various interacting forces in the market that determine the price of coins, it is an appropriate time to guide readers towards the various sources for numismatic material. There are three possible courses of buying coins; specimens may be purchased:

1 at auction
2 from a dealer
3 from a private individual

Auctions

It is not recommended for those who are new to the world of coins to bid at auction. Furthermore, I suggest that even when a reasonable grounding in numismatics has been acquired, two or three auctions are attended before bidding is contemplated.

At one London coin auction in the 1950s, 90 per cent of the lots were bought by just two London coin dealers. The remaining 10 per cent of the sale was acquired by just four other dealers. Times have changed. Today a good coin auction can attract hundreds of potential bidders, dealers and collectors alike. However, large attendances at coin sales are the exception rather than the rule.

It is often said that it is financially prudent to purchase at auction. The arguments is put forward that obtaining antiques or 'collectables' in this way ensures that the middleman – i.e. the dealer – is eliminated and thus his mark-up or profit avoided. Theoretically the argument may be sound, but it overlooks one essential factor – the bidders at an auction are human. Consequently, one cannot expect, and does not in fact see, a completely controlled rational behaviour pattern.

At any auction there are some prices that are considered low and others that are seen as high or even incredible. Contrary to popular opinion, there are few bargains to be had at auction. To say that coins sold through the sale rooms are inevitably cheaper than those available from dealers is a complete myth. Stories like that about the small London antiques dealer who purchased a marble bust of Pope Gregory XV at a country house sale for £85, only later to discover that it was a masterpiece by the great baroque sculptor Giovanni Lorenzo Bernini and possibly worth £500,000, may capture the public's imagination, but the odds against such strokes of good fortune are greater than those for winning a sizeable sum in a national lottery or the like.

Auctions are an important medium for both buying and selling coins. However, the newcomer to the world of coins must bear in mind that the sale rooms are not the dealers' wholesalers. The biggest danger for the public attending a sale is the catching of auction fever. Whilst the disease does not last long, and is seldom if ever fatal, the after-effects can be extremely painful on the bank balance. To be in a room with others wishing to obtain the same object can bring out the very worst in people. Rationality can be thrown out of the window and there is a desire to make the purchase almost at any price. After the fever has subsided and one has acquired the chosen lot or lots, there is always the consolation that one had paid, say, only £10 over the price paid by the 'unlucky' runner-up. However, if he or she was simultaneously suffering from the disease, then one is living in a fool's paradise. Meanwhile the dealers are either laughing up their sleeves or sitting in a state of bewilderment. Another potentially dangerous situation is when the item that is of interest is subject to the seller's unrealistically high reserve. In such cases, one is bidding into the vendor's hands.

Buying personally at auction is a time-consuming occupation and the time element must be carefully weighed against any potential advantage. Before contemplating purchasing at a sale there are some very simple rules to follow. As soon as the catalogue arrives, study it carefully and mark those items that appeal. If one is conversant with the market, then one has some idea as to the figure at which it will sell – other things being equal. It has become the custom in recent years for most auction houses to publish their estimate of realisations prior to the sale. These are a fairly useful guide, but there is a general tendency for them to be conservative. Further, it has to be appreciated that they are prepared considerably in advance of the sale itself, and thus whilst considered to be a reasonably, albeit conservative, expectation at the time they were compiled, circumstances may change.

Regardless of how detailed the description of the pieces, and even if the items of interest are illustrated in the catalogue, it is prudent to view the lots. As stated above, grading is subjective and there can be marginal differences of opinion between two experts. Whilst larger firms are generally conservative in their appraisal of a coin's state of preservation, it is not unknown for small firms of general auctioneers that hold the occasional coin sale, to be more than optimistic.

The catalogue will state when the coins are available for viewing. Potential bidders, under supervision, will be given an adequate opportunity to scrutinise the coins. Remember, however, that several people may wish to inspect the offerings. Whilst the auctioneer may make arrangements for the major dealers to view the material on a separate day, collectors and the smaller dealers will attend the public view. For security reasons, one will have to wait one's turn to scrutinise the items. The auctioneer's staff are there not only to keep an eye on the consigned lots, but will advise potential bidders. Dealers and sale room staff can be excellent tutors.

Having carefully examined the lots, either confirm or adjust the financial appraisal made when the catalogue was studied. There are three courses open to the collector who decides that he would like to bid for material.

1   To attend the sale itself and personally bid up to his assessment of the coin's worth.
2   To leave a bid with the auctioneer.
3   To commission a dealer to bid on his behalf.

1   Attending the sale and bidding

There are both advantages and disadvantages to this course of action. It may well be that the sale prices are generally higher than he anticipated and consequently he can adjust his own bids accordingly. Conversely of course, owing to adverse weather conditions or whatever, prices may be lower than those expected. Consequently, the funds available may buy more material than anticipated. Of course there is always the chance of purchasing a bargain. However, it is not prudent to bid blind. Whilst most auction houses give potential bidders seated at 'the table' in front of the auctioneer's rostrum a chance to have a last look at a lot as it is offered, for reasons of security, others in the room are assumed to have scrutinised all the coins in which they are interested at the public view. Whilst at some auctions all those present are seated at 'the table', it will be appreciated that in the majority of cases, owing to the lack of space, or as a result of a large number of people attending the sale, only a select few are invited to take their place in this prime position. Naturally the dealers with large businesses are at the top of the auctioneer's list. The disadvantages of personally attending a sale – the possibility of catching auction fever and the fact that it is a time-consuming occupation – have already been outlined above.

2   Leaving a bid with the auctioneers

The majority of auctioneers will execute bids, free of charge, for buyers unable to attend a sale. Every effort is made to obtain the lot or lots as cheaply as possible. Thus, if one leaves a bid of £1,000 on a particular coin and bidding from the floor and commissions only reaches £800, assuming the lot is not subject to a vendor's reserve, it will be knocked down for the latter figure. Auctioneers generally do not hold themselves responsible for failing to bid on behalf of clients.

3   Commissioning a dealer

A charge, normally in the region of 5 per cent of the hammer price, will be made for this service. Dealers will also offer independent advice to a collector and many consider the extra few per cent paid for this additional guidance to be well worth while. When a good business relationship has developed between a dealer and a collector, the latter may give the professional more or less absolute discretion to bid on his behalf. Thus the collector is saved the trouble of viewing the coins offered for himself and after a telephone consultation with the dealer will give the necessary instructions to the dealer. It will be appreciated that this situation is only possible when each party totally trusts the other; when the collector has absolute faith in the dealer's opinion and the dealer is confident that his judgement will be accepted by the collector. Some collectors establish a similar relationship with auctioneers.

There are other matters to consider when buying at auction. Remember that the hammer price may not be the payment required for taking possession of the goods. For example, a coin auctioneer may add a buyer's premium, and, in certain circumstances, a local and national tax. It is therefore necessary to read the 'Condition of Sale' in each sale catalogue. For example, the auctioneers may only hold themselves responsible for the safe custody of any lots left for more than three days after the sale. Further, a storage fee may be levied if lots are not collected within a stated period of time.

Auctions are fun, but, they can be minefields to the inexperienced collector. We therefore recommend that the newcomer to the world of coins does not buy at auction. His best source for coins is the dealer.

Dealers

Undoubtedly dealers are the main suppliers of coins to the collector. There are thousands of coin dealers world-wide. As in any trade, some are just one-man bands with a small general stock, whilst others specialise in a particular series. The medium-sized concerns may sell a reasonable range of material from ancient times to the present day. On the other hand, the leading dealers in a country may have several specialist departments and can therefore offer collectors an even greater cross-section of numismatic items. Whilst the latter category of dealer may have plush offices in the capital city, the vast majority operate from small offices, shops or even from their homes.

Some rely on word of mouth for their name to reach the collector, whilst others advertise in the trade press. As mentioned earlier, details of any list of coins offered for sale that they may publish are included in their advertisements. When a relationship has been established the dealer may forward coins on approval. The terms and conditions of sale are normally stated at the beginning of the list of items offered.

One can also visit the dealer to view his stock. It will be appreciated that a desired specimen will not always be obtainable. However, most dealers operate a 'Wants List'. The dealer will then endeavour to obtain, without obligation, a particular coin for the collector. It is also prudent to advise dealers of one's specialised collecting field. This is particularly so when seeking items either in choice condition, or which are rare, and thus are not readily available in the market. If a dealer knows a customer's especial interests, he will naturally bear this in mind whilst buying for his stock. Also, being desirous of a quick turnover, it is quite normal for a dealer to offer an item to a customer who has expressed an interest in the series. A quick turnover, as opposed to the inclusion of the coin in his next published list, can be reflected in an advantageous price. Further, a collector is far more likely to return to a dealer who has treated him well. A prudent dealer will think long term.

Needless to say, the standard of dealers varies considerably. Some are very knowledgeable individuals and a few only have a smattering of basic numismatics. Whilst many may treat the customer as a friend who should be encouraged in the pursuit of forming a worthwhile collection, it has to be stated that others, and thankfully these are a small minority, view the new collector as a means by which to fatten their own bank balances. It is therefore essential that the new collector only deals with a reputable dealer.

How does one know that a dealer is of good repute? Obviously a recommendation or personal introduction from an established and experienced known collector speaks for itself. However, not everyone is fortunate enough to have this form of initial guidance. You can be sure of some protection if you choose to deal with an individual dealer or firm of numismatists that belongs to an established trade body such as the International Association of Professional Numismatists (I.A.P.N.); the American Numismatic Association (A.N.A.); the British Numismatic Trade Association (B.N.T.A.); the Canadian Association of Numismatic Dealers (C.A.N.D.); the Professional Numismatists Guild (P.N.G.), the Verband Schweizer Munzenhandler, and so on. Many dealers do not belong to any such organisations. This does not mean that they are not honest or professional. However, it is recommended to deal only with those who will unconditionally guarantee that the coins purchased from them are both genuine and accurately graded. Members of the above trade organisations are bound by codes of practice and thus their guarantee is implied. I suggest that a written guarantee is incorporated into the receipt for material purchased from others.

BUYING COINS

However, I do stress the advantage of dealing with those who are members of a recognised trade organisation. Written guarantees and the like are only worth the paper they are written on firstly, if the dealer can be found when it is discovered at a later date that 'all is not well' and secondly, if he subsequently honours his guarantee – i.e. reimburses the purchase price if the coin proves to be either a fake or not accurately graded. It will be appreciated that difficulties can arise if the dealer is neither willing or able to put matters to rights. As a member of a recognised trade organisation has his reputation to protect, it is unlikely that he will not maintain a high standard of conduct. However, in the unlikely event of this happening, the aggrieved purchaser does have recourse to the trade organisation. It will act as an arbitrator in any dispute, and if a member is found to have breached the organisation's code, then clearly the ultimate sanction of dismissal from the association will be a suitable inducement to adhere to its recommendations.

There is no way that a dealer will want to incur the wrath of a trade association, for if the ultimate sanction is enforced, his reputation is damaged. Also, a reputable trade association will not want a member within its fold who brings the trade into disrepute. The trade organisation with world-wide membership is the I.A.P.N. It was constituted at a meeting held in Geneva in 1951 to which the leading international numismatic firms had been invited. There were twenty-eight foundation members. The objects of the I.A.P.N. are the development of a healthy and prosperous numismatic trade conducted according to the highest standards of business ethics and commercial practice, the encouragement of scientific research and the propagation of numismatics, and the creation of lasting and friendly relations amongst professional numismatists throughout the world.

Membership is vested in numismatic firms, or in numismatic departments of other institutions, and not in individuals. Today there are 110 numismatic firms in membership, situated in five continents and twenty-one countries. Membership of the Association is not lightly acquired as applicants have to be sponsored by three members, and the vetting of applications involves a rigorous and sometimes protracted procedure.

The ideal way of meeting as many dealers as possible in the shortest possible time, is to visit a fair, convention or bourse. The trade press gives details of forthcoming events. Some are grand affairs that attract dealers from many countries. Others are strictly regional events at which local dealers exhibit. Naturally, the larger dealers only place a selection of their stock on view. However, they are only too pleased to hand out copies of their latest list which gives an indication of the range of material they offer. Attending a major coin convention is an experience the newcomer to numismatics should not miss. It is an ideal opportunity to meet a good spread of collectors as well as members of the trade.

Earlier it was stated that the view that coins available from dealers were more expensive than those sold at auction was a complete myth

BUYING COINS

The reader may be confused by this statement. The explanation is quite simple. A dealer does not only acquire his stock from the sale room. It will be appreciated that if a vendor consigns material to auction he will probably have to wait several months before his coins are converted into ready money. In other words, the process of cataloguing (i.e. the auctioneer assigning it to a suitable future sale, describing the coins, possibly having them photographed, sending the manuscript of the catalogue to the printer and going through the various proof stages until the work is printed in its final form) all takes time. Additionally, for obvious reasons, a suitable period has to elapse before the appearance of the catalogue and the actual sale. If the vendor wants his money instantly, he has two courses open to him: to consign the material to auction, having previously agreed an advance to be paid by the auctioneer, or to sell to a dealer for cash.

In the former case, the lot will have to be sold without a reserve. In other words, the vendor will not be given the safeguard of protecting his material from the small possibility of adverse weather conditions, a transport strike or whatever, resulting in the coins being sold for a song. Even if the auctioneer is prepared to make a cash advance, it will be appreciated that, as the coins are effectively his security or collateral, he will only be prepared to advance a percentage of what he expects the pieces will realise at auction. Furthermore, the auctioneer will want reimbursement for what is in fact a loan to the vendor. This is generally achieved either by charging a higher than normal commission on the resultant hammer price or charging interest on the amount advanced. Faced with all these uncertainties, and the need for instant money, the vendor may decide to sell directly to a dealer for cash.

Assuming that the dealer and the vendor both have the same opinion as to the future auction price, the dealer will purchase the items at below the anticipated sale realisation. The vendor knows that the dealer will have to pay the auctioneer's commission and other related charges. These vary from auction house to auction house, but, where an advance is concerned will hover between about 15 and 20 per cent. Thus, by a process of subconscious arbitrage, the price at which the vendor will sell and the dealer buy, is based on a similar discount below the figure that both anticipate the coins will realise at auction. For simplicity, it has been assumed that their expectations are identical. Thus, if the dealer is prepared to on-sell for a quick turnover at, say 10–20 per cent, which is quite normal when he has a known buyer in mind at the time of purchase, his client will have acquired the pieces at below the anticipated auction price.

Readers will appreciate that this example only holds water if the lots actually reached the price that the parties anticipated. If for some reason, the realised price is much less, then clearly the dealer's customer would have fared better at the auction. However, we are entering the world of crystal ball gazing. Whilst it is quite possible for unforeseen

BUYING COINS

circumstances to affect the vendor's and the dealer's expectations (the former being influenced by the auctioneer's), it will be appreciated that in an actual situation, they will tend towards conservatism.

It is obviously impossible to cite an example of the price coins would fetch if a vendor sold them to a dealer *and* if he sold them in a sale room let alone to quote the price at which the dealer would on-sell to his client, but a general observation can be made. In the time when the market is particularly buoyant, auction realisations tend to be above the price of similar coins in the dealers' trays. In such circumstances, after a large auction which has attracted international dealers, the under-bidders at the sale swoop on local dealers and frequently buy more advantageously than at the auction. Conversely, when the market is not buoyant, the reverse may be the case.

Many newcomers to the world of coins are tempted towards dealing with those who only sell coins as a sideline to their main trade, e.g. antique dealers, jewellers and the like. Whilst their inexpertise may well result in their customers obtaining an item at a knock-down price, readers are warned that their lack of knowledge may well work to their customers' disadvantage. Quite innocently their opinion as to the value of a coin may be unrealistically high. Whilst leading dealers are seldom a source for real bargains, they do not suffer from over-optimism regarding a coin's worth.

Purchase from a private individual

This course of action is not recommended to the newcomer.
As with any collector's item, it is quite possible to purchase coins from fellow members of the general public. Contact with collectors at a coin club or society, or answering a classified advertisement in the coin press, may result in meeting a numismatist who wishes to dispose of some interesting coins. The asking price may be advantageous to both parties. In other words, the vendor may receive more than a dealer is prepared to pay, whilst the purchaser is charged less than the sum required to acquire the same coins from a professional numismatist. It will also be appreciated that the reverse may be the case. The purchaser could find that he has paid over the odds for the material. In such situations that there has generally been no intentional motive to over-charge. Quite simply, the vendor has an inflated opinion of the value of the material. This may be a result of over-grading. Whilst it cannot be denied that bargains can be acquired through private transactions, unless the potential purchaser is competent at grading and acquainted with the current market prices of any coins so offered, it is recommended that where coins of a reasonable value are concerned, an independent valuation be obtained. It could save a lot of aggravation and embarrassment at a later date. Do note that dealers generally make a charge for a

valuation. Whilst one can ask for an offer for the pieces, dealers are well aware of such attempts to obtain a free valuation and may well not oblige.

Conclusion

An experienced collector will buy from all three possible sources mentioned in this chapter. His knowledge is his safeguard for not falling into the many pitfalls that may trap a novice. Until one is armed with a good working knowledge of the world of coins, one should not meander from the clearly marked paths into the uncharted realms of coin purchase. Initially one should only buy from a reputable dealer, then, as one's knowledge expands, consider making purchases, with guidance, at auction. Only when one is completely competent at grading, identifying and valuing coins should one attempt to transact business with the coin world at large.

In appendices 1 and 2 respectively, the names and addresses of the world's leading auction houses that handle numismatic items and the more well-known coin dealers are listed. The latter are members of the I.A.P.N. It is stressed that non-inclusion in either list is not a slight on the character or integrity of any individual, firm or company.

4
Investing in Coins

'Successful alternative investment is only possible in areas where there is a hard core of dedicated collectors. Numismatics is one such area.' The Daily Telegraph, 1979.

Introduction

In February 1979, the Rt. Hon. Lord Hamilton of Dalzell, M.C., disposed of his collection of English milled silver coins. The sale, which was conducted by Spink Coin Auctions in London, realised a total of £222,000. The coins were acquired over a fifty year period and his Lordship estimates that he paid between £3,000 and £4,000 for the pieces. Lord Hamilton was a devoted numismatist. His collection, which was one of the most important of its kind in private hands, was not acquired as an investment. Nevertheless, gross of any taxes and the auctioneer's commission, he did profit to the extent of, say, £218,000 upon its disposal.

Until the early 1950s, a collector selling his cabinet of coins would be delighted if he received more for it than the capital outlay incurred in acquiring the individual pieces. The formation of the collection was an end in itself and the pleasure obtained from numismatics was the only expected reward. Today, matters have changed. A prudent collector disposing of a cabinet formed over a lifetime, would expect, and receive, a most handsome return on the sum spent on acquiring the collection.

With the Depression of the 1930s, followed by the general uncertainty of the War years, not surprisingly the art market in general was in the doldrums. The market for historic coins was no exception to this state of affairs. Furthermore, purchasers of objets d'art or whatever, acted for aesthetic as opposed to financial reasons. Naturally, there were exceptions. For example, an article published in *The Connoisseur* in 1903, indicates that our forefathers were purchasing stamps with an eye to a possible capital gain in addition to any philatelic reason.

Whilst investment in modern coins was promoted in the United States in the 1930s, the potential of historic coins did not receive wide publicity until three decades later. It was in the mid-1950s that prices for items falling into the latter category began to move upwards. This coincided with the sale of several major collections. The public's imagination was captured by the dispersal of the 'Palace Collections of Egypt', better known as King Farouk's collection. Sotheby's London auction of the numismatic items in 1954 received wide publicity.

During the 1960s interest in numismatics gathered momentum in almost every country in the Western world. It was as if the pastime had awoken from a deep slumber, and like fictional characters in the same circumstances, the public paid a great deal of attention to the 'new' phenomenon. A combination of events – economic prosperity, a greater awareness of collecting in general and more leisure – resulted in a greater interest in numismatics. New coin dealers seemed to appear from nowhere. The sale rooms, which were usually only attended by a handful of dealers and collectors, soon became great attractions even if the event was only a general coin auction.

In the U.K., the approach of decimalisation, or the demise of the £sd unit of account and the introduction of a new coinage based on a hundred as opposed to two hundred and forty pence to the pound, acted as a dramatic stimulant to a general interest in modern coins. The public were almost driven to a point of frenzy in trying to form complete runs of the recent coinage that would vanish as the new currency was introduced. Many were quite content to search their change for the required examples of the doomed coinage needed to complete a date run of a particular denomination. Others, anxious to obtain better specimens, hounded the established and new dealers for uncirculated examples.

Folders specially designed to hold date sets of the vanishing coinage were marketed. Booklets giving values of twentieth century British coins were published. The public, being totally ignorant of the grading criteria for coins, were convinced that every handful of coins given in change at the supermarket, was worth a small fortune to a collector. At the height of this hysteria, a friend encountered a middle-aged lady at a well-known London dealer's establishment. Outside, her taxi, with meter running, was waiting to whisk her to Harley Street. Inside she would not accept the expert's opinion of the value of her motley collection of currency coins that she had withdrawn from circulation only days earlier. The expert politely stated that they were worth no more than their face value; completely deaf to the reason for this shattering news, all she could do was point towards the values in her 'Check your Change' booklet. Only when the expert took a handful of loose change from his pocket and asked her to compare the two 'collections' was she partially convinced of her folly.

Meanwhile, those anxious to obtain near perfect date sets of denominations were storming the dealers' offices, to purchase coins that less than twenty or so years earlier were completely ignored. In 1970 uncirculated 1959 halfcrowns were changing hands at £25 each, or 200 times their face value. Ten years later examples could be acquired for less than half that sum. The public's enthusiasm to acquire modern uncirculated coins resulted in a dramatic increase in prices, as demand initially outstripped the supply in the market. Their rush to secure specimens. combined with their own lack of experience in grading and a similar lack of expertise plus the dishonesty of some of the nouveaux dealers, resulted in top prices being paid for coins in a second rate state of preservation.

Inevitably, the bubble burst. Having enjoyed the chase of forming their collections, those who entered the market early more or less simultaneously decided to liquidate their 'investments'. They loaded their wheelbarrows with their loot and proceeded to capitalise on their hitherto 'paper gain'. Alas, there were more seller than buyers, and prices plummeted. It was not only the nouveau 'collector' that burnt his fingers. Dealers too found that their stocks were only worth a fraction of their original cost. Many of those whose trade was solely based on the material that was subject to the boom, went out of business.

Nevertheless, not everyone who was lured towards coins in the boom years of the 1960s restricted themselves to very modern coins. Though this may have been their stepping stone to numismatics, many individuals acquired a permanent interest in the subject. This in turn led to an increase in the hard core of collectors. The past stability of the market had been said to be a result of the pastime of coin collecting being based on a solid collector foundation. Inevitably, the introduction of the investor into the market has resulted in quite marked price fluctuations. However, each 'boom period' has nearly always increased the hard core of coin enthusiasts and consequently the general trend of prices for numismatic items in the long term has been upwards.

Those who have purchased coins prudently, whether or not with an eye to a capital gain, have fared well over the last decade or so. In the 1970s, coins began to be recognised as a medium in which one could invest. The return was twofold; an interest in the fascinating world of coins and a possible capital appreciation to be realised on the disposal of an individual piece or the entire collection. Even those who were initially attracted by possible capital gains found the subject of numismatics attractive and learnt to appreciate the artistic merit of coins and their fascinating history.

In the 1970s the sharpest rise in coin values coincided with a period when conventional investments in the world's stock markets fell. Individuals, reluctant to place funds in financial securities, turned their attention to purchasing works of art, antiques, stamps, coins and even wine. The press fuelled the interest in what are now known as 'alternative investments'. Inevitably, the 1973/1974 flurry in the coin market was followed by a quiet period. Prices eased, some falling more than others, thus resulting in a disillusionment with the coin market for some individuals. The fall in prices was a result of investors realising, or attempting to realise, their gains. Their activities aggravated the price decline.

One of the first investment consultants to examine seriously the opportunities and dangers in investing in items as opposed to traditional financial media was Robin Duthy. His book *Alternative Investment* (Michael Joseph, 1978), analysed ten leading areas ranging from stamps to wine and from diamonds to coins. The author likens many fields of alternative investment to a game of Snakes and Ladders. The ladders represent knowledge, experience and so on, whether possessed by the investor himself or by one of the many dealers of integrity who will share all these advantages with their clients.

Clearly not all items meet the necessary criteria to make them suitable as an alternative investment. The three main qualities they should possess are:

1 Their appeal should be international. In other words they should be equally saleable, say, in North America and in Europe. However, it should be borne in mind that exchange rates play a large part in the level of international prices.
2 As a consequence of the above, they should be easily transportable. Thus, if an investment made in one particular country loses or looks like losing its attractions through taxation or for some other reason, it should be capable of being moved, subject to legislation, to a more favourable location.
3 The items should not call for any especial treatment in store.

Coins meet these three requirements admirably. However, before giving guidance as to how to invest successfully in numismatic items, it is first necessary to look at the concept of alternative investment and to highlight the main differences between placing funds in this as opposed to traditional financial investment media.

The difference between alternative and conventional investments

Funds placed into conventional investments produce an income. Other things being equal, the purchase of shares results in the receipt of dividends; land produces rent; and monies placed into bonds and bank deposits yield interest. Additionally, shares, bonds and land may result in a capital gain upon disposal. However, the purchase of coins, stamps, antiques, pictures or whatever does not result in any income flowing into the coffers. It is only when such items are sold that one is likely to be financially rewarded.

However, the net capital gain may well exceed the net realisable value of the aggregate of capital and reinvested income from conventional investments. The reason for investing in 'alternatives' is to achieve such a goal.

The world's financial markets are the closest one comes in the real world to the economists' theoretical concept of a perfect market. On the other hand, the world of antiques and collectables is far from perfect in any sense. The economist's concept of a perfect market is where, amongst other things, there are many buyers and sellers making numerous and frequent transactions against a background where both the buyer and the seller have perfect knowledge.

The price prevailing in such a market is readily available to all and one ordinary share in, say, COINS INC., is precisely the same as another. When an investor decides to buy 100 ordinary shares in a company or corporation quoted on any of the world's stock exchanges, he knows precisely what he is buying – a share, say, in COINS INC. Further, he can check the price he has paid against the daily published price prevailing in the market at the time of his purchase, by referring to the *Financial Times* (London) or the *Wall Street Journal* (New York) etcetera. (Note: the figure quoted in the press is the 'middle' price, i.e. half way between the buying and selling price.) The financial press will also publish information regarding the company that will help him decide the prospects of that enterprise. For example, major new orders received, events that are adverse for and the circumstances which are favourable to the organisation. Additionally, the entity is generally bound by law to provide information to shareholders. The available information, linked to press comment in the financial journals goes a long way in assisting a present or prospective shareholder in assessing the fortunes or fate of the company in which he is interested.

However, in the coin world, although there is a clearly defined market structure, there is no list of market prices produced on a daily basis. Coins and the like are simply sold at auction and by dealers the world over. The situation is aggravated by the fact that coins are not homogeneous – prices vary according to the state of preservation of individual items – and imperfect knowledge can result in identical specimens in comparable condition selling within a broad price band. Furthermore, there is a fraction of the demand for details of market movements, compared to the numbers of people who require information in connection with conventional investments, and, because transactions do not take place on a clearly defined market floor, it is neither economic nor possible to produce a daily list of average coin prices.

Additionally, rare coins, by virtue of their rarity, are infrequently on the market. Their price is determined by the interaction of demand and supply, as and when they appear. In chapter 2, I discussed how to keep up-to-date with market movements. However, because of the delays in the availability of information, it is not possible to be absolutely up-to-date with market trends without going to considerable expense. Therefore, unlike the buyers and sellers in the traditional investment market, the coin dealer and collector does not always have the very latest information available. This is particularly the case with the collector. His information-gathering technique is not based on a bush telegraph as is that of the dealers. Whilst the coin press publishes reports of sales and comment on market movements, there is a time lag between the occurrence of events and publication of the material, owing to lengthier copy deadlines and the longer periods between the publication of issues compared to the conventional financial press.

The lack of homogeny in the field of alternative investments is another major difference from those of the realms of traditional financial investment. Whilst two shares of a particular type in a company are identical in every respect, two coins of the same type may not necessarily be indistinguishable. As was seen in chapter 2, minor differences in their state of preservation, which are barely noticeable to the layman's eyes, can result in two otherwise identical coins having completely different values. Imagine an investor on the stock exchange, who having assessed all the information available regarding a particular purchase, then has to examine each share to ensure that there are no minor differences between those offered. Such 'differences', whatever they could be, would result in some shares being worth more and certain shares being worth less than others. Thankfully, shares of a particular class are homogeneous. In the market for historic coins, it is unusual to find two specimens that are identical in every respect.

The total volume of transactions, both in terms of value and in actual numbers, are many times higher in the conventional investment markets than in the art and collectables markets. This has an important financial consequence for those who choose to place funds in alternative investments. A stockbroker charges a commission for both buying and selling shares on behalf of a client. Because of the enormous volume of turnover, the commission charged, which is expressed as a percentage of the value of the transaction, is small. Additionally, the broker's 'turn', the difference between the buying-selling price is small. An individual who decides to realise his investment in a particular company can easily ascertain the price prevailing in the market and additionally he will be able to determine the costs, expressed in terms of the broker's commission, and so on, that will be incurred upon such a disposal.

By comparision to a stockbroker's turnover, a coin dealer's volume of business is minute. Added to the fact that a broker acts as an agent for individuals wishing to sell securities, as opposed to buying for his own stock-in-trade, this means that the coin dealer cannot merely charge a few per cent or a fraction of a per cent for his services. He is taking the risk of buying merchandise that may lie unsold in his trays for a long period. (Although the jobber does buy on his own account, he is generally dealing in fast-moving items.) Consequently, as a reward for this risk and in order to cover his overheads and make a profit, his mark-up is considerably in excess of the broker's. Remember that 1 per cent of

£50,000,000 is far greater than 20 per cent of £100,000 – especially when overheads have to be covered.

In the previous chapter it was stated that a dealer, in order to make a quick turnover, may only add between 10 and 20 per cent profit to the cost of a coin (even less where high value coins are concerned). This situation prevails when he has specific potential customers in mind. It will also be appreciated that where high value coins are concerned, he will be content with an even lower margin. However, when the coins concerned are run-of-the-mill specimens in the middle price range, and they are bought for stock, as opposed to satisfying any particular customer's wants, then a profit element of 30 per cent is the norm. Coins with a low commercial value, or which are not readily saleable, will be subject to higher margins. Auction houses charge between 10 and 20 per cent or more of the hammer price for their services in disposing of coins.

It will therefore be appreciated that during the period of holding a coin, its retail price, either at auction or when sold by a dealer, must have increased to a value greater than the likely costs to be incurred upon its disposal for the vendor to make a capital gain. Suppose a coin is purchased at £750 and the prevailing average market price a year later is £1,000, so that is has increased by one-third. The net realisable value, if sold at auction, is likely to be between £800 and £850. The price a dealer is likely to offer will range between £750 and, say, £900. Therefore, the possible capital gain could range from 0 to 20 per cent.

If the increase in the average price is less than 33 per cent, then, according to the actual increase, either a loss or smaller capital gain (which will be below 20 per cent) will be the rule of the day. Whilst an annual appreciation of one-third is not exceptional, it must be stressed that it is not the norm. Consequently, *all* alternative investments, including coins, must be viewed as a medium to long-term placement of funds – i.e. five to ten years or more. The costs of disposal are covered by the capital gains in the early years; later capital appreciation is pure profit. Other things being equal, the longer one holds alternative investments, the larger is the return in absolute and annualised percentage terms.

It will be appreciated that, compared to conventional investment media, a relatively small number of individuals can influence the market. I wrote earlier of the disposal acting as a catalyst. But what if two hundred individuals simultaneously decide to dispose of their collections of general run-of-the-mill material? If their accumulations comprise individual specimens that are neither of any great rarity or do not have the advantage of being in a choice state of preservation, then clearly the supply to the market could well exceed demand and thus prices will fall. If the same two hundred individuals decided to sell their portfolio of shares of a comparable aggregate value, the market would hardly notice their action and prices would not be influenced.

A splendid example of the consequences of treating alternative investment in the same way as one would conventional investment media was seen in the United Kingdom in the late 1960s. A combination of a belief that silver bullion was going to boom, the tax advantages of buying objets d'art with borrowed money, and certain anomalies in the duty imposed on the estates of deceased persons, resulted in the public clamouring to buy antique silver at almost any price. Needless to say, prices for such items rose dramatically. They fell equally sharply when the tax and duty loopholes were sealed by the government of the day and the price of silver bullion began to ease following a reappraisal of the metal's financial prospects. Almost simultaneously, those who had thrown themselves into the market with no guidance and purchased indiscriminately decided to liquidate their 'holdings. When they loaded their wheelbarrows full of beautiful objects and proceeded with smiling faces to the auction houses and dealers' establishments, they outnumbered those who wished to buy. They gaped in disbelief when certain objects were seen to have lost up to 70 per cent of their value in a short period of time. Happily the market did eventually return to normality. However, it did take some considerable time for confidence to be restored. May this extreme example serve as a warning to all.

Coin investment

It never occurs to many individuals whom are attracted towards alternative investment, that their purchases may decline in value. Certainly the world depression in the early 1980s left its mark on all areas of the fine art market. Whilst first-class rare items generally held their own, the price of average material eased in price. The explanation is basic: there was a general shortage of money and those wishing to sell at auction outnumbered buyers. As will be seen in the following chapter, the coin market suffered too.

By now it is hoped that readers will appreciate that alternative investments are not made by buying items indiscriminately. It never ceases to be a source of amazement that an otherwise prudent individual will seek guidance when making a financial investment, or will research the subject diligently, but will purchase antiques, coins or stamps, and so on with a view to making a capital gain, with no knowledge of the subject matter he is purchasing and without seeking professional advice. Earlier in this chapter the major differences between the market for alternative investment and conventional financial investments were outlined. The former field requires equal, if not more, skills than the latter and possibly contains more pitfalls to trap the investor than the conventional investment market.

Nevertheless, despite all the dangers drawn to the reader's attention, it has to be stated that prudent purchases of objets d'art, antiques and collectables have been most rewarding investments in the long term. In

1979, Editorial Comment in *The Daily Telegraph*, one of Britain's leading national newspapers, reflected that: 'Coin values have risen relatively slowly over the past few years, probably because of a much higher proportion of collectors and the smaller number of investors compared with other investments such as antiques and stamps. But this situation has begun to change. One reason is the growing demand for investment items which are small, portable and interesting as well as potentially valuable. Coins are a logical choice although they are nothing like as widely collected as stamps. But most coins have an historical interest and an aesthetic appeal and gold and silver coins have an intrinsic value as well.' However, it must be stressed that coins have had their stormy passages, as will be revealed in the next chapter.

The sale of the Lord Hamilton collection has already been cited as an example of good, albeit unintentional, coin investment. Another U.K. success was seen at the disposal of a coin collection acquired just before the Second World War. The anonymous collector purchased his material both at London sales and from leading dealers in the capital. The subject matter ranged from the earliest of times to the late nineteenth century. On average, individual coins sold at the auction at over one hundred times the price originally paid. However, even more impressive individual returns can be given. In 1978, Stack's of New York held a public auction of the United States gold coin collection of the dedicated numismatist and New York lawyer, Harold S. Bareford. A 1933 gold ten dollar piece, for which Mr Bareford paid US$310 in 1947 sold for US$92,500, or nearly three hundred times its original cost. The total collection sold for US$1.2 million against an acquisition cost of US$13,832.

The examples of the disposal of famous collections may not be situations to which the reader can relate. However, do remember that 'from little acorns mighty oak trees grow'. Although one may draw the conclusion that coin investment is only for the wealthy, such a view is far from the truth. For obvious reasons, individuals are reluctant to give full details of how they have fared at coin investment. However, providing anonymity rules, a few will reveal all. In the mid-1960s, Mr X decided he would make a modest provision for his two grandchildren. He decided to buy each of them a gold Cromwell broad. These British coins which bear the Protector's portrait were struck in 1656 by his order and with the consent of the Council. It is now accepted that the denomination was never placed into circulation and therefore must be classed as a pattern. The dies were prepared by the celebrated engraver Thomas Simon and the coins themselves were struck by means of Blondeau's machinery. Undoubtedly, the Cromwellian series of which this denomination is part, is an outstanding example of the British milled coinage.

In 1965 he acquired a Cromwell broad from B. A. Seaby Ltd. of London for £325. The coin was described as EF/FDC. The following year another specimen, also described as EF/FDC, was acquired from

Spink & Son Ltd. of London for £350. In February 1982 both coins were sold at auction by Glendining & Co. of London. They realised £8,200 and £9,200 respectively. Both pieces were purchased by a provincial dealer in the North of England. The net return on an annually compounded basis (i.e. after the deduction of the auctioneer's commission and Value Added Tax) was over 21 per cent. Their performance is typical of any quality coin over the same period. How, one may ask, does one go about securing similar returns? As with all investments, certain 'golden rules' have to be followed. These are now examined:

Buying from a reliable source

In chapter 3, I stressed the need for a new entrant to the world of coins to buy his material from a dealer of repute. I emphasise this again. Ensure that:

1. The dealer is a member of a recognised trade association and is thus bound by a code of practice whereby he had to guarantee that the coins he sells are both genuine and accurately graded.
2. If a dealer is not a member of such a trade association, obtain an unconditional guarantee as to the authenticity and state of preservation of the piece.
3. It is prudent initially to transact business only with those who are established dealers.

Successful buying is based on confidence, either in oneself or through the dealer on whom one relies for guidance. The basis for this confidence is knowledge, and until an individual has acquired a solid grounding in his subject I do not recommend that he throws himself unguided into the sale room. However, as soon as one is competent at identifying coins, grading them and has a good knowledge of the prevailing market prices, then one should look at all possible sources for material. Armed with knowledge one can acquire specimens at advantageous, if not bargain, prices. However, one should bear in mind that what may appear to be a bargain in a lesser-known dealer's list may in fact be an over-graded and thus expensive coin. On the other hand, it may be the buy of the year.

Quality

In chapter 2 it was stated that the importance of a coin's condition cannot be over-stressed, as it is crucial in determining its value. As a general rule, one should only buy for investment purposes coins that are in the best condition available. One has to be realistic. Whilst modern coins (i.e. from the early nineteenth century onwards) can be obtained with relative ease in an uncirculated state, ancient and medieval coins in near mint state are not readily available. Therefore, the best coins available may be in very fine, as opposed to extremely fine, condition. It is only from knowledge and experience of the market that one can ascertain what is and what is not choice or good material.

Common sense, one of the most uncommon of properties in man, also has to prevail. At certain times, particularly when the market is subject to heavy investment buying, the price of really choice material escalates. More and more people are chasing a diminishing commodity in the market and in their quest to obtain the best available at any price, rationality is often thrown out of the window. Whilst there is the danger of paying more than one should for a choice coin in an 'auction fever' situation, the biggest pitfall is to develop distorted vision. If some really choice coins have realised excellent prices, a general euphoria can ensue. In an attempt to secure similar pieces before prices rise further, individuals enter the market and start to bid against each other for similar, but not as choice, material. Consequently, they can pay top prices for second-rate material. Their folly is only realised at a later date when the fever, which they helped to create, has left the market. In blunt terms, they realise that they have paid too much for their purchases and this is made evident by subsequently lower auction prices.

Why should one strive to buy quality material? The answer is very basic. Because coins were made for use and not for ornament, the majority are worn and so the better specimens are found much more rarely. Examination of price movements since 1960 clearly show that material in the better states of preservation has fared much better than average material. When the market dips, and one must not fool oneself that the movement in prices is always upwards, then the average and below average material falls in value whilst coins in above average condition are more likely to hold firm.

However, just to buy quality material is not enough. One has to buy at the right price. Provided two individuals have the money, they can both enter a sale room and bid against each other to obtain the best known example of a particular coin. The resultant hammer price could be totally unrealistic. Therefore, in one's strife for quality, logic must prevail. Never get into a situation of buying quality at any price. If you do, you may find that only you consider the portfolio is worth what you paid, though the coins are of the ultimate quality.

Future saleability

Not only is it essential to buy quality material at the right price, but it is equally important, if one's sole object is a capital gain, to buy pieces that have a good investment potential. As one becomes familiar with the way the market is developing, one can make one's own judgements.

In time the situation will no doubt change and this is where a trusted dealer, who is acting in the capacity of 'investment adviser', comes into play. Interest in certain series of coins is very small. The secret of successful investment is to buy such specimens when the series is only attracting modest attention.

For example, whilst an incorrectly printed stamp can be worth a small fortune, a mis-struck coin does not raise a great deal of enthusiasm in the commercial numismatic world. This is so even when the legend is 'blundered' – i.e. the moneyer has spelt the monarch's name incorrectly or even placed the wrong indication of value when sinking the dies. Who knows though whether at some future date, it may not be fashionable to collect such items and this sector will then experience a rise in prices?

Period of investment

As indicated earlier in this chapter, all alternative investments have to be viewed as a medium to long-term placement of funds. The basic reason is that the cost of realising one's investment is higher than in the conventional financial investment markets. I recommend that coins should be held for at least ten years before disposal. Generally, the longer the items are held, the better the return. By 'return' I mean both the capital gain in absolute terms and when expressed as a compounded annual rate of return; i.e. the annual interest rate that would have been required to turn the original cost of the coin into the sum received upon its disposal over the same period of time on the basis that the interest is re-invested. Coins are therefore a medium in which to place capital as opposed to funds that may be required in case of need. Monies that fall in the latter category should be placed in deposits where there is an immediate access to the funds or where a short notice of withdrawal is required.

What to collect

Even if one's prime reason for buying coins is for financial gain, I suggest that only those items that actually appeal to the potential purchaser should be acquired. My reasoning is as follows. A coin does not yield income and the only reward derived from its purchase is the pleasure it can give the person who owns it. Whilst there are those who will invest in coins without any regard to the beauty or history of the pieces, such individuals miss a great deal. It is rather like making one's first trip to Agra on business and not visiting the Taj Mahal.

Investment strategy

It has been said that any market is no more than crowd psychology in action. In days gone by, the stability of the coin market was a result of its strong collector base. However, with the arrival of investors on the scene matters changed, although I hasten to add that numismatics is still very much collector-orientated. When investors enter the market en masse, demand increases instantly. Left to its own devices, the coin market would enjoy a steady influx of new collectors, which, if past experience is anything to go by, generally increases faster than the exit of collectors either by choice or from natural causes. Thus, the hard core of demand gradually increases because of an increase in the number of dedicated enthusiasts. Consequently, prices will also increase gradually under such conditions.

Let us make our imaginations work overtime. The following is not, I hasten to add, a real situation. For the sake of effect, it is a gross exaggeration of reality. If a band of investors were to enter the coin market with large funds at their disposal, it could set into motion a self-perpetuating price spiral in the short term. It could well be that they were attracted to coins following disillusionment with conventional investments and thought they would try their hand at profiting from 'Dead Money'. Possibly they were prompted to 'have a go' with coins following the publicity from the disposal of a famous collection ('formed between 1960 and 1975 at an outlay of £5,000 and sold yesterday for £150,000', according to the press report). However, for whatever reason, a small group of people start buying coins, prices rise and they are well pleased. The news spreads far and wide that 'coins are a good thing'. The press gets hold of the story that coins have potential. A few journalists write of recent price movements in the market and attract more punters. More disillusioned investors in the conventional financial markets move into coins. Prices rise further. The commentators write of their 'tip' being the things from which fortunes are made. Yet more punters join the race to swop their traditional investments for coins. The Stock Market falls further. The coin market rises. Everyone is suddenly extremely optimistic about coins, although they have been around for a couple of thousand years or so. Coin dealers' phones hardly stop ringing. Callers want coins for investment purposes. Individuals who have a smattering of knowledge about coins begin to buy and sell material. Demand increases, prices rise and the nouveau dealer suddenly finds he can make more money buying and selling coins than he can at his regular employment. He promptly resigns, goes to an auction, bids against new entrants into the market who have not a clue as to what they are doing and between them they set new auction records for several types of coin. The nouveau dealer on-sells to a group of new investors at cost plus 30 per cent (or more if he dares). Everyone is happy.

Then someone looks over his shoulder and notes that stocks and shares are at an unrealistic low. The investment potential is terrific. He sells his coins and returns to his stockbroker. One or two others do likewise and before we know what has happened, the supply of material into the coin market exceeds demand and prices begin to ease. Other punters decide to get out whilst the going is good and sell their coins. The dealers, for fear that they will not be able to gain entry to their offices if they buy any more stock, refuse to buy. All the nouveaux coin investors fly round to the auction houses and join the queue for consigning coins. The auction proves to be their biggest ever – unfortunately it attracts the smallest number of potential bidders and prices plummet even further.

The news that coins are cheap brings both newcomers and established collectors to the market, they begin to buy, and before we know what's happened, prices rise again. Hearing that the value of coins are increasing, more people join the merry band of coin enthusiasts . . . *Déjà vu?* However, let us move away from the realms of fantasy to the real world.

Although this scenario was exaggerated, the underlying principle as to why the coin market is no longer enjoying a gradual rise in prices cannot be denied. Whilst the general price movement for numismatic items has been upwards over the last two decades, it also has to be stressed that there have been varying degrees of price fluctuations too. Whilst external factors such as economic conditions can result in short-term price fluctuations, the overriding cause for volatile prices is the advent of the coin investor. It is a consequence of a lack of appreciation that investing in coins is not synonymous with traditional financial investment, linked to a deficient knowledge of coins, that causes prices to rise and fall. Certain series of coins appeal less to the investor than others; the more collector-orientated the series, the less marked are the price fluctuations.

The rises and falls in the market are by no means frequent events. A market may experience an upward trend in prices for a five-year period and fall during the following one or two years. From past experience, each market 'bottom' is higher than the previous low. A graph of market movements would thus look like the silhouette of a mountain range, with each mountain peak and valley being higher than the previous one. An observation of the general movement of coin prices over the past twenty years shows that an upward trend can last anything between three and five years, followed by a decline of eighteen to twenty-four months or more (see chapter 5).

The obvious ideal course is to buy at the bottom of the market and sell at a future peak. Indeed, this is the strategy to be adopted in all markets. However, it is easier to suggest such action than actually to put one's money where one's mouth is. The situation is summed up by Joe Granville, the American showman-cum-tipster, 'If buying seems the most hazardous and foolish thing you can do, then you are near the bottom that will end the bear market'. Nevertheless, it takes nerves of steel to go against the general consensus of opinion, i.e. to buy when everyone else is selling. However, it is how fortunes are made on the world's stock markets. To know where the market is in relation to the cycle of price increments is information that everyone wants to have.

Those who can see into the future with accuracy are in great demand, but, alas, cannot be found.

However, one does not need a crystal ball to read the signs that the market is nearing a peak. The more optimistic the market becomes, one can be reasonably confident that the peak approaches. What form does the optimism take? You will see what can only be described as a scramble for material; there will be a great deal of talk about how coins are rising in value; advertisements will appear in the press luring the public to invest in rare coins; the city pages in the newspapers will contain the occasional feature on coins as an alternative investment, and general euphoria will be in the air.

As to forecasting the timing of the actual peak – that is a matter of luck as well as judgement. However, when prices do begin to ease, the commentators will assert that it is only a temporary situation and that a rally will soon follow. However, it does not materialise. Prices ease even further as dealers only buy stock they know they can sell. Generally, this means either rare or choice material – in other words, there is not an across the board decline in prices. As stated above, if buying for investment, buy items in the best condition available. Although specimens falling within this category weather the storms of the bear market better, it is again stressed that it is imperative not to buy quality or rare items at whatever the price. As the market nears the peak, the price for quality specimens does tend to go out of control. Those who do strive for quality regardless of the price no doubt think that the downward price trend is out of control when their booty falls in 'value' to the realistic levels prevailing a few months earlier.

As the market nears the bottom, pessimism hangs like a heavy black cloud. Conventions lack the cheerful atmosphere of the boom period. Dealers adopt the countenances of directors of funeral parlours and talk nostalgically of the good old days. Whilst buying and selling does take place, the volume is less than it was a few months previously. However, although the market may appear to be at its weakest, it is a most opportune time for the investor to make his purchases. Many markets are safest when they seem the weakest, and weakest when they appear the strongest, and coin markets are no exception to this state of affairs. Why buy in a seller's market and sell in a buyer's market? To maximise profits one has to break away from the crowd and take advantage of the lost opportunities of others.

I again stress that coins are essentially a medium to long-term investment. The formation of a collection over two or three decades should prove to be an excellent investment as well as a source of pleasure, if past experience is anything to go by. Whilst the purchasing of material at a peak and the disposing of it at the next low will result in monetary loss, it will be appreciated that to buy at the top of the price cycle in Year 1 and to sell at the bottom of a cycle in Year 20, can nevertheless result in a sizeable capital gain. Whilst it is wise not to buy heavily when the market is at a peak, it may well be necessary to make purchases at such a time, to obtain that elusive coin needed to fill a gap in the cabinet. However, if such a need is realised, one is then a collector as opposed to an investor, and that can be no bad thing.

Diversification

At this stage, if writing on conventional investments, I would stress the need to diversify one's portfolio. Following the 'don't put all your eggs in one basket' syndrome, it would be recommended that, say, 10 per cent should be placed in oils, 5 per cent in teas, 15 per cent in property or whatever. I make no such recommendation regarding coins. Instead, the reader's attention is drawn to the fact that it is possible for a particular sector of the numismatic market to rise faster than another. It is also conceivable for a series of coins to fall in value, though I hasten to add that this is unusual in the really long term, though not impossible.

In deciding whether to form a diverse portfolio of coins or a coin collection, one has to examine one's long-term objectives against the funds available for coin purchase. Clearly to buy coins from numerous series does minimise the risk of placing all of one's funds into an area which performs badly. Thus, if monies are sunk into several branches of numismatics, one will be most unlucky if all are poor performers. Consequently, those that perform above average will, hopefully, compensate for others that fall short of the market's average trend. In other words, what is lost on the roundabouts will be gained on the swings.

However, unless funds are unlimited, at the end of the day one will have a mere assortment of coins and not a collection. If the intention is to sell the items individually or in small groups at some later stage, for example, to provide lump sums during retirement or whatever, then nothing will be lost. However, it should be noted that when a meaningfully formed collection appears at auction, the sale total is generally higher than the aggregate of its constituent parts sold separately. As mentioned earlier, when an important collection is sold at auction, it can act as a catalyst on the market. So, if buying coins with the intention of disposing of them 'en bloc', it may be considered prudent to form a collection based on a particular theme. If the collection is sufficiently important, the sale catalogue may even become a standard reference, so when an item from the collection next appears at auction, or in a dealer's list, it will proudly bear the tag 'Ex W.D.Smith' or as appropriate.

In the 1970s, one of the subjects that received attention from commentators on the alternative investment scene was the question whether it was the pure investor or the collector who made the largest capital gain. The debate came down in favour of the collector, as, in the opinion of those who participated in the discussion, his expert knowledge and love of the objects that he purchased, resulted in the formation of a desirable collection as opposed to an assortment of items. This tends to favour the collection as opposed to a portfolio.

The arguments as to whether to specialise or diversify can go on ad infinitum. If a collection is being formed for pleasure as well as for investment purposes, one will probably find that collecting, as opposed to accumulating, wins the day.

The 'golden rules' for coin investment are as follows:

1 Buy from a reliable source.
2 Buy items in the best condition available.
3 Bear in mind the future saleability of the material.
4 Note that investment in coins is not a short-term proposition.
5 Remember that the most opportune moment to buy is when the market appears weak.
6 Obtain a sound understanding of the subject and keep abreast of market movements.
7 Buy material that appeals – and have the advantage of gaining pleasure from its possession.

5
The Market: Past, Present and Future

There is no denying the fact that the coin market has lost some of its steam since the early 1980s. The buoyancy of the 1979–81 period is over and whereas one would have expected half a dozen potential bidders to clamour for a lot offered at a London auction just over half a decade ago, now only two or three possible buyers sedately catch the auctioneer's eye.

To understand the present situation fully, one has to have some knowledge of the past. However, as Charles Wolf Junior was reported as saying in the *Wall Street Journal* (1976), 'Those who don't study the past will repeat its errors; those who do study it will find other ways to err.'

Undoubtedly, the biggest mistake that has been made in the recent past is to treat coins, and indeed, any objets d'art, as investment media. Possibly dealers, buyers and journalists have expected too much from historic money in recent years. Having said all this, a report published in August 1985 still places coins top amongst assets that out-performed the U.S. Consumer Price Index over a ten-year period. Coins were respectively in fifth and third places over periods of five years and one year.

The days of the truly gigantic coin collections have passed, when one compares cabinets formed by our forefathers to those dispersed of late. Take Hyman Montague, a brilliant Victorian barrister, who loved collecting. The preface to the catalogue of his English collection, which Sotheby's began to disperse in November 1895, comments, 'What Mr Montague undertook, it was always the endeavour to accomplish thoroughly, and this dominant feature in his character was the keynote to his success.' Initially, Mr Montague concentrated on English coins. At the beginning he purchased cautiously, but as his knowledge and experience grew, he bought entire collections. Within years he had formed the most complete collection outside the British Museum and consequently there was little left for him to acquire. It normally took Sotheby's a day to dispose of a good collection. In Montague's case, as far as the English pieces were concerned, it took six, and that was after he had sold the 'later' pieces (from George I to Victoria) to Spink.

Mr Montague also turned his attention to Greek and Roman material. His Roman gold amounted to 1,300 pieces – the largest group ever to have been brought together by a private individual. However, that was only the tip of the iceberg. Although his executors (he died unexpectedly at the age of fifty) consigned the Roman material to be auctioned by Rollin & Fevardent in Paris, it took Sotheby's fifty-five days to auction the remainder for £48,860.

The largest purchaser at the sales of Montague's English coins was John G. Murdoch. His ambition was to own the best collection of British coins of all time. After his death, his executors consigned his collection to Sotheby's. From 1903, the six sales totalled £38,620. The major purchaser on this occasion was an eccentric Italian collector, Count P. Ferrari. Upon his death, his executors consigned his coin cabinet to Sotheby's where it was sold as 'the Famous and Remarkable Collection of British and Colonial Coins, Patterns and Proofs formed by a Nobleman recently deceased'. The first sale took place in 1922.

Sotheby's did not reveal the name of the owner of this 'mystery collection' until more than fifty years later. This was on the occasion of 'The Distinguished Collection of English Gold Coins 1700–1900, formed by Captain K. J. Douglas Morris', which was sold in November 1974. Sotheby's considered that this was the fourth sale of such quality which they had sold at Bond Street. It did not take fifty-five days to sell – just one. The 237 lots realised the then remarkable sum of £569,390. It was not until June 1983 that this London auction record was broken. This was when Spink Coin Auctions sold the R. Duncan Beresford-Jones Collection of English hammered gold coins. The 138 lots realised £586,230. So when I stated, 'the days of the truly gigantic collections have passed', the reader will now realise that one of the reasons why an individual cannot amass thousands and thousands of coins like his forefathers, is purely the cost. Note that the number of coins at the Beresford-Jones sale was less than 60 per cent of those at the Douglas-Morris sale, but nevertheless the decreased number sold for 2.96 per cent more. Having allowed for differences in condition and rarity, the underlying trend is indisputable; values had generally increased since 1974. Interestingly, it was not until 1985 that the likes of the Murdoch Collection was seen again in a London sale room. This was when Spink began to offer the Norweb Collection of English Coins.

However, we progress far too quickly. The 1930s and 1940s were relatively quiet numismatically. The Great Depression and Second World War left their mark. However, this does not mean that great sales did not take place. For example, in London Glendining & Co. offered coins from the T. B. Clarke-Thornhill collection in May 1937 (visitors to the Coin Room at the British Museum will appreciate that the bulk of this cabinet was bequeathed to the nation) and Lord Grantley's Collection (1944).

Nevertheless, during this period Bert Seaby was consolidating his business, which was founded in 1926 in a very small office on one of the upper floors of Oxford Circus House, London. To quote 'H.A.' from '1926–1976. Our Jubilee – Some Recollections', published in Seaby's *Coin & Medal Bulletin* in July 1976: 'The day I was demobilised in 1919, I walked from the Air Ministry in the Strand to Spink's, who were then in Piccadilly, and walked out with a job in their coin department at a wage of £3½ a week. Here I shared a desk with Leonard Forrer, Jr and was able to learn a great deal more about ancient coins from his father, Leonard Forrer, Sr, even at that time the doyen of European coin dealers.

In 1926, the opportunity occurred for me to start in business on my own. This was due to Valentine Ryan, the distinguished, if slightly eccentric, collector of Roman and British coins, for whom I had been buying coins at the London auctions. He arranged financial backing for me through Toler Roberts Garvey, the agent of the Irish estates, who became the first chairman of the company. At this time, there were only three numismatic firms in England: Spink's, Baldwin's and Lincoln's. I was fortunate at the outset to be able to purchase a very fine collection of some 6,000 British coins from the Revd. W. L. Gantz for the sum of £4,000. These priced out at about £5,000 and took many years to sell (today I suppose they would price out at nearer a quarter of a million pounds).' (Note that "H.A." was writing in 1976.)

It is interesting to note that whereas now all major collections are sold by way of public auction, in the past there was a tendency for some collectors to dispose of their treasures direct to a dealer. For example, in the summer of 1940, Seaby's bought the Major Philip Carlyon-Britton Collection of English milled and Raymond Carlyon-Britton's first collection of Ancient British, Anglo-Saxon and Norman coins. After the War, the company secured the S. R. Naish collection of more than 1,700 specimens. This was offered in its entirety in one list (the forerunner of the *Coin & Medal Bulletin*). 1,200 items sold within ten days and many pieces could have been sold ten times over. The coin business was very brisk after the War; Seaby's continued to buy entire cabinets. For example, in 1959, the company obtained the third and largest collection by Raymond Carlyon-Britton. It comprised some 10,000 English hammered, Scottish, Irish and Anglo-Gallic Coins.

It was not until the 1950s that a truly remarkable sale took place; the *Palace Collections of Egypt* formed by ex-King Farouk. It is also acknowledged that this acted as one of the post-war catalysts for the pursuit of coin collecting. The cataloguing was undertaken by Fred Baldwin of A. H. Baldwin & Sons Ltd., London. There were over 8,500 gold pieces and 164 platinum items – the latter number amounted to five times the quantity of any previous platinum coin sale ever held. As Frank Herrmann comments in *Sotheby's – Portrait of An Auction House* (London, 1980), 'In fact, when the coin catalogue eventually appeared, it was widely likened to a telephone directory, for nothing of that size had ever been produced for a single series of sales.'

Many stories have been told of this sale. There are accounts of the cataloguers working under armed guard, but my favourite tale initially has a 'ghostly' air. I quote Herrmann: 'A group of Sotheby experts stood chatting to members of the palace staff in the immense entrance hall of Koubbeh. Suddenly a portly figure in resplendent white uniform, accompanied by three uniformed officers, appeared at the top of the stairs. It could have only been Farouk. The Egyptians fell on their knees, while the Englishmen gasped. It was a moment of extraordinary tension which only relaxed when the figure in white winked. It proved to be an actor who was to play Farouk in a forthcoming film about the deposed monarch, who had donned Farouk's uniform to see whether he resembled the monarch. The likeness was staggering. It highlighted the prevailing tension of the period.'

In 1954 Mrs Emery May Holden Norweb attended the King Farouk sale in Cairo. She acquired many great coins and also met Mr David Spink of Spink & Son Ltd. Whether as a consequence of her meeting with David Spink, or not, Mrs Norweb developed a keen interest in adding to her English coin collection from the mid-1950s. As will be revealed later, this collection, which began to be sold in 1985 after Mrs Norweb's death, has been described as the best collection of its type to have appeared on the London market since the Murdoch cabinet was placed under the hammer at the turn of the century.

Before leaving Cairo, it is interesting to note from Bert Seaby's *Recollections*, that B. A. Seaby Ltd. had sold King Farouk many pieces, and that 'even during the War years, when Rommel's troops were almost at the gates of Cairo, we continued to receive lengthy cables marked "TOP PRIORITY" ordering coins from our list. He specialised in rare patterns and proofs, and we were somewhat put out when the Egyptians refused to withdraw from the sale two rare platinum pieces which had not been paid for, having arrived only a day or two before the King was forced to abdicate.'

Meanwhile, back in London, a fabulous collection of Ancient, English, Scottish, Irish and medieval European coins was being prepared to be placed on the auction block. This was the R. C. Lockett Collection. It was sold by Glendining & Co. in thirteen portions between June 1955 and October 1961. It realised a total of £367,365. At the time many collectors were staggered at the prices that individual coins commanded. The truth of the matter was that the offering acted as a catalyst and consequently stimulated demand. The result was higher prices.

One of the pieces offered at the Lockett sale was a 1644 silver crown struck at the Oxford Mint during the Civil War period of the reign of Charles I. Specimens are extremely rare. The obverse of the coin features the King on horseback – a view of the city of Oxford appears below. In 1956 it sold for £760. The same piece was offered at Spink Coin Auctions' first sale in 1978. It then realised £25,000. In 1970 the specimen had sold for £20,000.

It was in the 1960s that coin collecting really gathered momentum in the U.K. My own interest in coins developed in the early 1960s, when I was a schoolboy. I can remember one particular little event from those distant days. During a family holiday to North Wales I called at a jeweller's that also dealt in coins. The proprietor of this modest establishment informed my parents that it was a shame that I had not developed an interest in coins earlier (I was only nine at the time), for, 'prices had increased out of all proportion of late'! If only he had known what was in store over the next quarter century!

Increased leisure, economic prosperity and a greater awareness in general of items from the past, all combined to boost an interest in collecting coins. The situation in the U.K. was further stimulated by the country's decimalisation of its currency in February 1971. To quote H. A. Seaby's *Reflections* (1976) again. 'It was between 1966 and 1969 that the general public went slightly mad over modern coinage, hoarding coins from circulation in anticipation that fortunes were to be made after Britain decimalised her currency. With everyone doing the same thing it was eventually obvious that the fortunes were going to be very small. The same hysteria affected some collectors and at one time enormous prices were being paid for quite modern coins. Even before we reached "D" day the bubble had burst, but at this time there were some three hundred coin dealers scattered around the country, though some have now fallen by the wayside.'

Decimal Day passed, and although many had burnt their fingers with ultra modern coins, a considerable interest remained for antique and pre-1900 pieces. There were an amazing number of small-time dealers. Every town appeared to have at least one 'professional numismatist'. Some were purely mail-order; others worked from small shops, sometimes combining their coin dealing activities with general antiques. Others operated from market stalls. There was a very prosperous atmosphere.

This was an inflationary period and it was at this point in time that coins were looked upon as an ideal form of alternative investment. Advertisements appeared with such headlines as, 'Coins are probably the world's finest investment', and offered readers a free book, 'that tells you just why'. The sharpest rise in value came in 1973 and 1974 when the values of many conventional securities were collapsing. To quote Seaby's *Standard Catalogue* for 1975:

'Prices have again been the main talking point amongst collectors and dealers in 1974. A new world record price for a coin was established in May when an Athenian silver dekadrachm of about 470 BC realised Sw.Fr.820,000 (about £125,000) at a public auction held in Zurich. British coins have not yet attained this dizzy height but new records for

THE MARKET: PAST, PRESENT AND FUTURE

English coins were reached when a Henry VII gold sovereign and a specimen of the celebrated Charles I pattern silver crown sold in London in June for £20,000 each.'

However, these were not the highest prices that British coins achieved at auction. At the time that the *Standard Catalogue* was at press, Sotheby's offered the previously mentioned Captain K. J. Douglas-Morris R.N.'s collection of English milled gold. The top price at this sale was £26,000 paid for a 1703 VIGO five guinea piece. The catalogue description reads: 'light marks and minor surface blemishes but otherwise about extremely fine and extremely rare, probably one of the most desirable English gold coins and only about 20 specimens known'.

For the first time the 'View and Review' of Seaby's *Standard Catalogue* gave examples of price rises for specific coins. These make interesting reading: (see Table 5.1)

Table 5.1. Retail values extracted from Seaby's *Standard Catalogue*

Some hammered coins:	Condition	1970 £	1974 £	1975 £
Alfred, 'London' penny	F	110	225	260
William I, 'PAXS' penny	F	14	25	30
Edward I, penny	F	2	3½	4
Henry VII, young head groat	F	4½	12	16
Elizabeth I, 30s sovereign	F	225	500	1400
Elizabeth I, silver halfcrown	F	42	70	140
Some milled coins:				
Charles I, 'Briot' crown	VF	130	250	350
Charles II, 'elephant' 2 gns	F	80	175	350
George III, 'spade' guinea	VF	25	75	130
George III, Bank of England $	VF	17½	25	35
George III, 'cartwheel' twopence	VF	5	5	6
George III, sovereign 1817	VF	30	60	125
Victoria, £5, 1887	EF	120	450	525
Victoria, 'Gothic' crown 1847	EF	90	160	250
Victoria, 'Bun' penny 1860	EF	15	7	8
George V, crown, 1935	EF	6	5½	6½
Elizabeth II, sovereign 1962	EF	6¼	14	26

It will be noted that the only falls were recorded in copper and modern series. The reason for the latter has already been explained. Copper fell from popularity following just over a decade of increasing values. The appearance of C. Wilson Peck's mammoth work *English, Copper, Tin and Bronze Coins in the British Museum 1558–1958* in 1960 inspired many to collect this material. The popularity of the series, and hence of the standard work on the subject, is well-illustrated by the fact that a second edition of the tome appeared in 1964 and a photolithographic reprint in 1970.

ANCIENT GREEK: Gold stater of King Croesus of Lydia featuring the foreparts of a lion and a bull confronting each other, c.560–546 BC. The reverse of a 'punch mark' of co-joined incused squares of irregular size. This is probably one of the first gold coin types struck. Reproduced at twice actual size.
ANCIENT GREEK: Ptolemaic Kingdom of Egypt. Silver tetradrachm of Cleopatra VIII 51–30 BC (*the* Cleopatra). Undoubtedly the finest known specimen of this extremely rare coin. Sold for £65,000, October 1984. Reproduced at twice actual size. *Courtesy Christie's*.
3 ANCIENT GREEK: Dekadrachm of the artist Euainetos c.380 BC, from Sicily. The obverse shows a fast quadriga driven to the left by a charioteer who is crowned by Nike flying above. The reverse bears the head of Arethusa with four dolphins. *Courtesy Sotheby's*.

4 ANCIENT ROMAN: Galerius Maximianus as Caesar, AD 297. Medallion of 5 aurei. Of the highest rarity. Only one other example known. Ex Brand Collection. Sold July 1982 for Sw. Fr. 275,000 by Sotheby's. Reproduced at twice actual size. *Courtesy Sotheby's.* 5 BYZANTINE: Constantine VIII (1025–28 AD) gold histamenon minted at Constantinople. Reproduced at twice actual size. 6 ISLAMIC: A gold dinar of the Umayyad Caliph Abd al-Malik bin Marwan struck in the year 78AH (AD 697–698). This date is the second year in the Classical Islamic series and is the earliest one normally available to the collector. *Courtesy Spink.*

7 ENGLAND: A silver penny of Queen Cynethryth, wife of King Offa, struck in Canterbury c. AD 790. Actual size and obverse enlargement. *Courtesy Spink.*
8 ENGLAND: Henry VII sovereign 1489 – the first regular issue of the denomination. When auctioned in 1956 it realised £1,400 ... in June 1983 it sold for £36,000 at Spink Coin Auctions. *Courtesy Spink Coin Auctions.* **9** ENGLAND: Henry VII testoon or shilling of the profile issue (1502–4). This piece marks the beginning of England's modern coinage. Half a century after Pisanello's death, the English coinage, like the Continental, was becoming infused with Renaissance ideas. This was the first English coin to bear a realistic portrait. *Courtesy Spink Coin Auctions.*

10 ENGLAND: Henry III Gold Penny of 'Twenty Pence'. c.1257. Obverse: Bearded figure of the king holding an orb and sceptre and seated on a throne. Reverse: Voided cross. Reproduced at twice actual size. Very fine, of the highest rarity and one of the most spectacular coins in the entire British series. Sold at auction in June 1985 for £65,000. Reproduced at twice actual size. *Courtesy Spink Coin Auctions.* **11** ENGLAND: Elizabeth I gold half pound struck on Eloye Mestrelle's machinery from dies engraved by Derick Anthony, c.1565. Sold for £10,000 in June 1980. *Courtesy Spink Coin Auctions.* **12** ENGLAND: Queen Victoria's effigy as it appeared on the Jubilee Coinage of 1887–93. The work of J. E. Boehm, it was subjected to criticism, mainly because of the small crown perched on the top of the Queen's head. Nevertheless, place your finger over the crown and the portrait is perfectly proportioned. Clearly the headgear did not suit Her Majesty, but the Queen insisted on being portrayed wearing the piece, which can still be viewed at the Tower of London.

ENGLAND: The 'Oxford Crown' of ...44. This extremely rare piece is the ...rk of Thomas Rawlins. It is the only English coin to bear a city view. Reproduced at twice actual size.

14 AUSTRALIA: New South Wales Five Shillings or 'Holey dollar' 1813. The host coin is a Charles III 8 reales struck at Madrid in 1802. *Courtesy Spink (Australia)*.
15 AUSTRALIA: New South Wales, Fifteen Pence or 'Dump', 1813. Reproduced at twice actual size. *Courtesy Spink (Australia)*. **16** GERMANY: Brandenburg – Prussia. 1647 half-thaler of Frederick Willi struck in gold. Ex Brand Collection. S July 1982 by Sotheby's for Sw. Fr. 82 *Courtesy Sotheby's.* **17** SWITZERLA Undated double thaler struck at Ba c.1700. The obverse features a nor eastern view of the city. Ex Brand Coll tion. *Courtesy Sotheby's.* Half actual size

18 U.S.A.: 1834 silver quarter dollar. Engraved by William Kneass. Reproduced at twice actual size. **19** U.S.A.: Gold pattern four dollar, the 'Stella', struck in 1879 at the Philadelphia Mint from a design by Charles E. Barber. Reproduced at twice actual size.

20

20 A coin cabinet, formerly housing part of the Roman coin collection of His Grace the Duke of Northumberland. A fine piece in the George II style, made c.1850. Made of mahogany veneer, the rectangular moulded top is removable by a sliding action to reveal an open storage compartment. The whole is banded throughout with laburnum wood. The ten drawers have numbered ivory pulls. Each drawer is pierced to hold thirty-five coins. *Courtesy Sotheby's.*

Taking the coins illustrated in Table 5.1 as a portfolio, the statistically orientated will be interested to learn that it increased in retail value from 1970 to 1975 by 297 per cent. The price rises between 1970 and 1974 and 1974 and 1975 were, respectively, 123.6 per cent and 77.5 per cent. Note that the prices preceed the date of the catalogue by one year. Therefore, the 77.5 per cent annual increase relates to market movements from 1973 to 1974.

Appropriately, when in 1979 *The Daily Telegraph* invited B. A. Seaby Ltd. to compile the *Seaby Index* of English coin prices, 1974 was taken as the base year.

Although in 1974 prices collapsed in certain areas, the market was still relatively stable. The dip in values was viewed partly as a consolidation. With the almost meteoric rise from 1973 to 1974, some dealers and collectors/investors were so dazzled that they paid over the odds for average material. In other words, they secured only average coins, but paid the price of a choice specimen. The market consequently adjusted prices downwards for coins that had been enthusiastically 'bid up' by misguided participants at auctions in the previous year. The situation could be viewed as a readjustment of prices when rationality had returned. Downward pressure on values was further aggravated by investors selling their 'portfolios'. However, as can be seen from the *Seaby Index* of English Milled Coins (1662–1953) in Figure 5.1, the situation did not last long, for from 1974 to 1975 this series rose by an average of 29 per cent – a relatively moderate rise considering the situation in 1973 to 1974, but nevertheless a move in the right direction.

Generally coins gradually increased in value until towards the end of the 1970s. Matters altered dramatically in 1979. I quote my column in *The Daily Telegraph* for 30 August 1980:

Going for quality in coins
During the 1970–80 auction season, the London sale rooms sold nearly £6 million of coins, medals and related material. While this unprecedented sum reflects the magnitude of the trade in such items as historical coins, it does not tell the complete story.

The coin market has been extremely buoyant for choice specimens. Record after record was broken at auction. Although certain areas of the antique market became somewhat depressed towards the end of the season there was no sign of flagging in the demand for choice numismatic items.

Peter Seaby, the Chairman of the London dealers, B. A. Seaby Limited, said: 'Over the last twelve months, there has been a substantial movement in the prices of all choice English coins in all metals. Some items have increased by 40 per cent or more in value. On the other hand, inferior quality coins have moved very little.'

Undoubtedly the two-tier market structure has become more marked. There are coins that are keenly sought by the collector and those that are

THE MARKET: PAST, PRESENT AND FUTURE

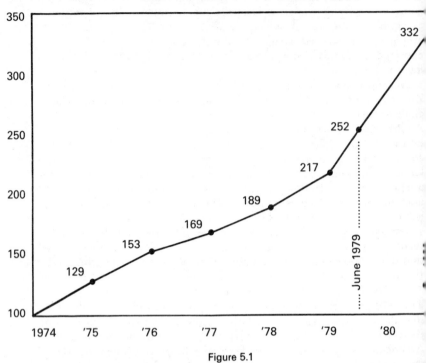

Figure 5.1

purchased by those seeking an alternative investment in addition to an interesting numismatic piece. The latter seek specimens in top-grade condition. The demand for such pieces is reflected in their price. In May, for example, Christie's sold an 1847 Gothic crown in absolute mint condition for £1,400.

Raymond Sancroft-Baker of the Coin Department comments: 'The price shows how significant quality can be. If it had had even the slightest mark, I feel sure it would only have realised half that sum.'

However, with the buoyancy of the market, the choicest specimens do not necessarily appear at auction. For example, Spink sold a Charles I gold 1642 Triple Unite (or £3 piece) of the Shrewsbury Mint in July 1985 for £45,000. This is considered the highest price ever paid for a British coin. The piece – the only other example of which is in the British Museum – was last sold in 1968 for £11,000.

The striving for quality is not just restricted to British coins. In February Sotheby's sold a silver stater struck at Thurium, circa 400–350 BC. Estimated at between £400 and £500, it sold for £1,050. Quality Greek coins have been scarce on the London market during the

68

1979–80 season – hence the high prices paid when they have appeared. A Sotheby spokesman said: 'On the other hand, medium quality Greek coins have fetched prices very much in line with estimates.'

Estimates have meant little where quality was concerned. For example, Spink Coin Auctions' June sale realised more than double the expected total. A 1746 crown in extremely fine condition (reverse better) fetched £4,200 against an estimate of £1,500.

One of the most dramatic European sales was held by Spink in Zurich. The two-day event realised more than £900,000. International dealers and collectors were prepared to pay almost any price for quality. An Australian 1864 half-sovereign sold for £4,200, or sixteen times the estimate. It must be stressed that these record prices are for coins in A1 condition. Specimens in average or below average condition have not fared so well. Indeed, some very rare but poor grade coins purchased at auction in February 1979 were resold at auction in June 1980. After the auctioneer's commission had been deducted, the seller made an average loss of 21 per cent.

The stability of the 'super' coin market is dependent upon the punters turning into dedicated, albeit wealthy, collectors. There is every indication that those who purchase coins for gain soon become fascinated by the absorbing subject of numismatics.'

The boom of the late 1970s and early 1980s caused the cynics to remark that there were no longer any coin collectors – just investors. Certainly there was a great deal of buying for financial gain in the States, for Americans could invest in collectables via retirement plans and receive various tax advantages into the bargain. Prices for U.S. material rose sharply. Indeed, the world auction price for a coin established at a Bowers and Ruddy sale of the Garrett Collection in November 1979, has as yet not been broken. The record is for a 1787 Brasher gold doubloon in MS-63. It sold for US$725,000.

The coin market was fuelled by the bullion boom of 1979–80. Silver reached US$52.50 an ounce in January 1980. The story of how two of the world's richest families – the Hunts of Texas and the House of Saud – tried to corner the silver market is excellently told in Stephen Fay's *The Great Silver Bubble* (London, 1982). Gold at the time was well over US$800 an ounce. Many coin dealers trade in bullion as an adjunct to their main businesses. Naturally, the profits they were generating from this activity was substantial. As the coin market was buoyant, the money was channelled in that direction.

Prices for U.S. material rose so sharply and suddenly that European coins looked extremely attractive by comparison. American dealers, flush with funds from their bullion activities, crossed the Atlantic and invaded the London and continental auction houses. As money was no object, prices for material boomed. Despite the Reagan Administration repealing the legislation which gave tax advantages to investors in

69

collectables, the demand did not wane. It was not just the Americans who were buying – the whole world was hungry for coins.

Then the economic recession took hold. Initially the coin market seemed impervious to the gloom that left its mark on the fine art market in general. However, it was not long before auction realisations for coins also began to fall. In September 1983 the Editorial in Spink's *Numismatic Circular* stated: 'It cannot be denied that the prices of coins has declined in recent months. This is the first ever significant fall.' Whereas falls in the value of numismatic material had been experienced in the past, such movements were generally viewed as little more than temporary hiccups.

The 'Guide to Market Trends and Investment' in the 1983 edition of *Coin Market Values* (A Link House Publication), which went to press in 1982, stated: 'Last year we commented on the collapse of the American market, and the effect that was having on coins in Europe. In the last twelve months, the booms in Australia and South Africa have also declined, and we have definitely seen the icy fingers of the world recession tighten their grip on the whole coin market.' The following year, under the heading 'Confidence Returns', the same column reported, 'We are happy to say this year that there are definite signs of improvement. At the time of writing we are almost seeing the light at the end of the tunnel. There has been a gradual trickle of decent prices being reported from auction rooms and the same thing is happening at the coin shows, dealers are now beginning to talk a little more optimistically, although they are not quite so ebullient as they were a few years ago.' Although the column was cautiously optimistic in the following two years, there was one common theme ... 'There is definitely a shortage of collectors, but, not of interest.'

The 'View and Review' in the 20th edition of Seaby's *Standard Catalogue* which went to press in August 1984, made some very good points:

'This last year has seen a widening gap between both the demand and the values of coins in a superlative state of preservation and those in a grade suitable to the needs of the average collector. Naturally, miniature works of art, into which category coins must fall, if in an exquisite state, will always be vigorously competed for by both collector and investor alike: this has always been and will rightly continue to be so.

However, we are surprised at the general slackness of demand for slightly lower grade (and consequently much cheaper) but still eminently collectable coins, and wonder whether some collectors may be failing to take advantage of a whole range of interesting and moderately priced coins which are available to suit individual pocket and interest.

To strive for perfection in a collection is laudable – if time and money are no object, but we do consider that there may be many keen collectors who, in their long and often fruitless pursuit of perfection, are denying themselves the actual pleasure of owning more than just a handful of coins. It is very easy for aspiring collectors to be conditioned or brainwashed into believing that only perfect coins should be collected because anything less is not worth buying, thus too often the accent on the pleasure and enjoyment of the hobby is forgotten in the desire to sell expensive coins as an "investment". It is not true that the high priced perfect coin is always the best investment (if that is what it is bought for) as a glance at the prices realised at some classic sales over the last five years will show when compared to what similar pieces might realistically expect to bring today.

Demand is always the keyword to value in any branch of the art market and a steady demand for coins in all grades will allow the collector to enjoy his hobby with a degree of financial security. After all, there are few hobbies in the world today which can be taken up, enjoyed with relish and satisfaction, and in which after a number of years the secondhand equipment can be sold at a profit, or indeed without some loss. Our advice is to buy the coins you like at a price you can afford and get the most pleasure from your collection.'

In the next edition, the Editor noted, '... there is nothing to report this year as it has been fairly difficult to note any major trends apart from specialist coins in what has been a fairly active scene.' Indeed, there were some very good realisations at London auctions despite the market being in a state of flux. For example:

	Hammer Price – i.e. excluding Buyers' Premium, etc.
An English silver penny of William, Earl of Gloucester, probably struck at Cirencester. About very fine, toned, UNIQUE. (Spink, March 1982)	£10,200
Ancient Jewish tetradrachm struck during the period of the Bar Cochba War (AD 132–135). With surface deposit, very fine and extremely rare. (Sotheby's, March 1983)	£12,000
Islamic dinar of the Post-Reform Umayyad coinage. Struck for Yazid II ibn 'Abd al-Malik at Ifriqiya in 103 AH. Virtually uncirculated and extremely rare. (Sotheby's, April 1983)	£24,000
Islamic Dinar of the Ayyubid Rulers of Egypt and Syria. Struck for al-Nasir Salah al-din Yusuf I ibn Ayyub at Dimashq in 583 AH. Bold extremely fine and of the highest rarity. (Sotheby's, April 1983)	£26,000

THE MARKET: PAST, PRESENT AND FUTURE

Hammer Price – i.e. excluding Buyers' Premium, etc.

An English sovereign of Henry VII.
Short of flan, but very fine and excessively rare, one of the most spectacular coins in the entire English series. (Spink, June 1983) — £36,000

An English sovereign of thirty shillings of Edward VI.
Slightly weak to right of King's face, but very fine and toned, excessively rare. (Spink, June 1983) — £28,500

An English triple unite of Charles I struck at the Oxford Mint in 1643.
In mint state, a superb portrait coin of the highest rarity, only one other believed known. (Spink, June 1983) — £32,000

An English George noble of Henry VIII
Very fine, extremely rare. (Glendining's June 1983) — £10,200

An English fifty shilling piece of Oliver Cromwell, 1656.
Graze in field by ribbon tie, and some minor hairlines, otherwise extremely fine and brilliant, excessively rare. (Spink, October 1983)
Note: This coin sold at auction in 1972 for £3,600) — £19,000

A United States quarter-dollar 1804.
Good very fine, rare. (Glendining's, April 1983) — £11,000

A German undated (*c.*1760) thaler *struck in gold* of Francis I (Regensburg). Of 20 ducats weight. Characteristic flaws both sides and at edge, a few faint scratches due to cleaning, otherwise good very fine and apparently unpublished in this weight. (Sotheby, July 1984) — £13,500

Egyptian tetradrachm of Cleopatra VII.
Reverse slightly off centre and weakly struck, otherwise nearly extremely fine. Undoubtedly the finest known specimen of this extremely rare coin. (Christie's, October 1984) — £65,000

Roman aureus of Clodius Albinus.
About extremely fine and extremely rare. (Christie's, October 1984) — £45,000

Ancient Greek stater of Taras. Struck at Calabria *c.*344–38 BC.
Minor spade damage on face, otherwise extremely fine. (Spink, December 1984) — £27,000

Ancient Greek tetradrachm struck at Naxos in *c.*460 BC.
A well-centred example with minimal wear, dark tone, extremely fine. (Spink, December 1984) — £31,000

THE MARKET: PAST, PRESENT AND FUTURE

	Hammer Price – i.e. excluding Buyers' Premium, etc.
English 1937 Proof sovereign of Edward VIII. Some hairlines in field, otherwise brilliant, of the highest rarity. (Spink, December 1984)	£40,000
English proof set, 1839, £5.1s.4d. (15 coins). Five Pounds with some surface and edge marks and Halfcrown with two scratches in obverse field, otherwise practically as struck, silver toned, copper with light spotting, in original velvet-lined case of issue. (Spink, March 1985)	£19,500
Portuguese portugues of D. Manuel I. Very fine and extremely rare. (Sotheby's, 16 May 1985)	£18,000
Guatemalan 8-escudos, 1768. Surface slightly stained on reverse and has probably been cleaned, good fine to very fine and rare. (Sotheby's, June 1985)	£18,000
English Henry III gold penny of 'twenty pence'. Very fine, of the highest rarity and one of the most spectacular coins in the British series. (Spink, June 1985)	£65,000
Roman aureus of Otho. Extremely fine and rare. (Christie's, October 1985)	£24,000
English penny, 1933. Extremely fine and lightly patinated, of the highest rarity. (Sprink, November 1985)	£15,000
English pattern crown of Oliver Cromwell in gold. Die flaw, a few minor surface marks on obverse, otherwise extremely fine and of the highest rarity. (Spink, November 1985)	£30,000

Patrick Finn of Spink & Son Ltd. was reported in *The Daily Telegraph* on 11 May 1985: 'It must be a good time to buy coins since in many people's opinion, prices for *certain* material are now at 1976 levels.' However, why the prices quoted above, which are way above sums that the pieces would have realised in 1976? The explanation is that in the second quarter of the 1980s, a few really superb collections found their way on to the market. For example, in July 1982, Sotheby's began to offer the collection of the American brewer, Virgil M. Brand. From 1900 to his death in 1926, he spent about US$3m amassing his cabinet. Half of the collection was sold a few years after his death. The second portion was sold in ten parts in both London and Zurich and the 23,361 coins, or 6270 lots, sold for £4,514,334 over a three-year period. The same kind of sum is expected for the Norweb Collection, the cataloguing of which is being undertaken by Spink. Spink Coin Auctions are offering the

English collection in London, whilst Christie's placed the American material on the auction block in the States. Emery May Holden Norweb's collection is believed to exceed 50,000 specimens. She began collecting in 1904. In 1984 Christie's offered, 'Highly Important Ancient Coins' which was, 'formed with discernment and taste over a period of almost 40 years beginning in the early 1920s'. The 313 lots realised £1,184,775, the highest figure yet for a one-day coin sale in the U.K. The high quality of material in these three sales, together with other choice offerings, have resulted in high prices being obtained when the market generally was in a state of flux. It emphasises that there is a demand for choice rarities. The problem has been with material not falling into this category.

Above it was stated that, 'there is a definite shortage of collectors, but not of interest'. This point is well illustrated by the fact that at the turn of the century, the membership of the British Numismatic Society was about 500 ... eighty-odd years later and the membership roll contains roughly the same number of names. Does this mean that the demand for material has remained static over the years? It does not. However, it emphasises that collectors are no longer as attracted to the purely academic aspect of the subject. For example, the Royal Mint Collectors Club has a six figure membership. If only the British Numismatic Trade Association could, through a concerted effort, lure a small percentage of those interested in modern issues to the more fascinating subject of old coins, its membership would benefit. Indeed, the market would be revitalised dramatically.

The long-term prospects for the coin market are by no means bleak. Admittedly, it suffered a set-back in the early 1980s and recovery has been patchy so far. In 1979 Editorial Comment in *The Daily Telegraph* reflected that

'Coin values have risen relatively slowly over the past few years, probably because of a much higher proportion of collectors and the smaller number of investors compared with other investments such as antiques and stamps. But this situation has begun to change. One of the reasons is the growing demand for investment items which are small, portable and interesting as well as potentially valuable. Coins are a logical choice although they are nothing like as widely collected as stamps. But most coins have historical interest and an aesthetic appeal, and gold and silver coins have an intrinsic value as well.'

Whilst it is the 'historical interest and aesthetic appeal' that is the crux of the lure of numismatics, one cannot discount repeats of *The Daily Telegraph*'s message appearing in the future. Unlike other collecting fields, numismatics has already attracted the collector for over 2,000 years and there is no reason why this should alter fundamentally. After all, numismatics is one of man's oldest collecting pursuits.

6
Protecting Coins

Having emphasised in chapter 2 that a coin's exact state of preservation is of prime importance in determining its value, the reader will appreciate that great care should be taken in storing coins. Having acquired historic or modern coins that may have miraculously escaped the rigours of circulation, one should not celebrate the event by throwing them into an old tin and shaking it to ascertain what kind of noise they make when jostled together. 'No one would be so foolish,' you may say, but having seen a proof set that had been cleaned with wire wool, I consider anything is possible. Remember that even the minutest scratches can reduce a coin's value, so care should be taken to ensure that coins in the collection do not become damaged. The careless handling of a specimen, or thoughtless storing, will result in financial loss to its owner.

Coins are generally sturdy objects, and no great skill is required to ensure that damage is not done. The following advice is given to help safeguard a collection:

1 Coins should always be held between thumb and finger so that only the edge is touched.
2 On no account touch the surface of the coin, for human fingers contain a corrosive salt which can cause silver coins to tarnish and can otherwise damage copper and bronze coins.
3 Dropping a coin on to a hard surface will damaged the coin. As accidents do happen, ensure that either a carpet is at one's feet or a padded tray or the like is on the table to cushion a coin's fall.
4 Store coins in moisture-free conditions.
5 Do not place items in contact with each other or with any metal.
6 If possible, isolate items from the air and remember that sunlight can tarnish a coin very quickly.
7 Only use a storage system from inert materials, i.e. those that are available from established accessory stockists and which have been well tried and tested and are not harmful to coins.

Furthermore, it is advised that coins should NOT BE CLEANED. However, surface *dirt*, which means dirt and not oxide, may be removed from gold and silver coins as follows:

Gold Bath in methylated spirits, but, on no account rub the surface of the piece.

Silver Loose surface dirt can be removed carefully with a soft non-man-made fibre brush. Deeper surface debris *can* generally be removed by bathing the offending piece in ammonia and carefully dabbing it dry with cotton wool.

Copper and bronze coins cannot be satisfactorily cleaned. Museums will advise how to preserve badly corroded examples. It is again stressed that numismatic items *should not be cleaned*. Nevertheless I know that more coins are ruined each year by injudicious cleaning than by any other means and I do not expect the situation to change, despite this warning.

Storing coins

Paper envelopes

The most economical method of storing coins is the use of small paper envelopes. However, although this method allows the collector to write a description of the piece on the exterior of the coin's abode, it is far from attractive visually, as the coin can only be viewed by removing it from the envelope. Special coin envelopes made from dried paper are obtainable from dealers. The use of ordinary small envelopes can damage the enclosed coin, for ordinary paper has a high water content. Furthermore, the glue on the flaps of commercial envelopes may cause metal within a close proximity to react chemically, which can damage the coin. Special cardboard boxes are marketed to hold coin envelopes and these provide a simple and unobtrusive means of storage.

Transparent envelopes

PVC plastic coin envelopes were introduced in the 1960s. Some of the leading dealers hesitated to recommend them as they felt that there might be possibilities of corrosion from long-term storage. They were later proved right, for PVC oozes a chemical plasticizer which reacts with a coin's copper content (a metal which is present in most coins; even gold and silver specimens contain it as an alloy). PVC plastic also reacts with water vapour in the atmosphere to form hydrochloric acid, which is another enemy of coins.

PVC envelopes should therefore be avoided, but the plastic industry does now offer acceptable alternatives: items made from acrylics, polypropylene and polystyrene. The coin accessory trade markets specially prepared envelopes, which are claimed to be 100 per cent free from harmful chemicals. Some have tabs along the opening edge which allow the collector to write a description of the coin. Others contain white cards with a punched-out coin recess designed to hold a specific denomination, whilst others contain a folding card with a clear-film-covered coin recess that seals the coin into place to combat the effects of oxidisation. Transparent envelopes may be stored in either plastic or cardboard boxes, like paper envelopes.

Coin albums

A wide range of coin albums are marketed today. They consist basically of transparent pages with pockets to hold the coins. The pages are housed in a ring binder. Care should be taken to ensure that they are manufactured from safe materials, so as with transparent envelopes, PVC is definitely to be avoided. As with all merchandise, some makes of coin album are better than others, and 'you only get what you pay for'.

Many people do not appreciate that a full album can be very heavy; therefore ensure that the one that you decide to buy is well-made. Check that the cover, 'hinges' and the pages of the album are adequately robust. Dealers will be pleased to give advice on the various makes and types of album available. Consider the size of coins it is destined to hold – in other words, select pages that have inserts which are suitable for the pieces in your collection. There is little point in purchasing pages designed for displaying crowns, if the collection mainly consists of small English silver pennies, and so on. Some collectors prefer only to half fill their albums and utilise the gaps for holding a description of the coins displayed. This is not necessary if the manufacturer has made provision for including a description of the contents. New types of albums frequently appear on the market and details of the range currently available may be obtained from dealers; or information may be gathered from advertisements or features in the coin press. Albums are relatively inexpensive.

Cabinets

The traditional method of housing a coin collection is in a wooden coin-cabinet. Basically this consists of a number of trays which are pierced to hold the collection. The trays are housed in a cabinet which may be fitted with doors that can be locked. Sizes can vary from a twelve-inch cube right up to a large cupboard.

Again great care should be taken to ensure that the material from which the cabinet is constructed is not harmful to coins. Well-seasoned mahogany, walnut or rosewood are recommended, and mahogany is generally preferred. On no account should cabinets be made from resinous softwoods, as the moisture content will have an adverse effect on the coins. Oak should also be avoided as it damages coins.

With the decline in the number of skilled craftsmen in recent years, and the scarcity of well-seasoned wood, coin cabinets have risen in price. Nevertheless, specialist manufacturers do manage to produce this traditional means of coin storage at a competitive price. The cost naturally depends on the size and aesthetic appeal of the cabinet. Details of the range available and prices may be obtained from dealers or from the advertisements in the coin press.

Choose a combination of trays containing the optimum size of insert for housing the coins. To prevent direct contact with the wood, each insert generally contains a felt or velvet disc. These are available from coin dealers. Not only do these discs prevent any chemical reaction from the coins being in contact with the wood, but they also alleviate 'cabinet friction'. If a tray is removed sharply from the cabinet, the coins will move in their inserts. If the felt is not in position, the coins will rub against the base of the tray, which causes wear. One does occasionally see a coin described as having 'cabinet friction'. It is therefore also essential that a tray glides easily upon runners. Some cheaper 'cabinets' have trays that stack upon each other. In this case, to prevent any damaging contact with coins stored in the tray below, the bottom of each tray should be padded with some suitable material. It is also essential that coins do not protrude above the top of the insert, for this can cause the coin to be damaged.

Some people are tempted to try their hand at making their own coin cabinet. I wish them luck. They will probably discover that it is not as easy a task as they thought. However, for those that do decide to follow this course, I emphasise that the chosen mahogany or rosewood must be well-seasoned.

An alternative to a new cabinet, of course, is a secondhand one. However, do not image that these are necessarily cheaper than brand new pieces. Admittedly, a relatively new cabinet can be purchased privately at below the price of a brand new item either by replying to a classified advertisement in the trade press or through a personal contact. However, there is great demand for the attractive 'old' cabinets, i.e. late nineteenth or early twentieth century, which appear at auction from time to time. This demand is reflected in the prices realised by such pieces. For example, the first portion of *The Pridmore Collection of 'The Coins of the British Commonwealth of Nations'* (sold by Glendining & Co., London, 21 & 22 September 1981) concluded with the following lot:

> 'An attractive burr-walnut cabinet, $20\frac{3}{4}$in. high, 12 in. wide and 11 in. deep, with double doors, lock and key, containing 31 trays with 471 finger-pierced, felt-lined holes (28 trays with 16 holes of $1\frac{7}{8}$in., two trays with 9 holes of $2\frac{1}{2}$in., one tray with 4 holes of $3\frac{1}{2}$ inches and one hole of $2\frac{1}{2}$in.) and a drawer $1\frac{3}{8}$in. *In very good condition, a most useful coin cabinet.*'

It realised £780. The reference to finger-piercing may confuse the reader. To assist the collector in removing his coins from the trays, each recess has a small hole through which the coin can be pushed upwards with a finger, say, of the left hand, thus allowing the piece to be picked up easily by the edge with the thumb and index finger of the right hand. This facility is most useful. Try picking up a currency coin by its edge from any flat surface and compare this action to picking up the same coin in a like manner when it is balanced on the finger tip. Finger-pierced recesses in a coin-tray are convenient, and also alleviate the danger of inadvertently touching the surface of a coin. If thinking of buying any cabinet, make sure that it has this facility.

The cabinet in the Pridmore sale was a most attractive example. It is quite possible for very acceptable coin cabinets to be purchased at auction for far less than this figure. Indeed, quite serviceable 'old' cabinets have been sold at London auctions for as little as £50. Remember that a broken cabinet can be repaired. The handyman will find it far easier to restore a damaged cabinet than to build his own entirely.

In recent years, coin cabinets have fallen a little from favour with collectors. Whilst the advent of transparent envelopes and coin albums can account for some of the proportionate fall in demand, the main reason is probably security.

Security

It is quite amazing how many numismatists do not insure their coin collections. Such individuals automatically insure their house, car and personal effects, but it never crosses their mind to insure their coins. It is recommended that whether one collects coins for pleasure or investment, that a reliable dealer or insurance company or broker be consulted and a suitable insurance policy effected. In the event of theft, the premium is a small price to pay for financial recompense.

However, money alone cannot replace a collection that has been slowly formed over the years. It may have taken ages to acquire an elusive coin, or a particular specimen in the collection may be the finest the collector has seen, and similar items available in the market, however good, are just not as good as the piece acquired. Perhaps, it is the toning as opposed to the state of preservation that makes a coin 'special' in an individual's eyes. In other words, the collector can become very attached to his own coins and any similar example would never completely satisfy. The pure investor may not become as attached to individual coins, nevertheless their replacement may not be assumed to be a matter of course.

Therefore, regardless of the insurance cover, care should be taken to ensure that the coins in one's possession are not stolen. Admittedly, when the value exceeds a certain figure, and this in turn depends upon the location in which they are stored, the insurers will insist that certain physical and other precautions are taken. For example, they may insist that when not being viewed, the collection is kept in a safe in the home, or that a burglar alarm system be installed.

However, the latter is not an alternative for good physical security. Such a system will warn of an intruder's presence, but it does not prevent him from entering the premises. Any form of alarm should therefore be backed by stout locks on doors and windows. These latter precautions are not especially for the coin collector, but for anyone, whether or not they have items of value to interest the thief. Quite frequently, intruders, disappointed at being unable to find some small items of value that can easily be removed, perform acts of vandalism that are distressing to the householder.

All external doors should be fitted with good quality locks, i.e. five-lever mortice locks produced by a well-established company that has an undoubted reputation for its merchandise. Similarly stout locks should be fitted to all easily accessible windows, and do not forget those on the first floor that are easily approached by way of flat roofs. Advice on home security is generally available from insurance companies and police authorities. The average home is far from secure; yet for very little capital expenditure you can ensure that your home is not easy game for the potential intruder.

The beauty of coins lies partly in the fact that they are small. This is an advantage both to the thief and to those that wish to give them protection. Whilst a large safe will be required for certain objets d'art, coins are extremely economical regarding storage space. Although a small free-standing safe may be required to house a coin cabinet, a coin album may be accommodated in a good sized wall safe. Coins housed in transparent envelopes can be stored in an under-floor safe. Don't forget to store coins in dry conditions; it is prudent to place the transparent envelopes in an airtight container if there is the slightest hint of dampness in an under-floor safe.

There are other obvious precautions that can be taken. Do not broadcast the fact that there are items of value in the house. 'Walls have ears' and careless talk may be very valuable information for the criminal fraternity. When away from home for a few days, or for a longer period, cancel the papers and any other daily deliveries. There is no need to advertise the fact that your home is unattended. It may be considered wise to remove the collection to a safe deposit for the period of extended absence; indeed many collectors always keep the bulk of their collection at their banker's or in a safe deposit. The small annual rental is considered well worthwhile.

It is also prudent to keep a record of each coin in the collection. In addition to recording a description of the items, a note should also be made of any distinguishing marks, the condition of each piece and the catalogue number of its type in the standard catalogue relating to the series. If possible, supplement these records wih photographic documentation of the collection. The cost of taking this step with the entire collection may be prohibitive, but the more valuable items should be preserved on celluloid. In the unfortunate event of theft, these records and any photographs can be invaluable. If purchasing an expensive coin from a dealer, it is well worthwhile asking if a photograph of the piece is available. In most cases, it is supplied with the dealer's compliments. For obvious reasons do *not* keep the records of the collection with the coins!

Finally, to record the prices paid for individual specimens is not only essential to see how one's 'investment' is progressing, but also makes interesting reading in years to come. Each year, just prior to renewing the insurance policy relating to the collection, it is essential to have the coins valued. This may be done either by a dealer (who will make a charge) or by the collector, who having kept abreast of market prices will know how much he would have to spend to replace the items in the case of total loss. Keeping the collection insured at correct replacement values is as important as effecting insurance in the first place. Care should therefore be taken to ensure that new acquisitions are insured. It is easy to overlook this in the enthusiasm surrounding a new purchase.

7
Selling Coins

> '*I have heard of a man who had a mind to sell his house, and therefore carried a piece of brick in his pocket, which he showed as a pattern to encourage purchasers.*'
> Jonathan Swift, The Drapier's Letters No. 2 (4 August 1724)

At some time the collector may wish to sell a coin or two. Certain specimens may no longer appeal, better examples may have been obtained, or simply there may be a need to raise some capital. Circumstances could mean that a decision is reached to sell the whole collection – the investor of course may consider that the time is right to realise his investment and sell his portfolio.

Disposing of a few coins, let alone a collection, should be approached with as much care as was taken in acquiring the pieces in the first place. Whereas the object at the time of purchase was to pay as little as possible, at the time of disposal, the goal is obviously to obtain the highest sum possible.

Selling may therefore be viewed as buying in reverse. The sources available to the vendor are precisely the same as for the purchaser of coins. Below, the advantages and disadvantages of sale by private treaty to the trade or by way of auction are outlined.

Private treaty

In chapter 3, 'Buying Coins', the purchase of material from a private individual was not recommended until a competent degree of knowledge had been acquired by the potential purchaser. When acquiring coins in this way, it was advised that an independent valuation be obtained in order to prevent any aggravation and embarrassment at a later date. The concern there was with the purchaser. However, it should be borne in mind that a vendor can under-price as well as over-price specimens, particularly if he has not followed the market for some time. However, do bear in mind that a dealer or auction house generally makes a charge for a valuation, if one is sought, and even if one has been out of touch with market prices for some time, it is easy to become acquainted with them relatively quickly. The 'retired' collector, unlike the new entrant, knows where to obtain the latest price information.

Whilst there are advantages in selling coins privately, it is felt that the disadvantages, particularly where coins of any value are concerned, cancel the 'plus' factors. The main advantage of course is a financial one. Disposal in this way avoids the auctioneer's commission and the profit element required by a dealer. It is possible for both the vendor and purchaser to benefit from private treaty sales if the sale price is above the net realisable value of selling through a third party and below the dealer's retail price or auctioneer's hammer price.

If a large collection is involved, the chances of being able to sell all of it privately, either as a whole, or in part, are slight. One may well find that the choice items go and one is left with the pieces that are difficult to sell on their own.

There is also a security risk. Whilst it may well be possible that known fellow collectors may wish to purchase the pieces, the likelihood of selling all of the collection to known collectors is small. The remedy is to advertise. Whilst a box number can be used, at some stage in the negotiations a prospective purchaser will want to see the coins. Instead of a keen numismatist, this could turn out to be a ruffian of the first order who is only too delighted to be invited in to ransack a collector's home and even to inflict personal injury in the process. Even if prospective purchasers are met on independent territory, there is still the risk of a personal attack, or of being followed home. For these reasons it is recommended that prospective vendors should seriously weigh up all the consequences of disposing of coins by private treaty sales to unknown persons.

Sales to the trade

When deciding to sell either a few coins or a whole collection, the collector will not be new to the market and so a number of dealers will be relatively well known. A special rapport may have been established with a particular dealer. If this is the case, and if the collection generally consists of material with which he deals, then an approach should first be considered in this quarter.

The advantage of selling to the trade is that the deal can be quickly concluded. In other words, if capital is needed quickly, it is best to sell to a dealer. If one is abreast of market prices all is well; if not, then become acquainted *before* contact is made. To save time the seller should list the coins and write down the price required for each specimen. The dealer is bound to ask what sum is wanted. On the basis that once revealed, the price can be brought down as opposed to being raised, be optimistic, but also realistic. If a dealer sells a coin at £100, he is hardly likely to pay that sum – he will want a profit. As mentioned earlier, the average profit margin is 33⅓ per cent, and the margin decreases for higher value coins and for specimens that are easily saleable. Conversely, it increases for low value material and 'slow-moving' items.

There are some obvious points which are sometimes forgotten, that should be borne in mind. When deciding to approach a dealer, chose one that is likely to be interested in the material. In other words, Ancient Greek coins should not be taken to a specialist in modern world proof sets. If the coins are individually in a high price bracket, do not attempt to dispose of them to a small-time dealer, as the time of both parties will be wasted. Similarly, if selling a large number of coins or a complete collection where the aggregate value is high, it is only productive to attempt to negotiate with a dealer who is in a financial position to buy.

The drawback of selling to the trade is a nagging feeling in the seller that the best possible price may not have been obtained. Sales by private treaty can also leave the vendor in the same state of mind. Human nature is such that certain individuals are never entirely happy with the price they obtain for anything. The situation can be alleviated by disposing of the pieces by way of auction. Then the vendor may be comforted by the fact that his coins have been effectively offered to the world at large. Unforeseen weather conditions and the like excepted, he knows that the hammer price is determined by all the market forces.

If the collection is both large and important, disposal by way of auction may indeed be suggested by the dealer. Indeed, it is the most adviseable course of action where an important cabinet is concerned. However, before looking at the plus and minus factors of consigning coins for auction, it is worth mentioning one further service that some, but not all, dealers offer. This is for the dealer to sell items for a client on commission. The advantage to the dealer is obvious; he increases his stock without having to outlay capital. The vendor may consider this method of disposal to be beneficial because he does have a say in pricing the coins and thus in determining the sum that he will receive when they are sold. However, no sale, no money. Thus, the advantage of having a hand in pricing the coins has to be weighed against the possibility of a non-sale. If a sale does not materialise (possibly because the price is too high) and the vendor decides to consign the material to auction, if the pieces are recognised (the coin market is not large and the coin fraternity are quite observant), the fact that they have lain in a dealer's tray for a period may be detrimental. Questions such as 'What's wrong with them?', or comments like, 'They've done the rounds', can destroy any desire to acquire them.

Disposal by way of auction

As previously mentioned in chapter 3, the period between consigning coins to an auction and the receipt of any proceeds can be one of several months. This time span is a result of the auctioneer selecting a suitable sale in his programme in which to place the coins, and the period taken to prepare, print and distribute the catalogue. Certain auction houses will advance the client a percentage of the sum that they anticipate the material will realise. In such cases, valuations are naturally conservative in order to safeguard their own interests as well as their client's. The cost of what is effectively a loan is reflected either by a higher commission charge or by charging interest on the amount advanced. In such circumstances, when an auctioneer accepts material for a sale, the consignor is not at liberty to stipulate any figure below which the coins cannot be sold. In other words, they are sold 'without reserve'. Wherever possible, it is prudent to place reserves on each lot consigned to an auction. Consequently, should unforeseen circumstances result in a lack of interest being shown at the sale, the vendor is safeguarded against the coins being sold at unrealistic prices. Whilst the reserve should not be too low, it should also not be too high either. The auctioneer will state what he considers the reserve should be. The consignor can either agree or disagree. It is not unknown for the vendor to stipulate a reserve, against the auction house's advice, that is out of line with the market. If he cannot be persuaded against this course of action, the auctioneer has no choice, assuming he still agrees to accept the consignment, but to adhere to his client's wishes. In the likely event of the auctioneer having to 'buy-in' the lots subject to unrealistic reserves, a charge will be levied. Generally this is calculated by applying a proportion of the normal commission rate to the 'bought-in-price' and by adding 'expenses'. The latter refers to charges for photography, insurance, packing, special advertising and the like.

To the public at large, one auction house is much the same as another. However, each has its own characteristics and varied range of expertise to be offered. It is possible to ascertain the basic commission charge by referring to the 'Terms and Conditions' found in each auction house's sale catalogues. It is prudent to enquire what additional charges will be made. For example, ask how much the insurance premium is for the period the coins are in the auctioneer's possession, is an additional charge made for photographing pieces that are to be illustrated in the catalogue, etc? The cost of selling material does vary from one establishment to another. However, whilst the cost is an important factor to be taken into account when deciding to which auctioneer one should consign a collection, a small group of coins or even the odd coin or two, it is not the only criterion on which to base the decision.

While a collector was actively acquiring coins he would have been acquainted with the catalogues issued by various auction houses. Some may have impressed him more than others. A catalogue can be viewed as an auction house's 'shop window', as potential bidders can be attracted towards an establishment that publishes well-presented catalogues. However, the presentation has to be backed by accurate descriptions, and of course the sale itself has to be conducted expertly. The reputations of auction houses do vary. During an individual's collecting career he will form his own opinion as to the merits of the various establishments. Those who acquire a few coins, for example through inheritance, and have no indication as to which auction house to use, are advised to write to a few and request details of commission and other charges and also a sample copy of a recent catalogue.

When a large and important collection is involved, the vendor is advised to invite two or three leading auctioneers to submit tenders for its disposal. It is stressed that this suggestion only applies where a choice and valuable collection is concerned. Clearly an important sale attracts attention both in the normal and specialised press and the auction house conducting the sale not only receives wide publicity but its reputation is also enhanced. The more important and valuable the collection, the finer the commission rates. However, as before, the cost in monetary terms, whilst important, must not be the only factor to be considered when deciding which establishment wins the consignment. Its ability to handle the pre-sale publicity is more important where a choice collection is involved than in the case of selling a group of coins. This is particularly so where a cabinet of world or ancient material is concerned. Thus another factor to be considered is not only the establishment's local reputation, but also its international standing.

Taxation

Benjamin Franklin (1706–90), the American printer and publisher, author, inventor, scientist and diplomat has been described as one of the best known and most admired men in the Western world during the last half of the eighteenth century. In a letter he wrote to Jean Baptiste Le Roy in 1789, he stated: 'But in this world nothing can be said to be certain, except death and taxes.' Two hundred years later his observation is equally applicable.

Ever since the advent of taxation, individuals have striven to avoid it. Governments, when discovering loopholes in a country's revenue laws, legislate to block the gaps through which the public legally escapes the clutches of taxation. Consequently, the law concerning taxes on income and capital gains is continually changing.

As a result, no attempt is made here to describe how the disposal of coins in various parts of the world can result in a tax liability. We advise those contemplating disposal of a collection of coins to seek guidance from an accountant or tax consultant. It is also worth bearing in mind that leading auction houses and dealers have their own expert tax consultants who are only too pleased to advise potential clients.

8
Forgery

Petronius, in the first century AD, compared the craft of a physician, 'who must know all about the anatomy of man', to the craft of a banker, 'who must know every detail of a coin'. Had Petronius lived in the twentieth century, he would no doubt have replaced the word 'banker' by 'numismatist'.

From the striking of the first coin way back in the seventh century BC, there has been a ceaseless struggle against the art and wiles of the counterfeiter. We know both from references in literature and from specimens that have survived, that forgery was a problem in the ancient world. Near the Roman fort at Halton Chesters in the U.K., a contemporary coiner's den has been discovered complete with moulds and forged Roman coins.

The penalties for counterfeiting have always been severe. In the ancient world the penalty was often death. The Anglo-Saxons severed the offending hand, and even more drastic mutilation was adopted when this failed as a deterrent. Later English penalties included hanging, transportation, and, as now, a heavy prison sentence. The Chinese had the most novel solution. Finding that the Government was losing the battle against the counterfeiters, the most skilled of them were rounded up and installed at the Imperial Mint, and paid a high salary!

However, so far we have only referred to the contemporary counterfeiting of current coins of the realm to deceive those who used the currency in their everyday lives. In the days when coin collecting was only a pastime for a select few, there were limited opportunities for the counterfeiter to turn his attention to the coinage of a past age. However, as more individuals became interested in the pursuit of numismatics, a small band of rogues turned their attention to producing old coins for the unwary collector. Imitations of ancient coins began to circulate as long ago as the mid-sixteenth century. These Renaissance pieces, known as 'Paduans', were mainly produced at Padua and other north Italian cities about the middle of the sixteenth century by reputable Italian sculptors. Albeit some were innocently intended to satisfy the Renaissance collectors' desire for articles that reflected Roman history and culture, and thus may be viewed as 'studies in the antique style', others were no doubt intended to deceive the unwary numismatists of the day.

Karl Wilhelm Becker

The most notorious forger of antique coins was Karl Wilhelm Becker of Frankfurt. He was born in 1772. His parents owned a vineyard and a wine-business, but the young Becker's interest lay in art rather than in the wine trade. Nevertheless, parental pressure resulted in making him enter the world of wine rather than art. His spare time was devoted to making drawings of ancient coins, and, according to his daughter, in experiments at making his own copies. We know little of his early life, but it is clear that before finding his true vocation he was in business as a draper. However, it was in Munich that he received the best training for his future career; he learnt the art of engraving steel dies at the Royal Mint.

According to an old tale, he was tricked by a Munich nobleman into purchasing a Roman gold coin from the latter's collection. It transpired that the piece was a modern forgery. When he tackled the nobleman he was told that he should not have meddled in matters which he did not understand. Becker was enraged and decided that he would turn forger in order to even the score. He thus began an intense study of numismatics, with special emphasis on the ancient art of cutting dies. In due course, Becker had the pleasure of passing off on the Baron an 'antique' coin that was of Becker's own making.

Becker was not only a perfectionist; he was also extremely prolific. He engraved at least 360 dies including Greek, Roman, Visigothic, Transylvanian and even siege pieces. Whilst it has to be acknowledged that Becker sold certain coins as copies, there is no way that one can give him the benefit of the doubt regarding all his activities. Interestingly, in 1824 Becker offered all his dies to the Imperial Coin Cabinet of Vienna. Although the original correspondence does not appear to have been preserved, we are able to ascertain Becker's explanation for his possession of the dies, from a draft of the original letter sent to a friend who was acting as an intermediary. This was that he produced copies of rare coins, the originals of which were beyond the financial reach of the average collector. He proceeded to elaborate upon their superiority over any previous imitations and told how sadly many had been passed as being original. It was suggested that the purchase and preservation of the dies by one of the leading European Collections would assist scholars and collectors in deciding whether certain coins were genuine or the work of Karl Becker! Prior to the making of this offer, suspicions began to mount regarding Becker. In 1825 Domenico Sestini supposedly issued a pamphlet warning the collecting fraternity of Becker's copies. They were certainly mentioned in a work on modern forgeries, published the following year. The master forger was apparently unmoved.

The sale of the dies to the Imperial Coin Cabinet of Vienna did not materialise. In 1829 Becker tried to arrange a sale to the King of Prussia, but again no sale took place. Becker died in the following year and the tools of his trade remained with his family. Eventually, they passed to the Saalburg Museum and in 1911 were transferred to the Kaiser-Friedrich Museum at Berlin. The items can still be viewed in that city. Whilst Becker's masterpieces have been well reported, it is still quite possible that some specimens lie undetected in some old collections.

The 'Manchester Mob'

Becker's demise did not result in counterfeit historic coins vanishing from the market. Other skilled forgers also made their living from producing numismatic items to satisfy the demand of the unsuspecting collector. However, as far as we know, no one surpassed Becker's excellence in forgery for nearly a century and a half. The dramatic rise in coin prices in the 1970s was an attractive proposition for the counterfeiter. This boom coincided with the perfection of a technique for making superb copies of original coins. Fate brought together a master forger and an international crook of the first order. The result was one of the most effective counterfeit conspiracies ever seen in the United Kingdom. At the time the swindle was broken, it was conservatively estimated that fake coins that would have been valued at £2 million had they been genuine, were scattered throughout the world.

The story began in 1969 when the scheme's creator, Harry Stock, a Korean war veteran, airline pilot, sometime priest, gun runner and confidence trickster, fled from the United States. He had been arrested and bailed out on a charge of selling fake three dollar gold coins. His flight from justice took him to Beirut, the traditional Western centre of the forgery business. There he met Said Chalhoub, a master coin forger who had perfected a method of sinking dies by using original coins (see 'Making false dies' below).

Stock was impressed. He considered that the fakes would fool not only the most experienced collectors, but also the world's leading dealers. Up to a point he was right. Had Stock and his recruited gang not become so active, the plot could have remained uncovered, but the perfect crime is reserved for novels. Although very disruptive and damaging for the coin trade in the short term, it did result in the establishment of a system that will safeguard against any future attempt to introduce counterfeit coins to the market.

In the summer of 1972, Stock took a consignment of Chalhoub's fakes to London and succeeded in selling a number to the leading London dealers. Some were also purchased by two dealers in the North of England. Before leaving the United Kingdom he informed both of the provincial dealers that the coins were in fact copies and suggested that they might wish to import similar examples on a regular basis. This was the beginning of the formation of a gang of eight individuals that were to organise the distribution of counterfeit historic coins in Britain. Stock returned to London later that year and attempted to sell Spink some five pound pieces. The company was suspicious at the appeareance on the market of so many good examples. As one London dealer stated: 'It was similar to large batches of Rembrandts appearing at auction each year — it was too good to be true.' Stock, who spent several months on remand in prison, was deported for importing fake gold coins.

He returned to Beirut and revised his plans. A system was formulated to smuggle Chalhoub's product by courier to Amsterdam's Schipol Airport. They were then placed in a left luggage locker to await collection. In order to avoid the metal detectors at the airport, the journey to the U.K. was completed by ferry. Once in th U.K. the 'coins' were distributed via a network of small advertisements in the coin press and by way of 'postal auctions'.

Dealers, the Royal Mint, the Bank of England and Scotland Yard Counterfeit Currency Squad were extremely concerned at the state of affairs. In 1973, two dealers at a coin fair in Cologne each bought a British 1738 gold two-guinea piece. Chance resulted in a comparison of the pieces, and to their horror, it was discovered that they were identical in every aspect. No two antique coins are ever exactly the same, for their surface marks can be likened to a person's finger-prints. The dealers realised that they were in possession of expertly faked items. Both pieces had been purchased from the same person and consequently Scotland Yard had the lead it required. It took the police three years of investigations across three continents before the gang was brought to justice.

Their trail led them to Chalhoub's workshop in Beirut. The 'coins' were being quite openly produced because it is not illegal to strike forgeries of foreign coins in the Lebanon. However, Stock, who was Chalhoub's agent, was not to be found. Close co-operation between European coin dealers and the police resulted in his being handed over to the authorities. He was caught whilst attempting to sell forged platinum roubles to an alert Swiss dealer in Zurich. Whilst in custody in Switzerland, he gave the police leads to the distributors in the United Kingdom.

The British police had to prove that the fakes, having been imported into the country, were in fact being sold as genuine items. One Flying Squad detective, disguised as a big-time coin buyer, called by appointment at the home of the gang's financier. After having been shown samples, he ordered £178,000-worth of what were in fact counterfeit coins. Having the necessary evidence on which to convict, the authorities rounded up the gang on 22 April 1975. On 11 November 1976 eight of the nine members of the gang were convicted at Manchester Crown Court. Seven were jailed, one was fined; the 'Revd' Harry Stock was not before the Court owing to prior engagements in Switzerland and the U.S.A.

The 'Manchester Mob' was broken. The fakes they distributed were produced by Chalhoub in batches of one hundred at a time. Stock dealt in at least fourteen different denominations and created havoc in the coin world. Clearly safeguards had to be established to protect both the trade and their customers.

When the activities of the 'Beirut Mint' were at their peak, there was a great deal of pressure within the London based International Association of Professional Numismatists to do something positive about the forgeries. The result was the formation in 1975 of the International Bureau for the Suppression of Counterfeit Coins.

However, before looking more closely at the activities of the I.B.S.C.C., and other organisations, it is useful to consider the principal methods of counterfeiting coins.

Methods of counterfeiting

1 Casting

This is the cheapest and commonest way of making forgeries. There are two methods of manufacturing items by this means. The first is when molten metal is poured into a mould made from the impression of a genuine coin. The resultant forgery is easily detected as such because the whole effect is 'fuzzy', i.e. the edges of the design are blunt and blurred. Furthermore, air bubbles are rife on the surface of the piece. The second and subtler method, said to have been discovered by an Egyptian dentist, is known as pressure casting. Here the mould is placed between the two poles of an electromagnet to draw the metal back into the recess of the mould to force out the air bubbles. The results of this method are very much more difficult to detect. However, the diameter of a forgery produced by the casting method is always less than that of a genuine original. This test of course cannot be applied to Ancient and medieval coins as they are not of uniform specification.

2 Electrotyping

This process of making a replica of a coin is somewhat similar to silver-plating. The process gives a faithful copy but there is a slight variation both in size and weight. Because the obverse and reverse are made separately, one is able to detect the join of the two halves on the edge. Naturally, this join can be plated or otherwise disguised. Whilst electrotypes will not pass the scrutiny of an individual who is reasonably competent at assessing coins, such pieces have been used by unscrupulous individuals as a means to delay the discovery of the theft of coins. An example of the celebrated Rawlins Oxford Crown of 1644, the only

'City Thaler' of the English series, was stolen from the view of the Archibishop Sharp sale in 1977 by the use of an electrotype as a decoy. The original coin has not been seen since.

3 Making false dies

The success of this method of course depends on the expertise of the counterfeiter. This was the method used by Becker, who of course engraved his dies by hand using traditional coining tools. Chalhoub the master coiner of Beirut used a more sophisticated method, known as the 'spark erosion technique'. This process used a copper or silver counterfeit made from a cast of an original coin, to sink the die. By passing an electrical current between the counterfeit and the steel used for the die the former cuts into the steel to leave its impression. As it is very difficult to distinguish between genuine coins and fakes struck from false dies manufactured by the 'spark erosion technique', I make no apologies for not being more explicit regarding this method.

4 Using genuine dies

Perhaps this method cannot be said to result in counterfeit coins. Nevertheless, a German mint master was convicted of this offence in 1975.

5 Alteration of a genuine coin

This means that a common type of coin is altered in an attempt to pass it off as an extremely rare piece. This might involve, for instance, changing the date of the common 1932 British Penny to read 1933 (a key date rarity in the British copper series). Such forgeries can always be detected without too much difficulty.

The I.B.S.C.C.

The I.B.S.C.C. has produced hundreds of reports on counterfeits of the coins of many countries, and also a periodical journal entitled *Bulletin on Counterfeits*. This has included articles on such subjects as the notorious Dennington forgeries of 1968 (twenty-four reproduction antique English coins, a counterfeit Athens tetradrachm, wax impressions of coins and coin moulds, together with counterfeiting equipment, were found at Dennington's flat) in addition to keeping readers informed of all the current research into forgeries.

Members of the public may send dubious pieces to the I.B.S.C.C. for an opinion. (Note that there is no legal responsibility in respect of any claim made as a consequence of the opinion.) There is a standard charge of £25 per item, regardless of value, plus postage, packing and insurance, except in cases where a consultant's fee may be charged (when the item(s) under scrutiny require specialised tests, in which case the I.B.S.C.C. will not proceed until the sender's permission has been acquired). Coins must be sent by registered post. The covering letter must state the full value of the piece(s).

Further details of the service may be obtained from:
   I.B.S.C.C.,
   P.O. Box 4QN,
   LONDON W1A 4QN

The International Numismatic Anti-Forgery Bureau

The best known professional opponent of the forger in the U.K. is E. G. Newman, O.B.E., formerly Chemist and Assayer at the Royal Mint. He has been providing an excellent service to dealers and collectors for many years. His organisation, the I.N.A.F.B., is a completely independent body.

Coins for authentication by the I.N.A.F.B. should be sent to Mr Newman at:
   M.N.C. Ltd.,
   P.O. Box 52,
   FARNHAM, Surrey GU10 4JR
   Great Britain

The I.N.A.F.B. charges are, per item:

Insured value of coin	Charge
Up to £100	£3
£101 – £1,000	3% of Insured Value
£1,001 – £2,500	£35
£2,501 – £5,000	£40
£5,001 – £10,000	£45
over £10,000	£50

A charge will be made for return registered postage, packing and in-transit insurance, which varies between £1.50 and £4 according to the value and destination.

The I.N.A.F.B. has an excellent track record. Its main expertise lies in modern coinages, i.e. from 1750 to date. It is generally felt in the trade that it has shown the public that the trade is concerned about forgeries. Its standing is reflected by the number of occasions that Mr Newman has been the chief prosecution witness at various trials in both the northern and southern hemispheres and by the fact that he has made several trips to coin conventions in the States which were financed by the American trade.

American Numismatic Association Certification Service (A.N.A.C.S.)

The A.N.A.C.S. is one of the services provided by the American Numismatic Association. The A.N.A.C.S. provide two types of service: authentication and grading. All items received at A.N.A.C.S. are given individual registry numbers, photographed and weighed for the permanent A.N.A.C.S. files. The items are examined by stereo microscopes and specific gravity tests are performed on those items that warrant additional testing. If the piece submitted is genuine, and if grading has been requested, the grade is determined at the same time by utilising the *Official A.N.A. Grading Standards for United States Coins*. If the item requires further examination by outside consultants for either authenticity or grade, the item will be forwarded to a recognised authority in that particular field, and the submitter will be notified of the delay.

When grading is desired for a coin that has already been certified, the grading fee and the A.N.A.C.S. photographic certificate must be sent with the item along with return postage and registered mail fees. Only authenticated coins will be considered for grading opinions.

At the present time A.N.A.C.S. is not able to:

a) Provide the basis and names of consultants used in arriving at the final decision.
b) Grade items that have not been or cannot be authenticated.
c) Estimated values, research background or history, or attribute numismatic items.
d) Recommend dealers or numismatic authorities.
e) Buy or sell any numismatic item.
f) Authenticate or grade any numismatic item on the basis of a photograph or rubbing.
g) Accept responsibility for the return of special holders. All items must be submitted in easy access holders.
h) Authenticate any legal tender currency.

Any coin sent to A.N.A.C.S. for authentication will be returned to the sender with one of the following opinions:

a) **Genuine** A photographic certification by A.N.A.C.S. will accompany the item.
b) **Cannot be certified** This means that the item has been altered, is counterfeit, or is otherwise not genuine.
c) **No decision** Occasionally, because of excessive circulation wear, corrosion, damage or other factors, a definite conclusion cannot be reached.
d) **Modern replica** A.N.A.C.S. defines the term 'modern replica' to be those items that are made of base metals, sometimes goldline or silver plated, and sold as souvenirs or novelties.

The services provided by A.N.A.C.S. are available to anyone, whether an ANA member or not. A schedule of fees and certification request forms are available from:

ANA Certification Service,
818N Cascade Avenue,
Colorado Springs, CO 80903,
United States of America

I.A.P.N. Warning System

The system is co-ordinated by Patrick Finn at Spink & Son Ltd.'s London offices. Within few hours of a report of a major theft or an attempt being made to place counterfeit coins on the market, all I.A.P.N. members and other dealers throughout the world will be contacted and duly warned. There is a pre-arranged communication system, using both the telephone and the telex. Each member must play his part by contacting the co-ordinator as well as his contact in his own area. Therefore, if the lead member in Amsterdam was advised of the theft of some important coins he would immediately telephone the co-ordinator and advise the next member of the I.A.P.N. via the communication chain in the Netherlands. Meanwhile, the co-ordinator would activate the whole communication network and the warning message would be relayed round the world. In addition to receipt of the message by I.A.P.N. members, arrangements are in existence in certain countries for all members of the National Numismatic Trade Association to be warned too. The system has proved to be most effective.

The I.A.P.N. is extremely modest about its successes. As the following account is now a matter of history, it can be revealed. A few years ago a number of coins were stolen from a major museum in the U.K. Their disappearance was not noticed, but nevertheless the person responsible for the theft decided it would not be prudent to offer them in London. He took them to Spink & Son (Australia) Pty. Ltd. The managing director, Jim Noble, was suspicious, for such rare items from the particular series to which they belonged seldom appeared on the market. Consequently, he stalled on making an offer, set the I.A.P.N. Warning System in motion and alerted the local police.

In a matter of hours, the museum and the whole of the trade, worldwide, had been alerted. It was only then that the museum discovered its loss. The man was duly arrested and brought back to the U.K. for trial and was subsequently sentenced to a term in gaol. Regrettable as coin thefts may be, the warning system does work in these cases, and in warning the trade of any attempt to introduce counterfeits to the market.

Coin dealers throughout the world are extremely vigilant in their fight against the counterfeiter. Although it is considered that one or two new forgeries are successfully passed on to the trade each year, I would not wish to give the impression that it is a serious problem. All leading dealers and auction houses guarantee their coins to be genuine and will naturally reimburse clients should it later be discovered that this is not the case. It is prudent to deal with established professionals as opposed to 'casual coin traders', for they have the expertise the latter may well lack, and the collector is safeguarded against financial loss.

Dictionary of Coins and their History

Account, money of A unit of reckoning, when there is no coin of the denomination. For example, no British guineas were struck after 1813, but professional fees and prices for certain goods were stated in guineas well into this century.

Adjustment marks Principally found on gold and silver milled* coins of the seventeenth and eighteenth centuries. They are the result of ensuring that the blanks* from which the coins were struck were of the correct weight. Ingots* of precious metal were passed through rollers in order to obtain a strip of metal from which the required blanks would be punched out. If a resultant blank was above the statutory weight, the disc would be filed until the required weight was obtained. Underweight items were melted. Scratches may be distinguished from adjustment marks, firstly as the striations are invariably closely parallel (unlike 'accidental' scratches), and secondly as adjustment marks lack the sharpness of scratches. Adjustment marks are naturally most apparent on the part of a coin that do not receive the full force of the dies, i.e. the raised surfaces, particularly those at the coin's centre.

AE (or Æ) The symbol derived from aes*, for any coin which does not contain gold or silver, i.e. which is struck from brass, bronze or copper. One may encounter AE I, II or III, which is a loose way of describing Roman bronze by size, i.e., AE I is a sestertius*, AE II a duopondius*, etc. Additionally the term AE 28 is used for a coin of this type with a diameter of 28 mm.

Aes Latin for bronze.

Aes Grave The earliest coinage of central Italy which was first issued at Rome by the Republic in c.269 BC. Denominations ranged from the as*, which weighed twelve ounces to the uncia of one ounce. The pieces were cast in bronze. Aes Rude is the earliest form of Roman metal money. It comprises unmarked crudely shaped bronze pieces of varying weights and shapes. This was followed by Aes Signatum (4th-3rd centuries BC), which are heavy bars or ingots of cast bronze which feature some device, for example, an elephant, bull or boar.

Aes Rude *See* Aes Grave.

Aes Signatum *See* Aes Grave.

Agnel A French medieval gold coin featuring the paschal lamb from which its name is derived.

AH The abbreviation for *Anno Hegirae*, or 'in the year of the Journey'. Some favour the single letter 'h'. It is the Muslim mode of reckoning time. It began in AD 622, the date that the Prophet Muhamad emigrated from Mecca to Medina. As the Muslim calendar is lunar, it is not sufficient to add 622 to an AH date to translate it to its AD equivalent. The following formula is to be used: $\frac{AH}{33} + 622$.

Alloy A mixture of two or more metals.

Amulet A charm worn in the belief that it has a psychic power which will protect its wearer from danger.

Ancients A term which embraces the coinage of Ancient Greece and Rome, or indeed any European numismatic currency struck prior to the collapse of the Roman Empire. 'Ancient' departments at the larger dealers also embrace coins of the Byzantine Empire, because of its Greco-Roman roots, although traditional Western medieval history is regarded as beginning at the fall of Rome and ending with the capture of Constantinople by the Turks in 1453.

Angel English gold coin introduced by Edward IV in 1465. It originally circulated for half a mark or a third of a pound sterling (6s.8d.). *Also see* Touch piece.

Anglo-Gallic coinage The name given to coins struck by English monarchs from the time of Henry II until the end of the reign of Henry VI, for use in their French territory.

Anglo-Hanoverian coinage The Hanoverian line of British kings, beginning with George I (1714–27) and ending with William IV (1830–7), struck a series of coins for their German possessions, Brunswick-Lüneburg and (from 1814) the Kingdom of Hanover.

Anglo-Irish coinage The term given to Irish coins issued during the period of British rule.

Anglo-Saxon coinage The term used for coins struck from the end of the Roman occupation of England until the Norman Conquest. It embraces copies of Roman coins, pure Anglo-Saxon currency and pieces with Viking influences.

Anna An Indian copper coin.

Annulet A symbol in the form of a small ring. It has been used on the

British coinage to signify the place of minting and to distinguish one issue from another. For example, the pennies of Edward the Confessor struck at York bear an annulet in one quarter of the reverse cross. During the years 1422–7, Henry VI adopted a similar identifying technique.

Anonymous bronze A coinage of the Byzantine Empire where the designs and inscriptions relate to religious subjects as opposed to the reigning emperor.

Antoninianus A third century Roman silver coin that circulated as a double denarius*.

AR (or Æ) The abbreviation for silver.

Archaic coinage Refers to the ancient Greek coinage struck between c.620 and 480 BC. The term relates to the style and execution of the coins.

As A copper coin of Ancient Rome. *Also see* Aes Grave.

Assay An analytical test to ascertain the purity of precious metals. *Also see* Trial of the Pyx.

Augg, Auggg An abbreviated plural found on Roman coins signifying the number of Augusti (plural of Augustus) in whose name the piece was struck. *Augg* signifies two; *Auggg*, three Augusti.

Aureus The standard gold coin of Ancient Rome first struck in the first century BC, equivalent in value to 25 denarii*. It was superseded by the solidus* in the fourth century AD. Note, plural is *aureii*.

Autonomous An autonomous coinage is issued independently of any state or other authority, i.e. a local type. Many Greek cities struck autonomous coinages.

AV or Æ The commonest abbreviation for gold.

Bag marks Refers to minor edge nicks and surface abrasions caused by coins knocking against each other while being transported from the mint to banks for distribution to the public. It will be appreciated that excessive bag marks have an adverse effect on a coin's value.

Bank of England Dollars and Tokens In 1804, following the widespread forgery of the countermarked 'pieces of eight'* issued in Britain (*see* Countermarks), it was decided to issue Bank of England dollars. These were struck on 'pieces of eight'. The obverse features a bust of George III and the reverse an effigy of Britannia. Upon close examination, traces of the original coin's design can sometimes be seen. In 1811 the Bank of England issued silver three-shilling, one-shilling and sixpence tokens. Dollars were also issued in that year, but still bear the date 1804.

Baronial coinage In continental European countries, the privilege of minting coins in the medieval period was extended to innumerable members of the aristocracy. The coins struck by the barons, counts and dukes etc., are collectively known as Baronial Coinage. In the reign of King Stephen, certain English Barons struck coins in their own names during the Civil War and Anarchy, 1138–53.

Barter The direct exchange of commodities without the intermediary of money.

Base metal Non-precious metals, e.g. bronze, copper, nickel, zinc, and so on, and alloys of such metals.

Bath metal A mixture of 75 per cent copper, 24.7 per cent zinc and 0.3 per cent silver which has a light brass appearance. It was invented by William Wood. The Rosa Americana coins and Wood's* Irish coins were struck in this metal.

Bawbee A Scottish denomination circulating at six Scottish pennies. First struck in 1542, it is considered that its name is possibly derived from the name of the Master of the Mint in office when it was first introduced – the Laird of Sillebawbee.

Becker, Karl A notorious German forger of ancient coins and metals in the early nineteenth century. His forgeries are known as *Beckers*. See p. 88.

Billon An alloy of copper and silver, with the former predominating.

Bi-metallic coins Are made from two separate metals, for example, the English tin farthing of 1684–5 has a central copper plug.

Bi-metallism A term to denote a currency system which is based on a fixed relative value of two metals, *viz.* gold and silver.

Bit Colloquial U.S. term for $12\frac{1}{2}$ cents. As no such denomination was struck, the expression 'two bits' is also used to refer to a quarter-dollar. Towards the end of the seventeenth century, it became customary in the West Indies to cut the Spanish-American eight reales or dollars, which circulated in the islands, into segments so as to alleviate the shortage of small change. The *bit* or *bitt* came into use to express the value of a real. *Also see* Nova Constellatio.

Blacksmith's halfcrown An Irish halfcrown struck at Kilkenny during the siege of 1649. It is so called because of its crude appearance. The design is based upon Charles I's Tower Mint halfcrowns.

Black money A general term for base-silver (i.e. billon*) coins.

Bland Dollar *See* Morgan Dollar.

Blank Also referred to as *planchet*, *flan* or *disc*. Metal cut to the shape of a coin, but which is unstamped, i.e. is waiting to be struck.

Blondeau, Pierre A Frenchman employed at the London mint during the second half of the seventeenth century to supervise the introduction of machinery into the English coining process. He invented a method of marking the edge of coins. In England, milled* coins finally replaced their hammered* counterparts in 1662.

Bonnet piece A Scottish gold coin first issued by James V in 1539. Its name is derived from the large flat bonnet in which the monarch is portrayed.

Boulton, Matthew An eighteenth-century British engineer responsible for improving steam power and introducing steam-driven machinery into factories. In 1777 he formed a partnership with James Watt, the famous engineer and inventor. He developed a steam coining press which was used at his Soho Mint, Birmingham. In addition to producing trade tokens, the Soho Mint also struck copper coins for the British and overseas Governments.

Box coins A box formed by joining together the obverse and reverse of two similar coins.

Bracteate The name given to thin pieces of metal impressed in relief with a die, on one side only. Owing to the thickness of the metal, the design appears on the other side in incuse*. The term originates from the Latin *bractea* (a thin piece of metal). It was not used until the eighteenth century.

Brass An alloy of copper and zinc. Sometimes one encounters the terms *Brass I* (or Æ I), *Brass II* and *Brass III*, which is a way of classifying Roman coins by size, i.e. a sestertius*, duopondius*, as* or its divisions. *Also see* Orichalcum.

Briot, Nicholas Celebrated coin engraver and medallist who was Chief Engraver at the Paris Mint from c.1606–25. He was an advocate of machinery in the coining process. His mechanical processes were not enthusiastically accepted by the French authorities so he moved to England and was patronised by Charles I. He was first employed as a medallist, but in 1633 became Chief Engraver at the London Mint. In 1635 he was appointed Mint Master in Scotland. He was faithful to Charles I during the Civil War, working at York and possibly Oxford.

Britannia The female personification of Great Britain.

Britannia groat A groat which features an effigy of Britannia upon its reverse. It was first issued in 1836. *Also see* Joey.

British Trade Dollar A silver piece struck at intervals from 1895–1935 at Bombay, Calcutta and London, specifically for trade in the Far East. It competed with Spanish and American dollars which circulated widely in the area.

BRITT An abbreviation found in legends for *Britanniarum* (i.e. 'of the Britains', meaning Great Britain and her overseas possessions). BRITT. OMN is the abbreviation for 'of all the Britains'. (The double 'T' is not an error, but is the peculiar form of abbreviated plural.)

Broad English gold piece of twenty shillings struck for Oliver Cromwell in 1656. It is classified as a pattern*.

Brockage A term applied to an imperfectly struck milled coin as a result of a previous coin jamming in the die. Subsequent pieces have one side struck normally in relief, and the other in intaglio, the design being a reverse mirror image of the side struck normally. The side bearing the design in intaglio is less distinct. *See* Incuse.

Bronze An alloy of copper and tin.

Bronze disease To be distinguished from patina* which enhances base metal coins. Bronze disease is a destructive corrosion of bronze, brass and copper coins as a result of oxidation. Not infrequently it acts under the visible surface of the coin and is therefore difficult to detect.

de Bruchsella, Alexander Possibly of Flemish origin, he was an engraver at the London mint from *c*.1494 to 1509. His superb profile portrait of the King on Henry VII's silver coinage gives him a prominent place among the founders of English medallic portraiture. *Also see* Shilling.

Bullion Precious metal in ingot form etc. The term 'Bullion coins' relates to coins that sell at a small premium over their gold content, e.g. Kruggerands, modern sovereigns, etc.

Bun penny The second type of Queen Victoria's 'Young Head' pennies struck from 1860 until 1894. The 'bun' refers to the Queen's hairstyle.

Bungtown Refers to counterfeit British halfpennies circulating in North America in the late eighteenth century.

Byzantine coinage Coins of the Roman Eastern Empire.

Cabinet Either a piece of furniture which houses a collection, or the collection itself.

Cabinet friction Slight surface wear caused either through specimens moving on the bottom of the tray when it is withdrawn abruptly, or, more likely, by the raised surface of the coin rubbing against the upper tray when the one below is withdrawn. See chapter 6.

Carat When applied to gold, the word indicates the metal's fineness*. Pure gold is 24 carats. Gold coins are generally 22 carat, i.e. 22 parts of pure gold to two of alloy. If coins were made from 24 carat gold, they would be too soft for the rigours of circulation.

Carolingian coinage This followed the Merovingian* coinage. The later Merovingian kings had become mere figure-heads, the actual ruling power in France having passed to the mayors of the palace, or chief ministers. In AD 751 the palace mayor, Pepin the Short, was crowned King.

He was responsible for introducing the *novus denarius*, or new denier*, which was a fraction larger and thinner than the deniers of the late Merovingian period. Although Pepin ordered the moneyers to make reference to his sovereignty on the coins, the actual design was left to their discretion. His son, Charlemagne, introduced a heavier denier, so that it could compete on the same level with the dirhem* of the Arab world. In 800 Charlemagne was crowned Emperor of France, Germany and Italy by the Pope, thus giving birth to the Holy Roman Empire. He completely re-organised the coinage, establishing a uniform design throughout his domain. As the power of the Carolingian kings declined, the feudal counts began striking their own coinages.

Internal struggles for power towards the end of the ninth century split the empire principally into the separate kingdoms of France and Germany, which developed their own separate coinages. The death of Louis V in 987 ended the rule of the Carolingian Kings.

Cartwheels The colloquial name for the large unwieldy copper British penny and twopenny pieces struck in 1797. The piece weigh one and two ounces respectively. The term was also adopted for American silver dollars struck from 1794 until 1935.

Cash Chinese copper denomination, being one-thousandth of the silver tael*. It has a central hole which facilitates stringing for carrying. Also refers to money as opposed to credit. This latter usage is derived from the French *caisse*, or cash-box.

Cast coins Refers to coins that are produced by pouring molten metal into a mould as opposed to being struck. Certain Ancient British coins were cast. This method was also adopted by the Chinese up until the late nineteenth century. *Also see* Geat.

Celtic coinage Coins struck by the ancient European tribes from sometime late in the second century BC until the middle of the first century AD.

Cent One hundredth part of a dollar*, etc.

Centesimo One hundredth part of the Italian lira*.

Centime One hundredth part of a franc* etc.

Check number *See* Die number.

DICTIONARY OF COINS AND THEIR HISTORY

Ch'ien The common Chinese term for money. Also written *Tsien* or *Tsen*.

Chisel cuts Small nicks found on the edge of Ancient coins which were probably made by merchants and money-changers to ascertain that the coins were not plated or that the metal was of the correct fineness (the piece being removed to analyse).

Chop mark A private punch mark* placed on a coin by a Far Eastern banker or merchant as a guarantee of genuineness. It is said that from experience, those chopping coins knew whether a piece was of the required fineness* according to the depth of indentation made by their mark. A coin which bears many punch marks, thus obliterating the design, is of little value. On the other hand, specimens bearing a few rare marks can sell at a premium over the value of a 'clean' or unchopped specimen.

Clad coinage Coins struck on blanks* made from two or more metals which are bonded together under pressure. Clad coinage is a post-1945 phenomenon. West Germany adopted bronze-clad steel pfennigs* in 1948 and brass-clad steel 5 pfennigs the following year. The U.S. introduced cupro-nickel-clad copper coins in 1965.
Note: Clad coinage is not to be confused with an alloy* of two or more metals.

Clashed dies Refers to dies inadvertently damaged by the dies being struck together with no blank* between them. If later used in the minting process, the resultant coins can bear traces of the design on the opposite side in intaglio and mirror-image.

Clipping In the days when coins were hammered* (hand-struck), the blanks* were literally cut from the sheets of metal by the moneyer* with a pair of shears. The resultant coins' edges were therefore not always clearly defined and perfectly round specimens were the exception rather than the rule. Unscrupulous members of the public would cut small pieces of metal from the denominations for their own personal gain, and then place the coin back into circulation. When a 'new' coin was clipped, it would probably go unnoticed unless the piece was weighed. Coins that were persistently clipped would not go undetected. Although clipping was a capital offence in many countries, this proved an ineffectual deterrent. To quote the entry in Evelyn's diary for 15 July 1694: 'Many executed at London for clipping money, now don(e) to that considerable extent, that there was hardly any money that was worth about half the nominal value.' (N.B. It should be remembered that until this century, the value of the metal content of a gold or silver coin was equivalent to its 'face value'*. Evelyn's phrase, 'worth about half the nominal value', therefore, refers to about half of the metal being cut away.) When coins were produced by machinery, the milled* or inscribed edges were intended to safeguard coins from clipping.

During the reign of Britain's Charles II, the Latin phrase DECUS ET TUTAMEN 'An ornament and a safeguard', was adopted on five guinea and crown pieces in place of milling. The phrase, which is a quotation from Virgil's *Aeneid* (Book V, 262), was supposedly suggested by Evelyn Although milled edges practically eliminated clipping, it was not unknown even in eighteenth century England for coins to be clipped – the milling of course being replaced once the deed had been done. Also *see* Long Cross penny.

Cob money Derived from the Spanish *cabo de barra* 'cut from a bar' describes crude silver coins minted in the Spanish colonies of the New World from the seventeenth to the early nineteenth centuries. Silver was cast into bars from which blanks* on which to strike coins were 'sliced' The resultant coins (multiples of the real*) are of crude appearance.

Coin A piece of metal impressed with an official mark guaranteeing its weight, fineness and value.

Coin weights Coins are struck to certain specifications: fineness of the metal, size and weight. In olden days, coins were weighed in order to ascertain that they were genuine, had not been subject to clipping*, and to assist money-changers dealing in foreign coins. It should be remembered that in the past, the bullion* value of a coin and its 'face value'* were equal. The weights are generally made of base metal*, and today are collectors' items, as indeed are coin scales.

Coiner and coining Today the words are synonymous with counterfeiter and counterfeiting (*see* Counterfeit). However, in time past they were words used to refer to an individual legitimately engaged in the process of striking coins. *Also see* Moneyer.

Colts The popular name for the silver coins of Ancient Corinth which feature Pegasus on the reverse.

Conjoined busts *See* Jugate.

Copy A *replica* of a coin, i.e. an item that is produced without the intention of deceiving. *See* Electrotype.

Counterfeit A forgery. Those producing such pieces are known as counterfeiters.

Countermark A punch mark* comprising a device, lettering, numerals, etc., officially stamped on a coin subsequent to its issue. The purpose of the countermark may have been to lower or raise the coin' value, or to render it current in a country other than the issuing state etc Countermarks have appeared on coins since time immemorial. *Also see* Bank of England dollars, Chop mark, Holey dollar and Host coin.

Cross Numerous forms of crosses are to be found on coinage. The four principal ones are:

DICTIONARY OF COINS AND THEIR HISTORY

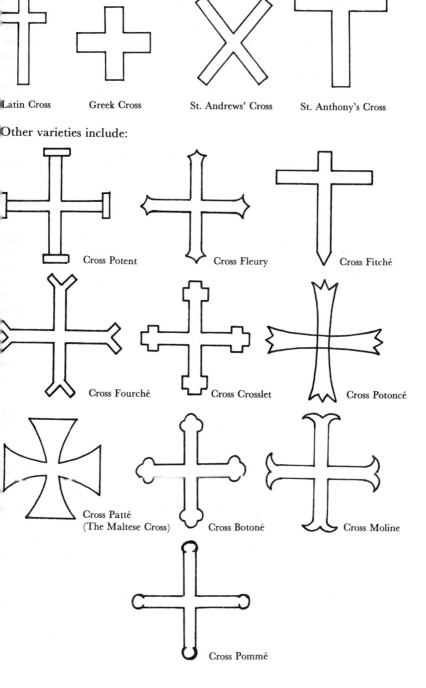

Latin Cross   Greek Cross   St. Andrews' Cross   St. Anthony's Cross

Other varieties include:

Cross Potent   Cross Fleury   Cross Fitché

Cross Fourché   Cross Crosslet   Cross Potoncé

Cross Patté (The Maltese Cross)   Cross Botoné   Cross Moline

Cross Pommé

Also see Long cross, Short cross and Voided cross.

Crown An English denomination of a quarter £1 first struck (in gold) during the reign of Henry VIII. Gold specimens continued to be struck until the early years of the reign of Charles II (1660–85). In 1551, during the reign of Edward VI, the denomination was struck in silver. Now struck in the UK to commemorate specific events. The last major issue of crowns for general circulation took place in the late nineteenth century.
Note: Following the U.K.'s adoption of decimal currency in 1971, the crown is officially a twenty-five pence piece.

Crown gold 22 carat gold. The term is derived from the fineness of England's first gold crown, struck in 1526.

Crux-type penny Refers to pennies of the English king, Aethelred II (979–1016), which have the four letters C R U X (Latin for cross), placed respectively in each of the four angles of the cross that features on the reverse of the pieces.

Cupro-nickel An alloy of copper and nickel. Most of the world's current 'silver' coinage is cupro-nickel.

Cut halfpennies and farthings Before Edward I (1272–1307) introduced fractional pennies into the English currency, pennies would be halved or quartered in order to obtain the equivalent to a halfpenny or farthing. Cut money refers to any fractional denomination obtained by cutting. *Also see* Bit and Voided cross.

d. British abbreviation for a pre-decimal (1971) penny. The abbreviation for a decimal penny is 'p'. *Also see* Denier.

Daler The Scandinavian equivalent of the Austrian and German thaler*, a crown-sized silver denomination.

Danegeld An annual land tax levied on the English people to buy off the Danish invaders. When the Danes became masters of the country they levied the tax on land-owning Anglo-Saxons. Payment was made in coin and consequently considerable quantities of Aethelred II (979–1016) pennies have been found in Scandinavia.

Daric A gold coin of the ancient Persian Empire. It was first struck by Darius the Great (521–486 BC), after whom it was named.

Debasement Until the twentieth century, the metal content of a coin was more or less equal to its 'face value'*. Debasement, or the lowering of the fineness* of the metal, was a means by which the issuing authority could fill its coffers in a time of financial crisis. Needless to say, it was not a popular measure with the public. Before the Hellenistic period, Greek coins were rarely debased. The Romans did debase their coinage from time to time. The first official debasement of the English coinage took place during the reign of Henry VIII (1509–47). Progressive lowering of the fineness eventually resulted in the 'silver' coins containing two-thirds alloy. Because of the amount of copper content, which was clearly obvious even to the lowest peasant, the king was nicknamed 'Old Copper-Nose'. During the reign of the 'Boy King', Edward VI (1547–53), debased coins were issued first in the name of Henry VIII and then in his own name. Sterling silver coins were also issued, and from 1551 debased silver specimens were no longer struck. The British silver coinage continued to be struck from silver of sterling fineness until 1920, when a 50 per cent debasement took place. The U.K. abandoned silver for its currency coinage in 1947.

Decimal coinage A system whereby the principal unit of account is divided into units of 100. For example, in the U.S.A. $1 equals 100 cents, and in the U.K. £1 equals 100 pence. The U.S. adopted their decimal system in 1792; the U.K. in 1971.

Decus et Tutamen *See* Clipping.

Dei gratia Latin for *By the Grace of God. Also see* Godless Florin.

Dekadrachm The silver ten-drachm* piece of Ancient Greece. Undoubtedly the most famous of this rarely issued denomination emanated from Syracuse. Its function was more medallic than monetary.

Demonetised A denomination is demonetised when it ceases to be 'legal tender'*. For example, prior to the U.K. introducing its decimal system of currency in 1971, the halfcrown was demonetised. This occurred on 31 December 1969. As the date approached advertisements stressed that the halfcrown 'can't be used as money' from the end of the year.

Denarius The principal silver coin of the Romans in Republican and Imperial times. *Note:* plural is denarii.

Denier The *novus denarius* (new denarius) was first struck by Pepin (751–81), the first of the Carolingian* kings. It was larger than the deniers of the Merovingian* dynasty which preceded the Carolingian rule, Charlemagne (781–814), influenced by the Arab dirhem, raised the coin's weight from 1.24 gms to 2.00 gms. 240 were coined from a pound of silver. It became the standard silver coin of Western Europe. The English silver penny was a derivative of the denier. Indeed until decimalisation in 1971, the abbreviation 'd.' was used for penny.

Device An emblematic design, such as a bird.

Diademed A diademed head or bust is one surmounted by a crown, fillet or headband.

Dicken A word used to describe certain Swiss coins modelled on the Italian testone*. It translates as 'thick', as the pieces are of greater thickness (and thus weight) than testones. They were struck from the late fifteenth century until about the first quarter of the seventeenth century.

Didrachm A two drachm* piece.

Die A minting tool made of hard metal, incuse engraved with one side of a coin's design. A blank* is placed between an obverse and a reverse dies and a coin is struck. The upper die is known as the *trussel*; the lower is called a *pile*.

In the days when coins were produced by hand (i.e. hammered*) the pile, which was fixed into a wooden anvil, was engraved with the obverse design. The trussel would receive the blows of the hammer necessary to transfer the dies' designs to the blank. As the trussel received the full force of the striking process, its life was not as long as the pile. A set of dies in the days of hammered coins comprised two trussels and a pile.

In ancient times each individual die was engraved by hand. In the medieval period the die was 'built up' by sinking punches bearing part of the coin's design in relief, into soft metal. When completed, the die was hardened. The advent of the mechanisation of the coining process in the seventeenth century brought another innovation; the *matrix*, which was used to produce working punches. Matrices are incuse-working punches in relief.

Today, much of the labour intensive aspect of die making has been superseded by the use of reducing machines. These produce a steel master punch (in relief) usually from an electrotype* copy of the artist's plaster model. The reducing machine traces the original design exactly to any reduced scale, i.e. the relief as well as the outline. The artists' models are usually six to ten inches in diameter.

The master punch is used to sink a matrix (incuse), which raises in a like way the individual working punches (in relief) which in turn are used for sinking the (incuse) working dies.

Die axis A term used to describe the relationship between the obverse* and reverse* of a coin. It is signified by the use of arrows. Thus ↑↑ means that the coin's reverse is upright in relation to its reverse. ↑↓ signifies the opposite. In ancient times, the moneyers were less concerned with die axes; therefore one encounters ↑→, ↑↗, etc. The first arrow always relates to the obverse.

Die flaw A raised mark or marks on the surface of a coin caused by a pit or crack in the die.

Die number A minute number on a coin from which the die can be identified.

Die variety A coin showing a *slight* variation of design.

Dime The U.S. 10 cent piece.

Dinar Arabian gold coin.

Diobol Ancient Greek silver coin, being one-third of a drachm*

Dirhem Arabian silver coin. The unit of currency for Morocco.

Disc *See* blank.*

Dodecadrachm A twelve drachm* piece. It is the largest Ancient Greek silver coin.

Dollar The monetary unit of the U.S. and numerous other countries.

Dorrien and Magens Shilling Name given to the 1798 shilling*; one of the rarest shillings in the British series. The London banking firm of Dorrien and Magens sent a quantity of silver bullion to be coined at the Mint. Although this was quite legal, the government of the day took offence and ordered that all the coins should be melted, on the basis that the issue had not been sanctioned by Royal Proclamation. Only a few specimens escaped the melting pot.

Double A Guernsey copper denomination equivalent to the British farthing*. It was first struck in 1830. Eight and four doubles were last issued in 1956. The Island's currency is now based on the U.K.'s £p system.

Double-struck Caused as a result of the blank* shifting between the dies when more than one blow is undertaken to strike a coin. Double-striking is generally associated with ancient and hammered coins, as opposed to specimens struck by machine.

Doubloon Initially a double excelente* struck for use in Spain and Spanish-America. In time the name was transferred to the eight-escudo piece.

Drachm The basic silver coin of Ancient Greece. Note: the plural is *drachma*.

Ducat A gold or silver coin, but usually struck in the former metal, which was current in various parts of Europe over many centuries.

Ducatoon A large Dutch silver coin, which is also known as a 'silver rider', as it features a mounted horseman, struck from the late sixteenth century until the end of the eighteenth century. *Also see* Rijder.

Dump Refers to any small, thick coin. For example, U.K. halfpennies and farthings of the reign of George I (First Issue) or the 'dump' from a Holey dollar*.

Duodecimal Currency which used denominations in units of twelve.

DICTIONARY OF COINS AND THEIR HISTORY

For example, the pre-decimal U.K. coinage where twelve pennies were equivalent to one shilling.

Dupondius   The two as* piece of Ancient Rome.

Durham House   Used as a temporary mint in 1548 and 1549. It was the London palace of the Bishops of Durham situated at the eastern end of the Strand, but has long since been destroyed.

EF   Abbreviation for *extremely fine*, a term relating to a coin's state of preservation. *See* 'Condition' in chapter 2.

E.I.C.   Provenance mark of the East India Company found on British gold coins of the reign of George II to indicate that the gold from which the pieces were struck was supplied by the Company.

Eagle   The U.S. gold ten dollar piece.

Ecclesiastical mints   In certain countries the ruling monarch allowed certain archbishops, bishops and abbots to issue coins. Their mints are referred to as *ecclesiastical*.

Écu   French for 'shield'. For a long period this was the 'crown' or 'dollar' of France. Until the mid-seventeenth century it was a gold piece; in 1641 Louis XIII struck the denomination as a large silver coin.

Edge   A coin has three surfaces. The obverse* and reverse* are two, the edge is the third. Measuring the edge will give a coin's thickness. *Also see* Graining and Milled coinage.

Edge-inscribed coins   *See* Blondeau and Milled.

Edge knock   An indentation to a coin's edge* caused by dropping or other mishandling.

Electrotype   A replica of a coin or medal made by a process that gives a faithful copy of the original. *See* chapter 8.

Electrum   A natural alloy* of about three parts gold and one part of silver and copper, from which the first coins of Ancient Greece were struck. Also applies to a man-made alloy of gold and silver.

Elephant or Elephant and Castle   The phrase "'Elephant' or 'Elephant and Castle' below (bust)", is found in catalogue descriptions of British gold and silver coins. The symbols are the marks of the African ('Guinea') Company and indicate that the bullion from which the coins were struck was provided by the Company. The elephant alone is found on coins of Charles II until 1675, and the elephant, with or without the castle, from that date on until nearly the end of the reign of George I. *Note:* After 1701, the symbols are only found on gold coins.

Emergency money   A general term which embraces all forms of currency issued when regular monetary media are in short supply. *Also see* Obsidional coinage and tokens.

DICTIONARY OF COINS AND THEIR HISTORY

Engrailed A coin is said to be engrailed when the edge* is decorated with a succession of dots or curved indentations.

Engraver The person who prepares the dies for a coin. The design is either cut by hand or mechanically using a reducing machine*.

Epigraphy The study of legends and inscriptions particularly with regard to their deciphering and interpretation.

Errors In ancient and medieval times when coins were hand-struck by a multitude of moneyers, the dies* could have been prepared by individuals who could neither read nor write. They would copy the legends and general design from either an actual coin or some form of pattern. Spelling mistakes were frequent, as the legends were often unintelligible to them. *Also see* Brockage, Mis-strike, Mule and Off-centre.

Escudo From the Spanish for 'shield'. Name given to various gold and silver Spanish coins from the early sixteenth century until 1868. Now the unit of currency for both Chile and Portugal.

Essay From the French *monnaies d'essai*, meaning a trial piece*. *Also see* Pattern; Proof; Piedfort.

Evasion A copy of a coin with sufficient deliberate variations from the original so as not to violate counterfeit laws.

Excelente Spanish gold coin struck from 1497 until 1537.

Exergue The lower area of a coin's design separated by a horizontal line. Generally found upon the reverse, it normally contains the date.

Exonumia Items which resemble currency, but which are not designed to circulate as such, e.g. amulets* and coin weights*.

Extremely Fine *See* 'Condition' in chapter 2.

F Abbreviation for *Fine*. *See* 'Condition' in chapter 2.

FDC Abbreviation for *fleur-de-coin*, which translates as 'bearing the bloom of the mint'. *See* 'Condition' in chapter 2.

Face value A phrase referring to the currency value of a coin as indicated on the 'face' of the denomination, e.g. one pound*, one dollar*, one rupee*, etc.

Falconer's Issues John Falconer was the son-in-law of Briot* and from 1636 onwards was joint Master of the Edinburgh Mint with the celebrated engraver. Falconer's Issues bear the letter 'F'.

Fantasy coin A coin which has the general appearance of a real piece, but which is simply an 'invented' item. It is not a forgery of an

111

existing coin. For example, one Reginald Huth had a silver four-peseta struck by Pinches & Co. bearing the date 1894. The piece features Queen Isabella II who was driven from the Spanish throne in 1868. A most peculiar fantasy purporting to emanate from 'Auracania-Patagonia' (a non-existent country) was struck by an eccentric Frenchman in 1874. The 'issuer' was styled King of Auracania-Patagonia.

Farthing U.K. denomination current for one quarter of a penny. Its name is derived from the Anglo-Saxon *feorthling*, or fourthling. It first appeared in 1279, during the reign of Edward I, as a silver coin. Prior to this date, a quarter of a penny was obtained by literally cutting a penny into four pieces. Owing to its small size it never proved popular with the public, and following spasmodic issues, no more were issued in precious metal after the reign of Edward VI (1547–53). Tin farthings were struck during the reigns of Charles II, James II and William & Mary and the first copper farthing was issued in 1672. Farthings continued to be produced in this metal until bronze was adopted for the base metal coinage in 1860. The last farthing was struck in 1956 and the denomination was demonetised in 1960. Fractional farthings were struck periodically from 1827 until 1902. With the exception of the half-farthing struck from 1839 through to 1856, they were issued for use in certain British colonies, for example the 1827 *third-farthing* was destined for Malta and the Victorian *quarter-farthings* for Ceylon (Sri Lanka). *Also see* Harington Farthings.

Fidei Defensor Latin title meaning 'Defender of the Faith', conferred on the English monarch Henry VIII by Pope Leo X in 1521. It was not until the reign of George I that it was permanently incorporated into the monarch's titles on British coins. It was generally abbreviated to F.D. *Also see* 'Godless' Florin.

Field The part of a coin not occupied by the main design or exergue. It may bear a letter, numeral or small symbol.

Filler One hundredth of the Hungarian forint*.

Find *See* Hoards.

Fine A term used for grading a coin's state of preservation. See 'Condition' in chapter 2.

In English numismatics, *viz.* during the Tudor and Stuart periods when the fineness of the metal used in the coinage varied, one encounters the terms *Fine Silver* (Edward VI) and *Fine Gold*. The former refers to sterling silver and the latter to the standard of the gold used. When Henry VIII introduced the Crown of the Double Rose in 1526, 22 carat as opposed to the normal 23¾ carat gold was used. The two standards were differentiated by the terms *Fine* and *CROWN GOLD*—the former is always the better quality. N.B. The standard of 'Fine' gold did vary at different periods.

DICTIONARY OF COINS AND THEIR HISTORY

Fineness   The percentage of precious metal contained in a coin.

Flan   *See* blank.

Fleur-de-coin   *See* FDC.

Florin   From the Italian *fiorino*, or 'little flower'. The European gold coinage began in Florence during the latter half of the thirteenth century with a coin featuring John the Baptist on the obverse and a lily, or *fleur-de-lis*, upon the reverse. The latter was the badge of Florence. This coin was imitated all over Europe. Edward III was the first British monarch to issue a 'florin' or 'double leopard'. As the alternative name indicates, it features a beast as opposed to a lily. An enthroned representation of the king flanked by two leopard's heads, is depicted instead of St John the Baptist. The British silver florin current for one-tenth of a pound, was introduced in 1849. *Also see* Godless Florin and Leopard.

Follis   A silver-washed bronze coin introduced into the Roman coinage by Diocletian (AD 284–305) and his co-emperor Maximian (AD 286–305). The striking of the piece was discontinued in *c*.AD 320. The coin was revived in the Eastern Empire by the Byzantine emperor Anastasius (AD 491–518). It continued to be struck until the late eleventh century. *N.B.* The plural is *folles*.

Forgery   An illegal copy of a genuine coin or medal manufactured for sale to a collector as a genuine item. *See* chapter 8.

Forint   Hungary's unit of currency.

Franc   Probably derived from the legend found on fourteenth-century French gold coins; *Francorum Rex*, or King of the Franks. Now the unit of currency for Belgium, France, Switzerland, etc.

Franklin cent   *See* Fugio cent.

Frosted proof   A most attractive form of proof* coin. The fields have a mirror-like finish while the design and lettering have a frosted appearance. Obtained by treating the die with a mild acid solution and then highly polishing the field.

Fugio cent   The name given to the first circulating coin issued by the authority of the U.S. government. It is so called because the word FUGIO ('I fly') appears in the obverse legend. The same side of the piece features a sundial. Struck in copper and issued in 1787, it is also known as the Franklin cent, as the motto MIND YOUR BUSINESS in the exergue was a saying of Benjamin Franklin. It should be noted that the name 'cent' for a U.S. denomination did not officially exist on a national level until 1792.

Galley halfpence   The name given to small base Italian and other continental coins that, resembling English coins, circulated illegally in England.

Geat or git Channel through which molten metal runs in the casting process. Cast coins*, for example Chinese Cash and Ancient British show traces of the geat in the form of small protrusions on the edge of the coin.

Gem An uncirculated coin that exhibits fewer marks associated with modern mass-production methods of minting than is generally found on other specimens in the same series.

George noble An extremely rare gold coin of the reign of Henry VIII. The noble, which was introduced by Edward III, was rated at the value of half a merk or one-third of a pound. The George noble was current at the same value. Its name is derived from the reverse type where St George is depicted slaying the dragon. Only one specimen of its corresponding half denomination is known.

Ghosting British one penny coins of the period 1911–27, are popularly known as 'ghost' pennies. The workmanship of the pieces was so poor that it is not unknown to find specimens where the obverse design shows on the reverse.

Gilt Gold-plated. Boulton* struck numerous gilt patterns* and proofs* N.B. These pieces were struck on gilded blanks, so that the specimens were not plated after striking.

Git *See* Geat.

Godless florin Also sometimes known as the 'Graceless' florin. In 1849 the British authorities introduced a new silver denomination, the florin, which circulated for one-tenth of a pound. The 'Gothic' bust of Queen Victoria appeared upon the obverse together with the legend VICTORIA REGINA 1849. The fact that the usual title 'DEI GRATIA FD'– By the Grace of God Defender of the Faith – had been omitted led to a great public outcry. An outbreak of cholera that year was even attributed to the anger of God at the non-appearance of that part of the Queen's title. The Master of the Mint, a Roman Catholic, was blamed for the omission and was dismissed from the post. The offending florins were called in and the next issue (1851) were struck bearing the customary DEI GRATIA FD.

Gothic crown or florin Victorian silver coins designed by William Wyon in mid-Victorian pseudo-gothic taste. The Queen is featured wearing a highly ornate dress and an Early English style of lettering is used for the inscriptions.

Graceless florin *See* Godless florin.

Grading Coins are graded according to their state of preservation. See 'Condition' in chapter 2.

Grain A unit of weight measurement. 1 grain equals 0.64799 grams.

Graining A technical term for a coin's edge serrations. *Also see* Milled coinage.

Greek Imperial A term for local bronze issues from Greek-speaking areas in the Eastern part of the Roman Empire, struck from the Christian era to the reign of Gallienus.

Gresham's Law In the baldest of terms, the law may be stated: 'bad money drives out good'. In other words, when an issuing coin authority in time past debased its coinage, the public would hoard the pieces struck from the superior (i.e. proper standard) bullion. Eventually only the debased coins would be left in circulation.

Groat This word and its equivalent in French, *gros*: in German, *groschen* or *grosch*; and in Dutch and Low German, *groot* and *grote*, is derived from the Latin *grossus*, meaning great. In continental Europe during the second half of the thirteenth century, improved economic conditions allowed a larger silver denomination than the bracteates and deniers to be struck. Because of its size, it was called *gros*, etc. The English groat was first struck in 1279, during the reign of Edward I, and circulated at four pence.

Groszy One hundredth of the Polish zloty.

Guilder The name given to the Dutch gulden* by the English.

Guinea A U.K. gold denomination first struck in 1663. Originally called the 'guinea-pound' the name was adopted as the bullion from which the pieces were struck came from the Guinea Coast in West Africa. Initially the face value was one pound sterling, but up until 1717 it circulated at a fluctuating premium. The peak was reached in 1694 when it was valued at 50 per cent more than its issue value. In 1717 its value was fixed at £1-1s (21 shillings). The last piece was coined in 1813, and in 1817 its place was taken by the gold sovereign. Nevertheless, until recently professional fees in the U.K. were generally reckoned in guineas.

Gulden Originally the north European equivalent of the Italian gold florin. Later the term was used for certain silver denominations.

Gun money An Irish emergency coinage struck in 1689 and 1690, when James II, ousted from the English throne, fled to Ireland. It was cast from scrap base metal, such as kitchen utensils, bells and cannons; hence the name *gun money*. One of the features of the coins is that they are dated by the month of issue, as well as the year. This was because James intended to redeem the pieces month by month. However, his cause was not successful. The total issue of £22,500 was redeemed in the reign of William & Mary for £640.

Halfcrown A U.K. denomination for one eighth of a pound sterling, first introduced as a gold coin in the regin of Henry VII. Although gold specimens continued to be struck until the reign of James I, Edward VI introduced the silver version in 1551. With the exception of the reign of Philip and Mary, it was struck in every reign until 1967. It was demonetised in 1970, the year before decimalisation.

Halfpenny U.K. denomination first struck by Edward I in 1280. Prior to this date, half of a penny was obtained by literally cutting a penny into two equal pieces. Until the reign of Charles II, the denomination was always struck in silver. In 1672 copper halfpennies were struck, and with the exception of the tin issued in the reigns of James II and William & Mary, this metal continued to be used until the adoption of bronze in 1860. Owing to the effects of inflation, by the 1980s the purchasing value of the coin was minimal. It was demonetised in 1984.

Hammered coins Prior to the mid-seventeenth century, coins were generally made by hand as opposed to by machine. The moneyers placed the blank between the two dies and struck the upper one with a hammer (hence *hammered*). The blow transferred the design of the dies to the blank and the coin was born or struck. Machine-made coins are referred to as milled*.

Hanover sovereigns The name given to brass medalets bearing the date 1837. They are similar to the Victorian sovereigns of the time, i.e. they portray Queen Victoria upon the obverse and a mounted figure on the reverse. However, the design differs from that of the sovereign, as the reverse does not feature St George and the Dragon, but Queen Victoria's unpopular uncle the Duke of Cumberland. The inscription* TO HANOVER suggests that she should succeed to this area of Germany. When the Queen ascended the throne she was barred from also becoming Elector of Hanover by the Salic Law which prohibited a woman from taking the title. Instead it passed to the Duke of Cumberland. The pieces were probably used as gaming tokens.

Hard times tokens Issued in the U.S.A in the 1830s and 1840s, they were generally struck in copper and modelled on the large cents of the day. They fall into two broad categories a) 'National' issues which are usually of a satirical political nature, and b) 'advertisement' types issued by retailers, etc. Both served as small currency.

Hardhead Scottish coin also known as a 'Lion' from the lion rampant found on its reverse. Struck in billon*, it was first issued during the reign of Mary Queen of Scots to afford relief to the poor, who suffered from the lack of small change. Originally, it was current for 1½ pence, but during the reign of James VI, the value was raised to 2 pence. Production of the coin ceased during the reign of Charles I.

DICTIONARY OF COINS AND THEIR HISTORY

Hardi The *hardi d'or* and *hardi d'argent* denominations were, respectively, gold and silver pieces in the Anglo Gallic series. The design of the coins are considered to have been derived from the *masse d'or* of Phillippe III Le Hardi, hence their name. The obverse features a half-length figure of the monarch holding a sword.

Harington farthings Also known as Haringtons, these are English copper regal farthing tokens struck under patent by Lord Harington. The patent was sold to the Duke of Lennox in 1615, and, upon his death it passed to his widow, the Duchess of Richmond. it was acquired by Lord Maltravers in 1635. The issue was ceased by Act of Parliament in 1643.

Harp or harper Irish sixteenth and seventeenth-century coins featuring a large harp on their reverse. The term especially applies to Henry VIII groats and half-groats struck for use in Ireland.

Hat piece *See* Bonnet piece.

Heaton Mint The former name of The Mint (Birmingham) Ltd. Since 1850, when, as Ralph Heaton & Sons, it first entered the minting business by buying at auction much of Boulton's* defunct Soho Mint*, it has manufactured currency for well over one hundred governments and issuing authorities in all parts of the world, including the U.K.'s Royal Mint. Various mint marks were used by the Heaton Mint. The most famous is simply a capital letter 'H', found near the date on British 1912, 1918 and 1919 pennies.

Heller An Austrian coin, being a hundredth part of the kreutzer*. Originally a small silver (later copper) denomination struck in Germany from the late thirteenth century.

Hiberno-Norse Literally 'Irish-Norse'. Describes the earliest Irish coinage, struck by the Viking invaders for about 150 years from the late tenth century.

Hoard An accumulation of coins hidden in time past.

Hog money Early seventeenth-century copper coins struck in the Bermudas. Four denominations were struck (1*s*., 6*d*., 3*d*. and 2*d*.), and all feature a hog upon the obverse; hence 'hog money'. In 1609 Sir George Somers' ship was cast ashore at the Bermudas. The islands were uninhabited, but swarms of hogs abounded, so this animal appears upon the coins.

Holey dollar An Australian emergency coinage issued in New South Wales in 1813. *See* chapter 1.

Host coin When a new design or a countermark is struck on an existing coin, the original coin is known as the 'host coin'.

DICTIONARY OF COINS AND THEIR HISTORY

i.m. *See* Initial mark.

Impaired A coin which has been mishandled or damaged in some way, as opposed to having been worn in circulation. Generally used for proof coins which have been badly scratched, have edge knocks etc.

Inchiquin money Irish emergency money* of 1642 taking the form of a circular stamp on irregular shaped silver. They bear no mark of value, merely the weight (e.g. 19 dwt 8 gr appears on the crown). In the past it was believed that they were struck by order of Lord Inchiquin, the Vice-President of Munster. However, it has now been proved that they were issued by the Lord Justices of Ireland and were never given the status of legal tender. Gold denominations were issued in 1646, but these are excessively rare.

Incuse Also referred to as *intaglio*. It is the opposite of relief*, i.e. the design is impressed into the coin as opposed to being in relief, or raised above the flan*.

Ingot Generally a *bar* of precious metal, but can be any shape. Usually marked with the fineness and weight of the metal.

Initial mark A mark on early medieval European coins to show where the legend began, usually in the form of a cross. The term has now become synonymous with mint mark*.

Inscription The wording or lettering across the field of a coin or medal. The term has become interchangeable with legend, but strictly this is the wording round the circumference of a coin or medal.

Intaglio *See* Incuse.

Islamic coinage Currency of the Muslim world. At one stage, Islam spread from Western Spain to Indonesia, so Islamic coins have been struck in Europe and Asia as well as in Arab countries.

Janus In Roman religion, the animistic spirit of doorways and archways. He is also regarded as the god of all beginnings. On coins he appears as a double-faced head. Janus is featured on the as*.

Jefferson nickel U.S. 5 cent piece featuring Thomas Jefferson, the third U.S. President, upon the obverse and Monticello, his home near Charlottesville, Virginia, on the reverse. First issued in 1938, the type is still being struck. It was designed by Felix Schlag. His work was chosen in a competition of nearly 400 artists. Although Schlag's obverse was largely retained, the mint's engraving staff prepared a new reverse. After a public campaign, it was not until 1966 that the small letters FS were placed below the bust. Schlag was the last private artist to design a regular U.S. currency coin.

Jeton Also spelt jetton. Derived from *jeter*, French for 'to throw'.

Originally used on the counting board of chequered cloth in medieval accountancy (hence *Exchequer*), they were later used in England as gaming counters. During the reign of Charles I, many fine jetons were produced. Today, seventeenth-century examples are still to be found in their original cylindrical silver boxes.

Joachimsthaler A large silver coin struck in Bohemia early in the sixteenth century, and named after the valley of St Joachim, where enormous deposits of silver were discovered in 1516. In 1520 the Counts of Schlick were granted the right by the King of Bohemia to utilise the silver to mint large silver coins known as *guldengroschen* The output was prolific. Indeed, it is estimated that within eight years, two million *Joachimsthalers*, as they became known, had been issued. Joachimsthaler means 'relating to St Joachim's Valley'. Eventually they were simply referred to as *thalers*. Large silver coins struck prior to 1520 are now also referred to by this name.

Joey The colloquial name given to the Britannia groat struck from 1836 until 1855 (pieces were also issued in 1888 for circulation in British Guiana). The introduction of the piece was campaigned for by Joseph Hume, the economist and politician. It was given the name 'joey' by the London cab drivers, for, as many short fares were four pence, they considered that they lost revenue when the piece was issued. Passengers would give the exact fare and not tender a larger denomination with the words, 'keep the change'. With the demise of the groat, the public called silver threepences 'joeys'.

Journey weight An English term from the days of hammered* coinage, when it referred to the quantity of coins that a moneyer* could coin in a day. The quantity for gold and silver were respectively 15lb Troy and 60lb Troy. *Also see* Trial of the Pyx.

Jubilee coinage In 1887 Queen Victoria celebrated her Golden Jubilee and J. E. Boehm was commissioned to redesign the coinage in honour of the event. *Also see* chapter 1.

Jugate Two or more busts joined together. Also referred to as *conjoined busts*. The reverse of the U.K. 1981 Royal Wedding Commemorative crown (25 pence) bears the jugate heads of the Prince and Princess of Wales. *Also see* Vis-à-vis.

Keping A copper denomination issued by the East India Company for use in Malaysia, in the late eighteenth and early nineteenth centuries. Also refers to the extensive series of copper tokens issued by Singapore merchants during the latter half of the nineteenth century.

Kilkenny money Irish emergency money struck by the 'Confederated Catholics' in 1642. The issuer's loyalty to the King, as opposed to Parliament, is represented by the obverse of the pieces featuring two sceptres in saltire* through a crown and the reverse a crowned harp between the letters CR. Comprising copper halfpennies and farthings, the coinage was poorly struck. *Also see* Blacksmith's halfcrown.

Kimon Considered one of the finest coin engravers of all time. His signed Dekadrachm* struck at Syracuse in *c.*405 BC, possibly to commemorate the Syracusan victory over Athens in *c.*413 BC, is a magnificent piece. It is thought that they were distributed as prizes at the Assinarian Games held to commemorate the victory. The obverse of the pieces features a victorious quadriga (chariot) whilst the reverse portrays the head of Arethusa, the water nymph daughter of Cerese, surrounded by four shimmering lively-looking dolphins.

King's Norton Mint Now known as Imperial Metals Limited, it is now a subsidiary of the Imperial Chemical Group. It is situated just north of Birmingham. With the exception of the Heaton Mint*, it has probably produced more coinages for more issuing authorities throughout the world, than any other private mint. Its mintmark is KN, to be found near the date on 1918 and 1919 British pennies.

Klippe The general name given to any square or lozenge-shape coin. They are common in the coinages of Germany and the Low Countries where it is possible that they were used on occasions as presentation pieces, for from time to time round and square examples of the same denomination were issued simultaneously. As the latter are often of finer workmanship, it is argued that they were not currency pieces. Multiple denominations of the standard klippes are frequently encountered throughout the world's emergency money*. *Also see* Klipping.

Klipping Derived from the Swedish *klippa*, i.e. to clip or cut with shears. The Scandinavian equivalent of klippe*.

Knife money An early form of cast bronze Chinese currency, struck from the ninth/seventh to the fourth century BC. It takes the form of a slightly curved blade with a handle mounted by a ring. The usurper Wang Mang (AD 9–23) attempted to revive knife money. These later examples have the ring of the handle replaced by a cash-like coin. Knives were also a popular form of currency in parts of Africa. *Also see* Spade money.

Koban Japanese gold coin; one-tenth of an oban*. Not only is it smaller than the main denomination, but it also bears no guaranteeing ink inscription, but only sundry stamped seals.

Kopek Russian denomination. It is one hundreth of a rouble*.

Korona Hungary's unit of currency until 1925.

Kreutzer or Kreuzer Central European denomination formerly circulating in Austria, Hungary and Southern Germany. Originally struck in silver, it later became a copper piece.

Krona The standard silver coin of Scandinavia from 1875 and Iceland since 1925.

Küchler, Conrad Heinrich Artist and engraver employed by Boulton* at the Soho Mint*. His most famous coins include the 1797 Cartwheels* and 1804 Bank of England Dollars*. He also produced pattern coins for Alexander I of Russia and Christian VII of Denmark. These beautiful examples assisted Boulton in securing contracts to supply mint machinery to both countries.

L.s.d. The abbreviation for the Latin *librae, solidi* and *denarii*, the words used by the medieval Lombards, the wealthy Italian merchants from Florence, Venice, Lucca and Genoa, to describe the English 'pound, shilling and pence' currency system. The 'L' eventually became '£', the symbol for *Pound Sterling*, the U.K's unit of currency.

Lafayette dollar Issued in 1900, this is the first and only U. S. commemorative silver dollar issued before 1975. It was struck in honour of the erection of a monument to General Lafayette in Paris as a part of American participation in the Paris Exposition of that year. The General was a French nobleman who fought with the American colonists against the British in the American Revolution.

Large cent U.S. copper cents, issued from 1793 through to 1857, were struck on 26 to 29 mm diameter flans according to the issue. In 1856 the size was reduced to 19 mm (the two sizes were issued in 1856 and 1857). Those with the 26 to 29 mm diameters are referred to as 'large cents'.

Laureate Used to describe a bust which bears a wreath of laurel leaves.

Laurel A twenty shilling gold coin issued by James I of England from 1619 to 1625. Its name is derived from the laurel wreath featured on the King's head.

Leather money The so-called leather money of the ancient world was probably nothing more than skins, possibly stamped, used as a medium of exchange. Leather has been used as a currency in various parts of the world, e.g. during the Siege of Leyden in 1574.

Legal tender A country's laws generally define what may be legally tendered in coins of that nation, to complete a transaction. The person who is destined to receive the money is duty bound to accept what the law states. For example, in the U.K., coins of the realm above 10p in value are legal tender up to £10; cupro-nickel coins below 10p, up to £5, and bronze up to 20p. Naturally, the recipient can receive larger amounts if desired.

Generally only the national coinage is legal tender. However, this may not always be the case. For example, up until the reign of George III, specified foreign denominations were declared legal tender in Britain. *Also see* Demonetised.

Legend The inscription to be found round the circumference of a coin. *Also see* Inscription.

Lennox farthings *See* Harington farthings.

Leonardo Da Vinci The versatile mind of this great Renaissance figure was directed towards coins on at least two occasions. He designed a machine for cutting blanks* which may be seen at the Smithsonian Institute, Washington D.C., U.S.A. Leonardo also designed coins for Milan from 1481–99. The dies were engraved by Cristofano Caradosso.

Leopard Also known as the half-florin. An impressive English gold coin introduced by Edward III in 1344. The design was based on the gold coinage of Philip de Valois of France, the obverse featuring the king er roned beneath a canopy with a crowned leopard's head to each side. It proved unpopular and was replaced later the same year by the heavier half-noble. Consequently, examples are extemely rare. A florin or double-leopard and a quarter-florin or helm were also struck, but likewise were replaced. A florin circulated at 6s, the noble* at 6s.8d.

Levant dollar A generic term for any crown-sized silver coin intended for trade in the Middle East. The most famous is the Maria Theresa thaler. *Also see* Trade dollar.

Liard Initially a base silver French coin, later struck in copper (1649–1792).

Liberty cap When a Roman slave was given his freedom he donned a hat known as a *pileus libertatis*, or liberty cap. This headgear has been a favourite symbol of certain revolutionary coinages, e.g. France and South America. The bust of Liberty is also capped on certain U.S. issues.

LIMA 'LIMA below' is a term encountered in British numismatics. Gold and silver coins minted in 1745 and 1746 have LIMA below the bust of George II. This signifies that the pieces were struck from bullion captured from a Spanish treasure galleon by Admiral Anson during his famous three-year voyage round the world. The vessel was bound for Spain from Lima in Peru. The booty was estimated at £500,000 – a king's ransom in those days. It took thirty-two wagons to transport it from the Port of London to the Tower of London.

The Spanish established their first mint in South America at Lima. Peru's present mint is located in the city today.

Lincoln cent U.S. one cent piece first struck in 1909 on the occasion of Abraham Lincoln's birth centenary. The obverse features Lincoln, the current reverse, the Lincoln memorial. The latter type was adopted in 1959. Previously, the reverse featured the words ONE CENT half encircled by two ears of corn.

Lion The proverbial 'King of Beasts' has appeared on coins since time immemorial. Not surprisingly, several denominations featuring the majestic animal are simply called *lions*. For example, Robert III introduced a gold lion to the Scottish coinage. The Scottish hardhead* was also known as a lion. France had its *lion d'or* in the reign of Philip VI; some of the silver denier of the Anglo-Gallic series are known as *denier au lion* and the Dutch struck *leuwendaalders* or 'lion dollars' from the 1570s to 1690s.

Lira   Plural *lire*. Unit of currency in Italy and Turkey.

Long Cross penny   Prior to 1247, the English penny featured a Short Cross* extending to inner circle, i.e. it did not break the legend. In order to help prevent clipping*, Henry III introduced the Long Cross. A coin ceased to be legal tender* if more than one end of the arms of the cross was missing.

Lord Baltimore's coinage   In 1659, Cecil, Lord Baltimore had silver shillings, sixpences and groats and copper pennies struck in England for circulation on his plantation of Maryland. The obverses bear his bust and the legend CAECILIUS DNS TERRAE MARIAE & CT (Cecil Lord of Maryland). The silver pieces feature his coat of arms; the penny a ducal coronet.

Louis d'argent   Silver crown-sized denomination introduced by Louis XIII of France in 1641.

Louis d'or   Gold denomination introduced by Louis XIII of France in 1640. Multiples were also issued.

Love tokens   A coin with one or both sides rubbed smooth and then re-engraved with an affectionate design such as conjoined hearts bearing initials. Others may just bear a simple inscription or a pair of initials. British examples date from the eighteenth century, whilst U.S. love tokens tend to be nineteenth century.

m.m.   *See* Mint mark.

Maltravers farthings   *See* Harington farthings.

Maria Theresa thaler   First struck at the Günzburg Mint, Austria in 1773, they continued to be issued from various locations for nearly two centuries after Maria Theresa's death. However, all those issued after her demise bear the date she died – 1780. They were struck for use in the Middle East where debased modern coinages were not tolerated by the locals. This century, Maria Theresa thalers have been minted at Birmingham, Bombay, Brussels, Paris, Rome and Vienna. *Also see* Levant dollar and Trade dollar.

Mark   The unit of currency for Germany. *Also see* Nova Constellatio.

Mascle   A voided lozenge, frequently used as a mint mark* in former days.

Matrix *See* Die.

Maundy money The Royal Maundy is one of the most interesting and colourful of Britain's ancient ceremonies. Held on Maundy Thursday, the day before Good Friday, the reigning monarch, or his or her representative, distributes the Royal Maundy to selected persons.

Today, as in time past, the recipients of which there are as many as the monarch has years, are handed their gifts in leather purses. They receive a clothing allowance of £3; a provisions allowance of £1.50; £1 for the redemption of the royal gown, and as many pence as the monarch has years in specially minted silver Maundy money. A Maundy set comprises a fourpence, threepence, twopence and penny piece. As many complete sets are given as possible. Only the recipients and certain officials receive the coins. They are not available to collectors from the Royal Mint (this practice was stopped by Edward VII). There has been considerable debate regarding what constitutes a Maundy coin. At one time, all small denomination milled silver coins were classed as Maundy pieces. Naturally the earlier numismatists excluded those items that were clearly struck for circulation. Although today it is generally accepted that the sets of Maundy money that the collector knows so well were first issued especially for the purpose, during the reign of George III, it is nevertheless customary to refer to the fourpences, threepences, twopences and silver pennies struck from 1662 onwards as Maundy money. *See* Wire money.

Medal The modern usage does not require explanation. However, in time past, the word 'medal' was synonymous with 'old coin'. The medal as we know it today was a fifteenth-century innovation.

Merk Scottish silver coin first issued by James VI in 1579.

Merovingian coinage Following the fall of the Roman Empire towards the end of the fifth century AD, the various barbarian kingdoms which became established in the former Roman province of Gaul (generally the area know today as France) gradually adopted the Roman gold solidi (*see* Solidus*) and triens* types into their own coinages. The area was divided amongst the Visigoths, the Burgundians and the Merovingians. All three kingdoms produced their own coinage: the first two for a relatively short duration, as they were conquered by the Franks in the sixth century.

The Merovingian kings of the Franks united most of France under their rule. Their kindgom was comprised of four sub-kingdoms and their coinage is a labyrinth for the scholar, let alone the amateur collector. Many of the rulers bore the same name, and were not distinguished on their coins. To complicate matters, much of the Merovingian coinage was issued by the ecclesiastics, and whilst the designs follow those of the regal issues, their inscriptions bear the names of bishops and monasteries.

Though solidi and triens were struck, they did not appear until after the Merovingians had conquered the Burgundian kingdom. Although their principal coinage was gold, they also struck the denier*, a small dumpy silver piece which they initially based on the rare silver coins attributed to the late fifth-century Roman generals in Northern Gaul. By the sixth century, the deniers, like their gold, were imitative of the coinage of the Byzantine emperor Justinian I. The quality of their coinage steadily declined and by the eighth century, bore meaningless inscriptions and almost unrecognisable designs.

Mestrelle, Eloye   Also referred to as *Meystrell* or *Menestrel*, responsible for the first trial of machine-struck coins in London. *See* chapter 1.

Milled coinage   Any coin struck by machinery, as opposed to being hammered*, is said to be 'milled'. The origin of the term is obscure, but, it is likely to be derived from the fact that horse-mills or water-mills supplied the power for the rolling mills used to turn the ingots into sheet metal of the required thickness from which the blanks* were cut.

'Milled' is also used to describe the serrations found on the edges of coins. However, graining* is a more accurate term. Not all milled coinage has a serrated edge. Some pieces are plain, others bear an inscription. The most famous edge-inscribed coin is Simon's Petition crown*. *Also see* Screw press.

Mint condition   A coin that is unused, flawless, without any wear scratches or marks. The numismatic term is *Fleur de Coin* (abbreviation 'FDC'). *See* 'Condition' in chapter 2.

Mint mark   A mint mark is a term borrowed from Roman and Greek numismatics where it was used to indicate the place of mintage. For example: HT – Heracleia Thraciae; K – Carthage. In more recent times we encounter: D – Denver; S – Sydney. Many of the symbols found on coins, which are referred to as mint marks, are strictly *privy marks*. Since the dating of coins was not usual in the medieval period – indeed, the first dated English coin appeared in 1548 – marks had a periodic significance, changing from time to time. When an heraldic mark is used to date a coin, it is known as a privy mark. When the dating of coins became the accepted norm in Tudor England, the tradition of the privy mark remained until the mid-seventeenth century.

Additionally, these marks were used to signify the mint master* responsible for the coinage. The abbreviation for 'mint mark' is *m.m. Also see* Initial mark.

Mint master   The U.K. term is the *Master of the Mint*. The title of the individual responsible for the entire coining process at a mint. Sir Isaac Newton* was probably the most famous Master of the Mint in Britain. Today, the Master of the Mint (i.e. the Royal Mint) is the Chancellor of the Exchequer. The day-to-day running of the operation is the responsibility of the *Deputy Master and Comptroller*. In recent years, the title *Chief Executive* has also been used.

Mis-strike   Refers to a coin that is struck 'off-centre' – i.e. the die comes into contact with the blank* when the latter is not in its correct, central position. *Also see* brockage*. In recent years *mis-strike* is increasingly being used to describe any error in the minting process.

Mite   In Mark xii, 42 we read 'There came a certain poor widow, and she threw in two mites, which make a farthing'. A mite is a colloquial term, *inter alia*, for any small coin of trifling worth.

Model coins   Produced during the Victorian era in the U.K., these pieces are midget imitations of currency coins. Struck from base metal, which was sometimes silver or gold plated, they were intended for children's games or Christmas crackers.

Module   Another term for the diameter, or width, of a coin or medal.

Mohur   Indian gold coin first struck by the Moghul emperors in the sixteenth century. Also issued by the British during their period of rule. Examples were last struck in 1891.

Money   An item, such as a coin or object, which is generally accepted as a medium of exchange. For example, cigarettes were money in some prisoner of war camps during the Second World War.

Moneyer   Either the person who actually strikes the coin (as in the Anglo-Saxon and Norman series of the U.K. coinage), or the official responsible for the mint.

Morgan dollar   Also referred to as '*Morgans*'. U.S. silver dollars designed by George T. Morgan and which were struck from 1878 through to 1904 and also in 1921. It is also known as the 'Bland dollar', after Representative Richard P. Bland, who introduced the bill authorising the coin.

Mule   A coin struck from two dies not normally used together. For example, it may feature the current type on the obverse and the previous type on the reverse.

Mullet   The heraldic term for a star.

Napoleon   The 20 franc gold pieces issued by Napoleon I and III.

Newton, Sir Isaac   The great mathematician and scientist who spent over thirty years of his life at the London Mint, first as Warden and subsequently as Master.

Nickel   A metal first used for coinage in the nineteenth century. It is also the name given to the U.S.A. 5 cent piece.

Nike   The Greek goddess of victory. Nike was depicted as a woman in a long chiton, usually winged, holding a wreath and palm and crowning the horses of a victorious charioteer or decorating a trophy.

Noble English gold coin current for 6s.8d., first issued by Edward III. It was also struck by order of later Kings, viz: Richard III, Henry IV, V and VI, and Edward IV. The obverse features the monarch holding a sword and shield and standing in a ship. The type is said to be symbolic of England's growing powers on the seas. It has also been suggested that it originally commemorated the English victory over the French off Sluys in 1340.

The name was also given to the Isle of Man's platinum coins first issued in 1983.

Northumberland shilling Name given to the British shilling struck in 1763. In that year, the Earl of Northumberland was appointed Lord Lieutenant of Ireland. Two thousand pieces were struck with the intention that they should be distributed to the inhabitants of Dublin. Owing to the scarcity of bullion, it was the only 'large' George III silver denomination struck prior to the shillings and sixpences of 1787. Silver fourpences, threepences, twopences and pennies were struck prior to the latter date. George III ascended the throne in 1760.

Nova Constellatio Copper coins struck in England in 1783 and 1785 for circulation in the American Confederation (shortly afterwards to become the U.S.A.). They bear no mark of value. The name is derived from the obverse legend.

Silver patterns* bearing the same obverse legend and a similar design were struck in America by Robert Morris, Superintendent of Finance. Three denominations were struck – the *bit, quint* and *mark*. They are unique.

Numismatics The science and study of coins and medals.

Numismatist A student of numismatics* as opposed to a collector who simply accumulates coins.

Nummus A generic term used by the Romans for money. Also the most important current coin in any monetary system.

Oban The largest of Japan's oval gold coins which were issued at various intervals during the period 1591–1860. Like the koban*, they are punched with seals. However, they also bear their value and the mint master's signature in Indian ink.

Obsidional coinage Term derived from the Latin *obsidionalis*, pertaining to a siege. Obsidional coins are therefore siege pieces, i.e. a branch of emergency money*. There are over one hundred recorded instances of such coinages in European history (*viz.* from the fifteenth to the nineteenth centuries). England struck obsidional coins in the Civil War during the reign of Charles I.

Obverse The side of the coin which normally features the ruler's head. When a coin is 'headless', the obverse is taken to be the more important side. It is appreciated that this can be a matter of conjecture.

Off-centre When a coin is incorrectly struck so that part of the design disappears off its edge, it is said to be struck 'off-centre'. *Also see* misstrike.

Officina mark A Greek or Latin letter found on a high proportion of Roman and Byzantine coins to indicate the *officina*, or workshop, that struck the pieces. If at some later date it was found that a coin was defective in some way (e.g. if bullion of the required standard had not been used), the superintendent responsible for the workshop could be traced.

On The Old English preposition having the mean of *in* or *at* in modern usage. Therefore, an Anglo-Saxon legend reading *Aelfgar on Lund(ene)*, translates as *Aelfgar at London*.

Öre One hundredth of the Scandinavian krona.

Orichalcum An alloy of four parts copper to one of zinc which is neither brass nor bronze. It was used for base coins throughout the Roman Empire.

Ormonde money Also spelt 'Ormond'. An Irish coinage struck in 1643 during the Great Rebellion, so named because it was thought to have been struck on behalf of Charles I by the Viceroy, James, Marquis of Ormonde. However, as he did not take over the duties of Lord Lieutenant until much later, it would be more accurate to refer to the pieces as 'The Lord Justice's 2nd Issue 1643'. *Also see* Inchiquin money.

Overstrike Term used to describe a coin struck on an existing piece as opposed to a blank.* *See* Bank of England Dollars and Host coin.

Paduans In the sixteenth century, Giovanni Cavino of Padua (Italy) the celebrated engraver, in conjunction with the scholar Bassiano produced a whole series of medallions and coins in the Roman manner. The pieces are not counterfeits, but fantasy* items. Although no doubt some were sold as 'originals' to collectors of the day, they were intended as 'studies in the antique style'. Indeed, they are Renaissance works of art. It is said that more forged Paduans than original ones exist today. Cavino's dies may be seen at the *Cabinet des Médailles* at the *Bibliotheque Nationale* in Paris.

Patina The incrustation on the surface of bronze formed by oxidisation. Whilst this can look unpleasant it can also enhance the look of a coin. Good patina considerably increases a coin's value. On no account should such pieces be cleaned. *Also see* Tone.

Pattern An unofficial design for a coin struck as a suggested type.

DICTIONARY OF COINS AND THEIR HISTORY

Pax penny *Pax* is the Latin for peace. The word is found on certain English pennies struck from the reign of Cnut (1016–35) to Henry I (1110–35). It either appears across the reverse field or one letter appears in each of the four angles of the cross. In the latter case, it is rendered PAXS. One encounters the term 'Pax type'.

Peace dollar The name given to the U.S. silver dollars struck from 1921 through to 1935.

Penny The principal coin of England's Middle Ages. It was introduced in the eighth century. Struck on silver, multipes were not issued until 1279, when Edward I introduced the groat*. The first copper penny was not struck in England until 1797. Silver pennies still form part of the present Maundy money*.

Henry III issued a gold penny of twenty pence in 1257. However, only a few were struck and only six specimens have survived. *Also see* Denier.

Peseta The unit of currency for Spain.

Peso The Spanish dollar or 8-real* piece. The figure '8' appears to the right of the reverse shield, hence their name 'pieces of eight'.

Petition crown Arguably the most spectacular coin in the entire English milled silver series. It is known as the 'Petition' crown because of the following wording found on its edge*: THOMAS SIMON MOST HUMBLY PRAYS YOUR MAJESTY TO COMPARE THIS HIS TRYALL PIECE WITH THE DUTCH AND IF MORE TRULY DRAWN & EMBOSS'D MORE CAREFULLY ORDER'D AND MORE ACCURATELY ENGRAVEN TO RELIEVE HIM. It was presented by Thomas Simon to Charles II, in an unsuccessful attempt to regain his position as Chief Engraver at the London Mint. *Also see* Roettier.

Pfennig One hundredth part of the German mark*.

Pheon The heraldic term for a downward pointing arrow-head. Pheons were used as privy marks. *Also see* mint marks.

Piastre The former unit of currency, or denomination, in Egypt, Turkey, Morocco, Tunisia, etc.

Pièce de plaisir Refers to a coin struck in very small quantities, for example, specially for a monarch's or nobleman's collection. They were often struck in a more precious metal than the corresponding currency piece. Many of the patterns* of Louis XIV are *pièces de plaisir*.

Pieces of eight *See* Peso, Real.

Piedfort or piefort Piedforts are coins which have been struck on thicker than normal blanks*. As their name suggests, they are closely associated with France, where from the reign of Henry II (1547–59) they were apparently issued by the monarchy as presentation pieces. The Paris Mint still strike piedforts today.

The U.K. Royal Mint, started to strike piedforts specially for collectors in 1982. In that year, 25,000 twenty pence pieces in sterling silver were made available. The following year, 10,000 piedfort English pound coins were struck and in 1984, 15,000 piedfort Scottish pound coins were issued. Both were in sterling silver. Until these issues, British piedforts were extremely rare; indeed, none had been struck in the country for some considerable time.

It has been suggested that piedforts were originally struck for moneyers* to copy when making coins; their extra thickness is their distinguishing feature from currency pieces. In other words, they are patterns*. On the other hand, they may also be regarded as proofs*.

Pierced coins *See* Plugged coins and Touch pieces.

Pile *See* Die.

Pin money Not a numismatic term, but nevertheless an interesting phrase to include in a work such as this. In the fourteenth century, pins were not only expensive, but according to Brewer's *Dictionary of Phrase & Fable*, they were only allowed to be openly sold on 1 and 2 January. Ladies were given a specific allowance for the purchase of these objects so essential to dress-making. When pins became cheap, the term 'pin money' remained to describe a lady's allowance for her personal expenditure.

Pine tree coinage The name given to Massachusetts shillings, sixpences and threepences dated 1652, the obverses of which feature a pine tree. *Also see* Willow tree coinage.

Pingo, Lewis Assistant Engraver at the London Mint from 1776 and Chief Engraver from 1779 to 1815. The spade guineas* of 1787-99 were struck from dies he engraved.

Pioneer gold *See* Territorial gold.

Pistole The name given by the French to the Spanish gold double escudo.

William II of Scotland issued a gold pistole and its half in 1701. Some German states struck denominations bearing this name in the eighteenth and early nineteenth centuries, for example, Saxony-Weimar in 1764 and Brunswick-Luneburg in 1803. Excessively rare pistoles occur in the Irish series; *see* Inchiquin money.

Pistrucci, Benedetto Arguably the last of the really great coin and gem engravers. Born in Italy in 1784, he settled in London in 1815 having worked in Rome, Florence, Pisa and Paris. His 'St George and the Dragon' reverse which has appeared on many issues of British gold and silver crowns since its first appearance in 1817, is still used on British sovereigns today.

Plack A Scottish billon* piece which was struck from the late fifteenth to the late-sixteenth centuries. Its face value* was extremely low.

Planchet Another term for blank*.

Plate money Large rectangular copper coins issued in Sweden from 1644 through to 1722. A shortage of silver resulted in the striking of a high value copper currency. In the first year of its issue, a 10 daler piece was placed into circulation. Weighing 44lbs and measuring 24″ × 14″ and ¼″ thickness, it is the largest coin ever issued. Of the 26,552 pieces struck, only three remain today. Subsequent issues, although smaller, are nevertheless still large.

Plated coins Coins which are either struck from a base metal and later coated with a thin layer of gold or silver, or which are struck from copper, etc., blanks* which have been plated. The art of plating was known to the Ancient world. Whilst such specimens are generally associated with counterfeits*, official plated coins have been produced, e.g. Roman denarii from the second half of the third century AD. *Also see* Clad coinage.

Platinum This metal was discovered in Spanish South America in the 1720s and in Russia in the early 1820s. Albeit now prized, it was initially held in relatively low esteem. Prior to 1836 in Russia, during the reign of Nicholas I (1825–55), it was used for coinage. As it has a high melting point and is hard, not to mention rare, which was only discovered later, it was found to be unsuitable for currency. The Prussians experimented with the metal again in the 1860s and 1870s.

In 1983, the Isle of Man introduced a platinum bullion* coin known as the noble.

Plugged coins In the latter half of the seventeenth century, the English monarchs struck tin farthings* and halfpennies*. A copper plug was inserted at the centre of the pieces to help prevent counterfeiting*.

From time to time one encounters coins that have been pierced, perhaps to be worn as jewellery. At a later date the resultant hole may have been filled in or plugged. Pieces so treated are of little numismatic value, unless of course they are extremely rare. Some plugging is more expert than others, but can be easily detected by the naked eye or a low-power magnifying glass. *Also see* Touch pieces.

Pocket piece A coin kept in the pocket as a talisman. Pocket pieces are quite frequently worn from rubbing.

Portcullis money Name given to England's first colonial coins struck in 1600 and 1601 for the then newly formed East India Company. Comprising a crown, halfcrown, shilling and sixpence, the reverse of the pieces feature a crowned portcullis or drop-gate.

Pound The unit of currency for the U.K., Egypt and Malta. The U.K. pound is known as the pound sterling, or just as sterling.

Pound coin During the Civil War, Charles I issued silver pounds at the Shrewsbury Mint (1642) and at Oxford (1642–44). They are the largest silver coins in the English series.

Although the gold sovereign* is the most famous pound piece, other coins which circulated at one pound were issued from time to time, e.g. the broad*, laurel* and unite*. After 1915, no sovereigns were struck for internal use in the U.K., but the main British Commonwealth gold producing countries, e.g. Australia and South Africa, continued striking the denomination until 1930–2. Banknotes then prevailed. However, in 1983, the British government issued one pound coins to replace pound notes. Struck from an alloy of 70 per cent copper, 5.5 per cent nickel and 24.5 per cent zinc, the pieces are pale yellow in colour. Scottish and Welsh variants were issued in 1984 and 1985 respectively.

Note: Although sovereigns ceased to be struck for circulation in the U.K. during the First World War, they have been, and indeed still are, issued. In recent years the Royal Mint has also struck limited edition proofs* from time to time for the collector.

Private gold *See* Territorial gold.

Privy mark *See* Mint mark.

Proclamation coins From 1701 through to 1808, a series of Spanish-American commemorative coins proclaimed new rulers. they are known as 'Proclamation' coins. In Australia, the term has a different meaning. During the late eighteenth century, there was a shortage of coin in the U.K., therefore the British were not in a position to supply their colonies with currency. In Australia, foreign as well as British coins circulated freely, at the value of their metal content. In 1800, a Proclamation was issued at Government House, Sydney, fixing the value at which certain coins should circulate. For example, a British guinea (£1 1s.) was fixed at £1 2s. It was policy for higher values, compared to those prevailing in Britain and elsewhere, to be proclaimed so as to encourage the retention of the precious metal currency in the country. The denominations named in the Proclamation are known as 'Proclamation' coins.

Proof A coin which is carefully struck from special dies which since the nineteenth century feature mirror-like or matt surfaces. *Also see* Frosted proof.

The rule of thumb for identifying a British eighteenth century proof coin is: 'If the bases to the legend letters are square (as opposed to 'fish tailed') and the edge beading is well-defined (as opposed to being 'fugitive'), the piece is a proof as opposed to a currency coin'. Naturally, there are exceptions.

Provenance mark A symbol or word to indicate the source of the metal from which a coin is struck. Provenance marks in the British series include: Prince of Wales's plumes – Welsh silver; roses – West Country silver; SSC – South Sea Company, and WCC – Welsh Copper Company.

Puffin In 1929, Martin Coles Harman, the owner of Lundy, an island in the Bristol Channel off the English coast, declared himself 'King' of Lundy. He issued Puffin and Half-puffin pieces bearing his portrait and a puffin. Harman was prosecuted, as his action breached the U.K.'s Coinage Act 1870. The pieces were withdrawn.

Punch *See* Die.

Punch marks The early Greek coins were uniface (only had a design on one side). To hold the blank* firmly on the pile* during the striking process, the trussel* featured a raised geometric design – usually a square, sometimes divided. The resultant incuse* pattern is known as a 'punch mark'. *Also see* Chop mark and Countermark.

Quadrans The quarter as* in the Roman Republican Coinage

Quadriga A chariot pulled by four horses, elephants or other animals. It is a type frequently encountered on Ancient Greek or Roman coins, usually signifying a triumph.

Quan Unit of currency of Annam.

Quarter The U.S. quarter-dollar. First struck in 1796, it has featured numerous designs. Today the types are referred to as 'Draped Bust', 'Liberty 'Capped', 'Liberty seated', 'Barber' (after Charles E. Barber, the Chief Engraver), 'Standing Liberty' and 'Washington' quarters, etc.

Quid British colloquial term for a pound* sterling.

Quint *See* Nova Constellatio.

R The abbreviation for rare. Degrees of rarity are indicated either by RR (very rare), RRR (extremely rare) or R^2, R^3 etc.

Radiate Denotes beams or rays emanating from the head.

Rawlins Thomas A coin and medal engraver and also a playwright. Said to have been a pupil of Nicholas Briot*, with whom he possibly worked for some years at the London Mint. During the Civil War he served Charles I at various mints. His most famous work is the excessively rare 'Oxford Crown' of 1644. The obverse features the King on horseback and a distant view of the city of Oxford.

Real One eighth of the Spanish peso*. The silver real was introduced into the Portuguese and Spanish currencies almost simultaneously in the mid-fourteenth century. In the former country, it became a copper coin in the sixteenth century. The denomination survived as a *reis* up until the early years of the twentieth century. Multiples of up to 10,000 reis were struck in silver and gold. In Spain, the silver real, together with multiples in gold as well as silver, continued to be issued almost until the introduction of the Second Decimal Coinage in 1864. The 8-real pieces, or Spanish dollars, are the famous Pieces of Eight.

Rebel money Part of the series of Irish siege money* of 1642–9. Comprising undated crowns and half-crowns featuring a distinctive cross potent upon their obverses and bearing a mark of value (in shillings and pence) on their reverses, the pieces were supposedly struck by the Confederate Catholics in 1643 in imitation of Ormonde money*. Another theory is that they were issued by Colonel Michael Jones, the Deputy Governor of Dublin Castle appointed by the English Parliament. If this is the case, they would have been issued in 1648.

Reddite crown This piece, which is also by Thomas Simon, is identical to his Petition crown*, save that the edge is inscribed REDDITE QUAE CAESARIS CAESARI – Render unto Caesar the things that are Caesar's.

Reducing machine *See* Die.

Relief The raised part of a coin, i.e. the legend and the design, is referred to as the *relief*, and can be defined as 'low relief' or 'high relief'. Whereas the design of medieval and later coins are generally in low relief, the coins of Ancient Greece are in high relief.

Remedy The allowable tolerance for loss of weight and fineness* in the minting process. *Also see* Trial of the Pyx.

Restrike A coin which is struck at a later date from original dies. For example, the dies, machinery and plant, etc., of the Soho Mint* were auctioned in 1850. The dies were acquired by W. J. Taylor, a London die-sinker, who used them to restrike examples of the coinages produced by Matthew Boulton*. Occasionally, restrikes emanate from official mints, for example, modern restrikes of the Calcutta Mint proof 1862 half anna and restrikes exist in the Austrian series.

Reverse The opposite of obverse*.

Rider A Scottish gold coin introduced by James III in 1475. Its name is derived from the obverse design; the King, clad in armour, helmeted and crowned, with sword drawn, riding a horse to the right. The design may have been inspired by the French *franc à cheval*, issued by John the Good in 1360, for this also features a knight, in full armour, mounted on a galloping horse.

Rijder The name given in the Low Countries to any coin bearing a horseman. *Also see* Rider.

Rim The raised thin line found on milled coinages* where the edge* joins the obverse* or reverse*.

DICTIONARY OF COINS AND THEIR HISTORY

Ring dollar   *See* Holey dollar.

Ring money   One of the earliest metal media of exchange. Ancient Egyptian printings show merchants weighing gold rings. Rings were also used as currency in Ancient Britain, Scandinavia and Japan, and in many primitive countries until relatively recent times.

Rocker press   The dies used in the rocker press were curved. They were pivoted together and operated by a seesaw bar attached to the upper die. A blank* would be placed between the two dies and the bar depressed and thus the coin struck. This machine was not ideal, sometimes producing mis-shapen pieces, and the uneven pressure of the dies made certain parts of the coin's design weak. The superior screw press* became the established coining machine when the world's mints were mechanised. Rawlins' 'Oxford' crown was struck in a rocker press.

Roettier   The Roettiers were a famous Flemish family of coin and medal engravers who befriended Charles II of England when he was in exile. They advanced him money in return for the promise that he would find positions for the three Roettier sons at the London Mint should he be returned to the throne. Charles was true to his word and John Roettier was appointed one of the Chief Engravers in 1662 and sole Chief Engraver in 1670. His brothers Joseph and Phillip were appointed at the Royal Mint prior to that date. John was responsible for much of England's coinage from 1662 until 1697. Descendants of the Roettiers worked at the Paris Mint until the end of the eighteenth century.

Roller press   A coining machine that impressed both the obverse and reverse designs on a strip of metal drawn between two rollers. It was invented in the mid-sixteenth century and used in Austria, England, Germany and Spain. However, the roller press had many disadvantages and the superior screw press* became the established coining machine when the world's mints were mechanised. Only Richmond farthings* were produced by this method in England.

Rosa Americana   In the period 1722–4, William Wood struck, under Royal Patent, twopenny, penny and halfpenny pieces intended for circulation in Britain's North American colonies. The series is struck from bath metal*. It proved unpopular, and although the contract was not revoked by the Crown, Wood apparently did not exercise his rights under it after 1723, although later patterns exist. The obverse features the bust of George I and the reverse a Tudor Rose (sometimes crowned). *Also see* Wood's Irish coinage.

Rose noble   *See* Ryal.

Rouble or ruble   The unit of currency for Russia.

Royal farthing tokens   Another name for Harington farthings* and

135

farthings struck by subsequent holders of the patent: the Duke of Lennox, the Duchess of Richmond and Lord Maltravers.

Runic alphabet Early Anglo-Saxon coins and certain early English coins sometimes bear runic lettering which is angular in shape. In the case of the latter, Latin and runic letters are intermingled. As at the time reading and writing were considered a form of white magic, the runes became associated with spells and charms and were frowned upon by Orthodox Roman Christianity. The origin of the runic alphabet is not certain. It is considered to have been devised by the Scandinavians from a form of the Greek alphabet. The angular shape of the letters made them easy to carve on wood or stone, etc. Runes are even found on the Norman coins. The runic p is the equivalent of a Roman W, so one encounters PILLELM for 'William'.

Rupee The unit of currency for India. The name is derived from the Sanskrit *rupa*, i.e. cattle, thus indicating that in Ancient India, as in Ancient Greece and Rome, cattle were at one time used as currency, or an indication of wealth.

Ryal An English gold coin introduced by Edward IV in 1465. It was then current for 10s. Its design was similar to the noble*, but the side of the ship on the obverse bears a rose. The flower also features at the centre of the reverse cross. Ryals were also struck during the reigns of Mary, Elizabeth I and James I (the last known as a *rose-ryal*, worth 30s or 32s.). The denomination is also known as a *rose-noble*.

Ryals were also issued in the Scottish series from the mid-sixteenth century. However, they bear no resemblance to their English namesakes. Gold three pound pieces, also known as ryals, were issued by Mary, Queen of Scots in 1555 (specimens dated 1557 and 1558 are known, but are extremely rare). They bear the portrait of the Queen on the obverse and the crowned arms of France and Scotland on the reverse. From 1565, the Scottish ryal was only struck in silver. The first issue features the facing busts of Mary and Henry Darnley and examples are excessively rare. The second and subsequent issues bear no portraits, but a tortoise climbing a palm tree. James VI also adopted this type, but in addition had ryals struck featuring a crowned sword and a pointing hand. These were also known as 'sword dollars'.

s. Abbreviation for shilling*.

S.C. The abbreviation for *Senatus Consulto* (by Order of the Senate) found on base metal Imperial coins struck at Rome.

S.S.C. The abbreviation for *South Sea Company*. The letters are found on 1723 U.K. silver denominations to indicate that the metal from which the coins were minted was supplied by the Company. The bullion originated from Peru. *Also see* Provenance mark.

Saint-Gaudens, Augustus Celebrated U.S. sculptor who also turned his attention to medallic art. He designed the U.S. $20 gold piece first struck in 1907 and which continued to be issued at intervals until 1933. These are known as 'Saint-Gaudens'. He also designed the Indian Head Eagles ($10) struck periodically from 1907 through to 1933.

Saint Patrick's coinage The circumstances surrounding these Irish halfpennies and farthings remain uncertain. Featuring the standing figure of St Patrick on the obverse preaching to a gathering and St David playing a harp upon the reverse, they are considered to have been struck by the Dublin Corporation in the 1670s. A quantity of them were taken to New Jersey, U.S., by Irish emigrants under the leadership of Mark Newby, where they were declared an official circulating currency.

Saltire The heraldic term of St Andrew's cross, which takes the form of an 'X'. Saltires were occasionally used in the English medieval period as legend stops. A pair of sceptres (i.e. highly ornamented staffs) crossed are known as 'two sceptres in saltire'.

Sassanian coins Currency struck by this Persian Dynasty from AD 226–641.

Sceat A small Anglo-Saxon* coin, originally struck from base silver and later in copper. *Note:* Plural *sceatta*.

Scissel The technical term for the scraps of metal left after blanks* have been cut from sheet metal.

Screw press The first coining machine, the invention of which is usually attributed to the Italian Donato Bramante, an architect who played a significant role in the design of St Peter's and was also a seal-maker to the Popes. It had an upper and lower die*; the latter was fixed. The two were brought together by turning a bar which operated a screw to lower the upper die. This 'squeezing' process resulted in both dies simultaneously leaving their impression on the blank*, and the coin was born.

In the mid-sixteenth century, Henry II of France installed an improved screw press for coin production into the Paris Mint. However, the traditional moneyers*, fearing the loss of employment at the introduction of machinery, rebelled and coin production reverted to the traditional hammered* method. The screw press was retained for medals and certain minor coins. An attempt was made in the 1560s to introduce the screw press to the London Mint (*see* Mestrelle). It was not until 1640 and 1662, at Paris and London respectively, that this machine finally replaced moneyers wielding their hammers. Towards the end of the eighteenth century steam-powered machinery was being conceived. *Also see* Milled* and p. 6.

Scudo The Italian for 'shield'. Originally it referred to any gold or silver coin bearing an heraldic device upon its reverse. By the mid-sixteenth century it became associated with the silver crown-size struck at various Italian mints, irrespective of whether a shield featured upon the coin's reverse.

Scyphate Any coin of concave-shape. Scyphates are encountered in the late Byzantine coinage*. However, the term is improperly used in this context, for in the East such coins are referred to as *trachea* or 'not flat'.

Sede vacante Encountered on ecclesiastical coins issued during the interregnum between the death of one ruler and his successor. Papal coins from the sixteenth century issued when the see was vacant bear this phrase.

Semée An heraldic term meaning an indeterminate number of little pieces. Although an adjective, it is often used in numismatics in the context of 'with semée of hearts'. The term is encountered in connection with the U.K.'s 1787 shilling or sixpence which are described as either with or without a semée of hearts.

Semis An early bronze coin of the Roman Republic, namely one half of an as*. In the Roman Imperial series it was a gold piece, first being a half aureus* and later a half of a solidus*. (N.B. the latter are more frequently referred to as *semissis*).

Sen One hundredth of the Japanese yen*.

Serrated coins Pieces with indented or 'nicked' edges (N.B. *no* grained). They first appeared in the Roman coinage just before the turn of the second century BC. Exactly why they were produced remains a mystery. One theory is that they were issued to the Celtic tribes, for whom the serrations possibly had some religious significance. Celtic ring-amulets also feature a form of serration. *Also see* Graining.

Sestertius A Roman coin current for a quarter of a denarius*. In the Republican period it was struck in silver and during the Roman Empire in bronze.

Sextans One sixth of the Roman as*.

Shekel The principal silver coin of the Jews. It was also a unit of weight in Babylonia which was adopted by the Phoenicians, Hebrews and other Semitic races.

Shilling The English silver shilling, or twelve-pence piece, was first issued by Henry VII in 1504. At that time it was known as a 'testoon', as it was inspired either directly or indirectly by the Italian *testone*. Featuring the profile bust of Henry VII, it is the first English coin to bear a realistic portrait. It is the work of Alexander de Bruchsella*. By the reign of Edward VI (1547-53) the piece took the name 'shilling', the derivation of which is uncertain. When the U.K. adopted the decimal system of currency in 1971, the denomination survived as a five-pence piece.

In Scotland, testoons, which circulated at four Scottish shillings each (roughly equivalent to one English shilling), were introduced by Mary Queen of Scots in 1553. Irish shillings were first issued by Edward VI in 1552.

Short Cross penny   A reverse design introduced by Henry II in 1180. As the phrase implies, the feature of such coins is a short cross, i.e. the angles extend only to the minor circle, or to the 'base' of the legend. It was adopted by subsequent monarchs; Richard I, John and Henry III, until 1247. Interestingly, regardless of the reign of issue, all of the pieces struck for circulation in England bear the name *Henricus* (i.e. the Latin for Henry). The coins of Richard and John are identified by variations in the lettering and style of bust, etc. *Also see* Long Cross penny.

Siege coinage   *See* Obsidional coinage.

Simon, Thomas   One of England's greatest coin and medal engravers. His masterpieces include Oliver Cromwell's milled* coins, the Petition crown* and the Reddite crown*.

Sixpence   The English sixpenny piece first issued by Edward VI in 1551. It was last struck in 1967. After the U.K. introduced a decimal coinage in 1971, the denomination continued to be current for $2\frac{1}{2}$ pence, until it was demonetised in 1980.

Skilling   Low value base metal denomination of Denmark until 1813, and of Norway prior to 1874. Large multiple skillings were struck in silver.

Slug   In general terms, any pieces of metal in its natural, unrefined state. However, in the States, it is the colloquial term the Territorial gold* 50 dollar pieces issued from 1851 to 1855.

Soho Mint   Matthew Boulton's* private mint located at Birmingham, England.

Sol   The name for a denomination by various continental European countries, from solidus* (Note: German – *solidus*; Italian – *soldo*; Spanish – *sueldo*). Although originally struck in gold, in the sixteenth century it became a base metal piece, though multiple sols were struck in silver (e.g. the Geneva 3 sols of 1791, etc, and the French 6 sols of 1782 and 1783, etc). Until the French monetary reform of 1794, 20 sols equalled a livre and during the Revolution the denomination became known as a sou. The phrase 'not worth a sou' still survives.

French sols also circulated in Canada during the seventeenth and eighteenth centuries. The Bank of Montreal issued one sou tokens in 1835 as did the Banque du Peuple in 1837.

Peru's decimal system, introduced in 1863, includes the sol (N.B.

plural *soles*). 100 centavos equal 1 sol, and 10 soles equal 1 libra. The sol was originally struck in silver, but from 1943 multiple soles have been issued in gold, silver, cupro-nickel and aluminium bronze.

Solidus First struck in AD 312 or AD 309 by order of Constantine the Great, this denomination soon superseded the aureus* as the standard gold coin of the Roman Empire. It was slightly heavier than its predecessor. It was also the standard gold denomination of the Byzantine coinage* Note: plural is *solidi*. *Also see* Sol.

Sou The colloquial name for the French 5-cents. *See* Sol.

Sovereign The gold sovereign, which circulated at twenty shillings or one pound sterling, was first introduced into the English series by Henry VII in 1489. The obverse of the first specimen features a magnificent enthroned figure of the monarch holding an orb and sceptre. Sovereigns continued to be struck at intervals until the end of the sixteenth century. Edward VI, Mary and Elizabeth I also issued sovereigns of thirty shillings. James I's first coinage of 1603-4 included the issue of a sovereign and later coins with a face value of twenty shillings, e.g. the unite* and laurel*. This situation continued until 1663 with unites and broads* emanating from the mint. In 1663, the guinea* became the country's standard gold coin. It was not until 1817 that the sovereign reappeared. *Also see* Pound coin.

Spade guinea The name given to George III guineas* struck from 1787-1809 (excepting the years 1792 and 1799). The term is derived from the 'spade-shaped' shield featured upon the reverse of the coins.

Spade money An early form of Chinese currency cast in bronze in the form of a spade, said by some to date from the ninth century BC and by others from the seventh century BC. *Also see* Knife money.

Specie The term 'to be paid in specie' means to be paid in coins as opposed to paper money.

Spur-ryal Name given to James I of England's half rose-ryal (*see* ryal) which circulated at fifteen shillings. Its name is derived from the large sun with sixteen rays which is featured upon its reverse. This was said to resemble a *spur rowell*, hence spur-ryal.

Spurious A coin that is not genuine, thus counterfeit*.

Stater The name given to the principal coin of any Ancient Greek city or state, whether it is struck in gold, silver or electrum*. The principal Celtic coin is also referred to as a stater. Rome's first gold denomination struck in the period 222-205 BC, is also known as a stater.

Stella A U.S. pattern four-dollar gold coin dated 1879 and 1880. Its name is derived from the central star which is the feature of the reverse design. (*Stella* is Latin for star.) It was intended that the denomination would link the U.S. to the Latin Monetary Union formed in Europe in 1865. The object of the Union was to standardise currency systems.

Sterling This word has several meanings. pennies (or their continental equivalent) of good weight and standard were referred to as 'sterlings' during the Middle Ages. For example, Burns, in his standard work *The Coinage of Scotland* (1887), refers to Scottish pennies as 'sterlings'. In *House of Fame* (1315), Chaucer mentions 'nobles* and sterlinges'. It is also a standard of fineness*. Sterling silver contains 925 parts per 1000 of pure silver. This is the lowest legally acceptable standard for silver in the U.K. Sterling also means anything of a fixed authorised value. Consequently, the English pound is referred to as the 'pound sterling' or simply 'sterling'.

Stiver The British struck stivers for use in British Guiana and Ceylon in the early years of the nineteenth century. The word is the English rendering of the Dutch stuiver*.

Stuiver A denomination struck by the Republic of the United Netherlands. Twenty stuivers equalled one gulden*. Stuivers were also issued in certain of the Dutch colonies.

Styca A term used inaccurately in former days to refer to the copper or base silver sceatta* issued in Northumbria from c.670 to c.900. The pieces bear no resemblance to the silver pennies struck elsewhere in England from the latter half of the eighth century.

Sweating An illegal method of obtaining metal from coins which is less obvious than clipping*. A quantity of gold or silver denominations are placed in a box or bag and shaken vigorously for a period. Minute particles of the coins are removed by this process.

Sword dollar *See* Ryal.

Tael *See* Cash.

Talent Derived from the Greek *talenton*: a balance, or pair of scales. No denomination of such a name was ever struck. It was used by the Babylonians, by various Semitic races (including the Jews) and by the Greeks as a weight and unit of value.

Talisman An object endowed with magical power, either to protect the wearer from harm or to attain certain results. Not necessarily a coin.

Tanner, John Sigismund A German coin and medal engraver who arrived in England in 1728. Very shortly afterwards, John Conduit, the Master of the Mint, offered him a post as engraver. He worked under John Croker, the Chief Engraver. Upon the latter's death in 1741, he was appointed to the position. Consequently, he was responsible for much of the coinage of George II. He continued working at the Mint until 1773. He died in 1775. Using Simon's* original punches*, he made dies to strike copies of Cromwell's coinage.

Tealby type   Henry II silver pennies struck from *c.* 1158–80, featuring a facing bust of the King upon the obverse and a cross circle containing a cross pattée with a small cross in each angle on the reverse. The issue, which is crudely struck, is so-named as a large hoard of these pieces were discovered at Tealby, Lincolnshire in 1807. There are six main varieties*.

Territorial gold   A term used to describe currency struck privately from locally mined gold. They were generally issued by pioneers or those (individuals and companies) involved with mining, smelting or bullion etc. The series is also referred to as 'Private' or 'Pioneer' gold. It evolved from the shortage of official coin in the frontier areas.

The most prolific issues were in the U.S.A. from 1830 through to the 1870s. Prior to 1864, federal law, whilst barring a state from coining, allowed individuals to strike coins, providing the pieces did not resemble the official coinage. The first Georgia territorial gold was issued by Templeton Reid of Gainesville in 1830. Norris, Grieg & Norris issued the first of the Californian issues in 1849. In the same year, the Oregon Exchange Co. issued pieces in Oregon, and the Mormons items in Utah. Companies in Colorado only produced pieces in 1860 and 1861.

In South Australia, crude small circular or rectangular ingots stamped with the issuer's name, weight and fineness of the gold, circulated in the early nineteenth century. However, this series is not extensive. *Also see* Slug.

Testone   *See* Shilling.

Testoon   *See* Shilling.

Tetradrachm   A four-drachma piece. Like the drachm*, it was struck in silver.

Thaler   *See* Joachimsthaler. The continental European equivalent of England's silver crown*.

Thistle crown   A gold crown issued by James I of England from 1604 until 1619. It initially circulated at four shillings. In 1611, its value was raised by 10 per cent, thus it circulated at $4s\ 4\frac{3}{4}d$. It did not feature in James's third coinage of 1619–25 or in the issues of subsequent monarchs.

Thistle dollar   Name given to the double merk*.

Thistle noble   A gold coin of James VI of Scotland struck from 1588 to 1590. It circulated at eleven merks*. The obverse features a crowned shield on a ship with a thistle below whilst the reverse type is a thistle plant with crossed sceptres and lions rampant in a panel surrounded by eight thistles.

DICTIONARY OF COINS AND THEIR HISTORY

Three-farthings This odd silver denomination made its first appearance in Edward VI's Irish coinage when it was issued from 1547 to 1550 as part of Henry VII's 'Posthumous' series (coins featuring the bust of Henry). It was not struck by later monarchs for use in Ireland; however, Elizabeth I issued the denomination in most years from 1561–77 for use in England. It is distinguished from the penny by a rose which was placed behind the Queen's head.

Three-halfpence An Elizabethan silver coin current in England for three halfpennies. Issued during most years from 1561 to 1577, it was struck to fulfil the need for a halfpenny denomination. Had such a coin been struck in silver, it would have been too small to be practical. It was not until the following century that a copper coinage became acceptable. To purchase an item costing a halfpenny, a three-halfpence would have been tendered and a penny received in change.

The silver three-halfpence was revived during the reign of William IV for use in certain British colonies. It was also struck for colonial use in certain years of Queen Victoria's reign up to and including 1862.

Threepence This English silver denomination current for three pennies, first appeared in 1551. In 1937 it was struck in nickel brass and was dodecagonal in shape (twelve-sided). It was last struck in 1967.

Thrymsa An early Anglo-Saxon gold coin struck in various parts of England from cAD.630 to 675. Originally in the style of Merovingian tremises* or copied from obsolete Roman coinage, the later pieces are purely Anglo-Saxon in style.

Token A token is not a coin as it is not issued by a government. When small currency was in short supply, private individuals (e.g. shopkeepers), manufacturers and towns issued tokens to enable commercial transactions to take place. Although tokens have the same function as coins, they are not copies of the official currency. Also, tokens were not generally acceptable (e.g. they would circulate in a limited geographical area) and they were not legal tender*.

Mainly struck in base metal and occasionally in silver, the intrinsic worth of the pieces was lower than their face value*, so consequently the issuers profited from placing tokens into circulation. Tokens have circulated in most countries. England had three periods when they were issued: 1648–72, 1787–97, 1811–12.

Token coinage A coinage where the intrinsic worth of the metal content of the coins is less than their face value*. Today, all of the world's currencies are token coinages.

Tone Just as one may refer to a musical instrument having a 'rich tone', so a coin which is deepened and enriched in colour by time may be said to be *toned*. See chapter 2.

143

Tooling A coin is said to be *tooled* when worn areas have been re‑engraved at a later time. This detracts from the piece's value.

Note: Certain cast metals were tooled after being produced. This hand-finishing was part of the process. German late Renaissance pieces made from a wooden mould were usually tooled afterwards.

Touch piece In the past it was frequently held that metal had a magical power. In Roman times, the Emperor Vespasian cured many by 'the touch' or by distributing a coin or medal to sufferers. The English monarchy also 'touched'. It is thought that Edward the Confessor 'touched' for curing the King's 'Evil or scrofula (a form of tuberculosis). However, there is no documentary evidence that he bestowed his healing by way of coins – he did, however, give food to his 'patients'. There is an interesting reference to 'touching' in Shakespeare's *Macbeth* (Act IV Scene 3). Malcolm refers to the King, 'Hanging a golden stamp' round the necks of the sick and saying 'holy prayers'.

Edward I is the first English monarch known to have used coins as *touch pieces*. We read in the Household Accounts (1277–8) that, 'On Monday 4th of April to broth Rudolph Almoner ... for 73 persons sick of the King's Evil 6s.1d.' A quick calculation will reveal that each 'patient' received one penny.

However, it is the gold angel* that had a special place in the healing ceremony. Introduced by Edward IV in 1465, the obverse features St Michael defeating Satan. When used as a touch piece it would have been pierced and suspended from a ribbon. When angels ceased to be struck, special medalets bearing St Michael and the devil were produced specially for the ceremoney.

Tower Mint From c.1300 to 1810, London's mint was located within the Tower of London, hence Tower Mint.

Trachea *See* Scyphate.

Trade dollar Dollars struck for the purpose of trade outside the territory of the issuing authority. The most famous example is the Maria Theresa thaler. The U.S.A. struck trade dollars regularly from 1873 to 1878, and the British intermittently from 1895 through to 1935. *See* Levant dollar.

Treasure trove The U.K. law relating to the discovery of precious metal which has been deliberately concealed. Anyone discovering such treasure has to inform the police immediately. If the original owner cannot be found, it belongs to the Crown. However, in practice the treasure trove items will be offered to the national collections and the finder rewarded with their full market value. Alternatively, should the museums not wish to add the pieces to their collections, the pieces will be returned to the finder. Whether a find is treasure trove is decided by an inquest held by a coroner and a jury.

Tremissis A Roman gold coin first struck in the fourth century AD. It was current for one-third of a solidus*. Also a gold coin of the Byzantine Empire. The Merovingian Kings also issued tremisses, which were based on the Byzantine pieces. *see* Thrymsa and Triens.

Tressure An heraldic term for the framework of a shield. It is used in numismatics to refer to any florid or ornamental border framing the main device on a coin.

Trial of the Pyx The Trial of the Pyx takes place annually at Goldsmith's Hall in the City of London. It is an examination by jury to ascertain that the gold, silver and cupro-nickel coins made by the Royal Mint are of the correct weight, diameter and composition required by law.

The Trial of the Pyx is of very ancient origin; there is reason to believe that an examination of the fineness of the English coinage by assay and comparison with trial plates was practised as early as Saxon, or perhaps even Roman times, and there is record of a public Trial in the year 1248 before the Barons of the Exchequer by a jury of 'Twelve Goldsmiths of the same place'. The earliest known writ ordering a trial is dated 1282.

The Trial, which is presided over by the Queen's Remembrancer, is carried out in accordance with a direction issued by the Treasury. The jury consists of Freemen of the Goldsmiths' Company. For the purposes of the Trial a specified number of coins is required to be placed in the Pyx, or box, and produced by the Officers of the Mint. In the case of cupro-nickel coins, for example, from every 5,000 coins manufactured, one must be put in the Pyx. Officers of the National Weights and Measures Laboratory of the Department of Trade produce the standard trial plates of gold, silver, copper and nickel and the weights for use in the Trial.

The jurymen first check the number and denomination of the coins to see that the proper number has been produced, and then weigh the coins in bulk, as well as selected specimens, to ascertain that the average weight of the coins is within the 'remedy' or tolerance allowed by law. They then carry out assays to test accurately the fineness or composition of the metal by comparison with the standard trial plates, and to ensure that it is within the prescribed tolerance. They also measure the diameters of selected coins to ascertain whether they are within the tolerances allowed.

The verdict of the jury is delivered to the Queen's Remembrancer in May in the presence of the Chancellor of the Exchequer, who is Master of the Mint, or of his Deputy, and is subsequently published in the *London Gazette*. *Note:* The Trial is not open to the public.

Trial piece A piece struck at any point in time during the preparation of a die, so the engraver or designer may have an indication of its appearance.

Tribrach A cross with three limbs. It is found from time to time on Anglo-Saxon coins.

Triens Latin for 'one-third'. Numismatically, it refers to one third of an as*. None were minted after *c.*120 BC. The Roman tremissis* was also referred to as a triens.

Trime Name of the U.S. three cent piece struck in silver from 1851 through to 1873, and in nickel from 1865 through to 1889. In certain years proofs only were struck.

Triobol The name given to the half-drachm* of Ancient Greece.

Triple unite Dimensionally the largest English gold coin ever issued. They were struck at Shrewsbury in 1642 and at Oxford from 1642 until 1644.

Truncation The 'break-off' point of the bust, i.e. the base of the neck.

Trussel *See* Die.

Tsien or Tsen *See* Ch'ien.

Type The general design found on the obverse or reverse, for example, a bust, an eagle or a shield.

Type set or collection A collection comprising an example of each coin in a series. Varieties* of types* and date runs, are not a feature of the type set or collection.

Uncia *See* Aes Grave.

Uncirculated *See* 'Condition' in chapter 2.

Unicorn A Scottish gold coin introduced by James III in 1484. It takes its name from the unicorn featured upon its obverse. The denomination ceased to be struck after 1526.

Uniface A piece with the design on one side only, the other remaining blank.

Unit *See* Unite.

Unite This gold coin takes its name from the reverse legend FACIAM EOS IN GENTEM VNAM – *I will make them one people.* In 1603, James VI of Scotland succeeded to the English throne as James I. The unite was struck the following year. It features the half-length crowned figure of the King holding the orb and sceptre on the obverse. The crowned shield on the reverse bears the English arms and the first and fourth quarter with the Scottish and Irish in the second and the third respectively. The denomination was struck during the reign of Charles I and the

Commonwealth period. Its Scottish equivalent which was also first struck in 1604, was called the *unit*. *Also see* Triple unite.

Variety   A coin showing a *slight* variation of design.

VIGO   In 1702, the British, in conjunction with the Dutch, attacked the French and Spanish fleet off the Portuguese port of Vigo. Vast quantities of gold and silver bullion were captured. English coins struck in 1702 and 1703 from the booty have VIGO below the bust of Queen Anne.

Vis-à-vis   Portraits are said to be *vis-à-vis* when they face each other. The portraits of Spain's Ferdinand and Isabella and England's Philip and Mary are *vis-à-vis*.

V.O.C.   The abbreviation for *Vereenigde Oostindsche Compagnie*, or the United East India Company. The monogram VOC is found on the Company's coinage.

'Voce populi' coinage   This Irish copper coinage is strictly a token issue as it was never legally sanctioned. It was struck in Dublin in 1760, during the reign of George III, to remedy the shortage of small change. The dies were prepared by Roche, the button manufacturer. The obverse features a bust together with the legend VOCE POPULI, meaning 'By the voice of the people'. Nine distinct portraits have been identified. They appear to resemble George II as opposed to George III. However, as they are not the true likeness of either monarch, it has been suggested that the portraits are either of the exiled 'James III' or his son Prince Charles Stuart. The reverse of the pieces bear the figure of Hibernia. The issue consists of halfpennies only. Pattern* farthings exist, but these are very rare.

Voided cross   Before Edward I (1272–1307) introduced fractional pennies into the English currency, pennies would be halved or quartered in order to obtain the equivalent of a halfpenny or farthing. In 1180 a cross consisting of double lines so that it appears that the limbs are hollowed out, was placed on the reverse of pennies. This 'voided cross' as it is called, facilitated the equal dividing of the piece into either two or four, according to whether a halfpenny or farthing was required. *Also see* Cut halfpennies and farthings.

W.C.C.   The abreviation for *Welsh Copper Company*. Certain shillings of George I dated 1723–6 were coined from silver supplied by this company. To signify the provenance of the metal, the letters WCC are found below the King's bust. *Also see* Provenance marks.

Willow tree coinage   The name given to Massachusetts shillings, sixpences and threepences dated 1652, the obverses of which feature a willow tree. Only three examples of the threepence are known. *Also see* Pine tree coinage.

Wire money   Name given to Maundy* coins dated 1792 because the large numerals featured on the reverse of the pieces to indicate their value, are of a thin 'wiry' appearance.

Wood's Irish coinage In 1722, the Duchess of Richmond, George I's mistress, was granted a patent to coin copper halfpennies and farthings for circulation in Ireland. She sold it to William Wood, an English entrepreneur, merchant and ironmonger for £10,000. Wood struck the pieces in bath metal* and made a fortune. However, there was strong opposition to the coinage and he was forced to resign the patent in 1725. The pieces were shipped to Britain's North American colonies, where they circulated alongside the Rosa Americana* coins. Wood's Irish coinage features the bust of George I on the obverse and Hibernia upon the reverse.

Wyon family A most talented family of coin engravers. The first Wyon to leave their native Cologne, arrived in England during the reign of George I. Forrer's *Biographical Dictionary of Medallists* devotes over 100 pages to the Wyons and 75 per cent of these relate to William Wyon and his son, Leonard Charles Wyon. William was Chief Engraver at the Royal Mint, London from 1828 until 1851, and Leonard held the office from 1851 until 1891. Working at a time when the sun never set on the British Empire, their work extends far beyond Britain. William's output included coins for Australia, British Guiana, British West Indies, Ceylon, Gibraltar, Ionian Islands, Malta, Mauritius and Penang.

Xeraphin A silver coin struck for the Portuguese Indian colonies from 1570 to 1841. Gold multiple xeraphins continued to be struck until 1841.

Yen The unit of currency for Japan since 1870.

Yeo, Richard Assistant Engraver at the Royal Mint, London, from 1749 and Chief Engraver from 1775, until his death in 1779.

Zinc Coins are seldem struck in this metal as in its pure state, it is too soft and oxidises quickly. However, it was used by the Germans in both World Wars in occupied Denmark, France, Belgium and the Netherlands.

Zloty The unit of currency for Poland.

Zodiacal coins Although signs of the Zodiac appear on ancient and some modern coins, the most famous zodiacal pieces are a series of twelve mohurs* struck by order of the Mogul Emperor Jahangir of India between 1618 and 1622. Each piece shows a different sign of the zodiac. Similar rupees* were also issued. In recent years, forgeries have appeared on the market.

Appendix 1
Major Coin Auctioneers

Australia

Spink Auctions (Australia) Pty. Ltd.,
A.P.A. Chambers,
53 Martin Place,
SYDNEY, NSW 2000.
Tel: 27 55 71

England

Christie's,
8 King Street,
St. James's,
LONDON SW1Y 6QT
Tel: 01-839-9060

Glendining & Co.,
7 Blenheim Street,
New Bond Street,
LONDON W1Y 9LD
Tel: 01-493-2445

Sotheby's,
34/35 New Bond Street,
LONDON W1A 2AA
Tel: 01-493-8080

France

Emile Bourgey,
7 Rue Drouot,
F-75009 PARIS.
Tel: (1) 770-88-67 and 770-35-18

Germany

Albrecht & Hoffman GmbH,
Rubensstraße 42,
D-5 KÖLN 1.
Tel: 0221/230848

Netherlands

Jacques Schulman B.V.,
Keizersgracht 448,
NL-1000 GN AMSTERDAM.
Tel: (020) 23 33 80 and 24 77 21

Norway

Oslo Mynthandel AS,
Kongens Gate 31,
N-OSLO 1
Tel: (02) 41-60-78/41-60-79

Spain

X & F. Calico,
Plaza de Angel 2,
E-BARCELONA 2.
Tel: (03) 310 27 56/310 55 12/310 55 16

Switzerland

Bank Leu AG.,
Numismatik,
Bahnhofstraße 32,
CH-8001 ZÜRICH.
Tel: (01) 219 24 06

Galerie des Monnaies S.A.,
6 Rue Adhémar-Fabri,
P.O. Box 294,
CH-1211 GENÈVE 1.
Tel: (022) 31 41 35

Munzen und Medaillen AG.,
Malzgasse 25,
Postfach 3647,
CH-4002 BASEL.
Tel: (061) 23 75 44

APPENDIX I

Schweizerische Kreditanstalt (*Credit Suisse*),
Numismatische Abteilung,
Bundesplatz 2.
CH-3001 BERN.
Tel: (031) 66 94 07/66 94 10/66 94 11.

Spink & Son Numismatics Ltd.,
Löwenstraße 65,
CH-8001, ZÜRICH.
Tel: (01) 221 18 85

Frank Sternberg,
Bahnhofstraße 84,
CH-8001 ZÜRICH.
Tel: (01) 211 79 80

United States of America

Bowers & Marena Galleries Inc.,
Box 1224-B,
Wolfeboro, NH 03894.
Tel: (603) 569-5095

Numismatic Fine Arts Inc.,
342 North Rodeo Drive,
P.O. Box 3788
BEVERLY HILLS, CA. 90212.
Tel: (213) 278-1535

Rare Coin Company of America Inc.,
31 North Clark Street,
CHICAGO, IL. 60602.
Tel: 312346-3443

Superior Stamp & Coin Co., Inc.,
9301 Wilshire Boulevard,
BEVERLY HILLS, CA 90210.
Tel: 213 272-0851 or 213 278-9740

Appendix 2
Dealers

The following companies and individuals are all members of the International Association of Professional Numismatists.

Australia

Spink & Son (Australia) Pty. Ltd.,
A.P.A. Chambers,
53, Martin Place,
SYDNEY, N.S.W. 2000,
Branch Office in Melbourne
Tel: 27 55 71

Max Stern & Co.,
234 Flinders Street,
P.O. Box 997.H.,
MELBOURNE 3001,
Tel: 63 67 51

Austria

G. Herinek,
Josefstädterstraße 27,
A-1081 WIEN VIII.
Tel: (0222) 434396

Münzhandlung Lanz,
Hauptplatz 14,
Postfach 677)
A-8011 GRAZ
Tel: (0316) 79345/79346

Belgium

Albert Delonte,
4 Avenue Jette,
Boîte n. 1,
B-1080 BRUXELLES
Tel: 02/426 32 35

Jean Elsen,
Avenue de Tervuren 65,
Bte 1,
B-1040 BRUXELLES
Tel: 02/734 63 56

B. Franceschi & Fils,
10 Rue Croix-de-Fer,
B-1000 BRUXELLES
Tel: 02/217 93 95

Pierre Magain,
Rue de Lennery 17B,
B-6340 WALCOURT
Tel: 071/32 63 94/31 94 96

Jean René de Mey,
6 Rue du Culte,
B-1000 BRUXELLES.
Tel: 02/219 07 24

Denmark

Johan Chr. Holm,
Landemaerket 45,
DK-1119 COPENHAGEN K.
Tel: 01-115418

Mønthandel Gert Hornung,
Vimmelskaftet 47,
DK-1161 COPENHAGEN K.
Tel: 01-150620

Egypt

Pietro Bajocchi,

151

APPENDIX 2

45 Abdel Khalek Sarwat Street,
CAIRO
Tel: 919160

England

A. H. Baldwin & Sons Ltd.,
11 Adelphi Terrace,
LONDON WC2N 6BJ
Tel: 01-930-6879

Lubbocks,
315 Regent Street,
LONDON W1R 7YB
Tel: 01-580-9922/01-323-0676/
01-637-7922

David V. Perry
P.O. Box 92,
New Bond Street,
BATH, Avon.

B. A. Seaby Ltd.,
8, Cavendish Square,
LONDON, W1M 0AJ.
Tel: 01-631-3707

Spink & Son Ltd.,
5-7 King Street,
St. James's
LONDON SW1Y 6QS
Tel: 01-930-7888

V. C. Vecchi & Sons,
Church House,
23 Great Smith Street,
LONDON SW1P 3BL
Tel: 01-222-4459

France

Gérard Barré.,
8 Grande Rue,
F-35400 SAINT-MALO.
Tel: (99) 40-89-58

Jacques Bonvallett,
64 Rue de Richelieu,
F-75002, PARIS.
Tel: (1) 297-47-50

Emile Bourgey,
7 Rue Drouot,
F-75009 PARIS.
Tel: (1) 770-88-67/770-35-18

Claude Burgan,
68 Rue de Richelieu,
F-75002, PARIS
Tel: (1) 296-95-57

Maison Florange,
17 Rue de la Banque,
F-75002, PARIS.
Tel: (1) 260-09-32

Maison Platt, S.A.,
49 Rue de Richelieu,
F-75001 PARIS.
Tel: (1) 296-50-48

Numismatique et Change de Paris,
3 Rue de la Bourse,
F-75002, PARIS.
Tel: (1) 297-53-53

Etienne Page,
16 Rue Milton,
F-75009 PARIS.
Tel: (1) 878-80-75

Claude Silberstein,
39 Rue Vivienne,
F-75002 PARIS.
Tel: (1) 233-19-55

Jean-Paul Vannier,
6 Rue des Remparts,
F-33000 BORDEAUX.
Tel: (56) 81-34-80

Jean Vichon,
77, Rue de Richelieu,
F-75002 PARIS.
Tel: (1) 297-50-00

Alain Weil,
18 Rue Saint-Mare,
F-75002 PARIS.
Tel: (1) 236-27-06

Germany

Egon Beckenbauer,
Maximilianstraße 31,
D-8 MÜNCHEN 22.
Tel: 089/29-52-30

Frankfurter Münzhandlung,
Freiherr-vom-Stein Str. 9.,
D-6 FRANKFURT 1.
Tel: 0611/727420

Galerie Für Numismatik, A. Ringberg
 GmbH.,
Achenbachstraße 3,
D-4000 DÜSSELDORF 1.
Tel: 0211/66-10-77

Giessener Münzhandlung Dieter Gorny,
Maximiliansplatz 16,
8000 MÜNCHEN 2.
Tel: 089/226876

Ludwig Grabow,
Lietzenburger Straße 64,
D-1 BERLIN 15.
Tel: 030/881-83-93

Gerhard Hirsch Münzhandlung,
Promenadeplatz 10/11,
D-8000 MÜNCHEN 2.
Tel: 089/29-21-50

Fritz Rudolf Künker Münzhandlung,
Leger Straße 13,
D-4500 OSNABRÜCK.
Tel: (541) 2192

Kurpfälzische Münzhandlung,
Augusta-Anlage 52,
D-6800 MANNHEIM 1.
Tel: 0621/44-88-99

Numismatik Lanz,
Maximiliansplatz 10,
D-8000 MÜNCHEN 2.
Tel: 089/29-90-70

R. Laugwitz,
Xantener Straße 15a,
D-1000 BERLIN 15.
Tel: 030/88-19-363

Niels Menzel,
Eckerstraße 6A,
000 BERLIN 41.
Tel: 030/855-52-96

Münz Zentrum,
Albrecht & Hoffmann GmbH,
Rubensstraße 42,
D-5 KÖLN 1.
Tel: 0221/23-08-48.

Dr Busso Peus Nachf,
Bornwiesenweg 34,
D-6000 FRANKFURT.
Tel: 0611/59-70-281

Münzhandlung Ritter,
Bastionstraße 10,
Postfach 200 629,
D-4000 DÜSSELDORF 1.
Tel: 0211/32-50-24/5

H. J. Schramm,
Lindenallee 21A,
D-5000 KÖLN 51.
Tel: 0221/37-83-36

Schulten & Co. GmbH,
Klingelpütz 16,
D-5000 KÖLN 1.
Tel: 0221/121777

Tietjen & Co.,
Spitalerstraße 30,
D-2000 HAMBURG 1.
Tel: 330368

Greece

E. Sepheriades,
Havriou 5,
ATHENS (125).
Tel: 021/3233574

Ireland

Coins & Medals (Regd)
10 Cathedral Street,
DUBLIN 1.
Tel: 01/744033

Israel

Shraga Qedar,
P.O. Box 520,
91004 JERUSALEM.
Tel: 02-630-302

Italy

Giulio Bernardi,
Via Roma 3,
P.O. Box 560.
I-34121 TRIESTE.
Tel: (040) 69086/69087

Carlo Crippa,
Via degli Omenoni 2,
I-20121 MILANO.
Tel: (02) 878-680

APPENDIX 2

G de Falco,
Corso Umberto 24,
I-80138 NAPOLI.
Tel: (081) 206-266

Fallani,
Via del Babuino 58a,
I-00187 ROMA.
Tel: (06) 6789-700

Renato Giannantoni,
Via Farini 31,
I-40124 BOLOGNA.
Tel: (051) 23-21-74

Gino e Figlio Marchesi,
Viale Pietramellara 35 (Scala A),
I-40121 BOLOGNA.
Tel: (051) 55-52-64

Walter Muschietti,
Galleria Astra,
P.O. BOX 125,
I-33100 UDINE.
Tel: (0432) 207754

M. Ratto,
Via G. Pisoni 2 (ang. Via Manzoni),
I-20121 MILANO.
Tel: (02) 659-2080 and 659-5353

Rag. Mario Raviola,
Corso Vittorio Emanuele 73,
I-10128 TORINO.
Tel: (011) 546-851

O. & Figlio Rinaldi,
Via Cappello 23 (Casa di Giulietta),
I-37100 VERONA.
Tel: (045) 38-032

P. & P. Santamaria,
Piazza di Spagna 35,
I-00187 ROMA.
Tel: (06) 679-0416

Luigi Simonetti
Piazzadella Stazione 1,
I-50123 FIRENZE.
Tel: (055) 215-831

Dr Giuseppe Toderi,
Sdrucciolo de Pitti, 22r,
I-50125 FIRENZE.
Tel: (055) 604-400 and 295-367

Japan

Taisei Stamps & Coins Co.,
Ohno Bldg,
1-19-8 Kyobashi,
Chuo-Ku,
TOKYO.
Tel: (03) 562-0711

Luxembourg

Lux Numis,
20 Rue J. P. Kommes,
OBERANVEN.
Tel: 48 78 77/34487

Monaco

Victor Gadoury,
38 Boulevard des Moulins,
MONTE CARLO.
Tel: (93) 50-84-49

Netherlands

Jacques Schulman B.V.,
Keizersgracht 448,
NL-1016 GD AMSTERDAM.
Tel: (020) 23 33 80 and 24 77 21

Van der Dussen B. V., A. G.,
Hondstraat 5,
NL-6211 HW MAASTRICHT.
Tel: (043) 15119

Norway

Oslo Mynthandel AS,
Kongens Gate 31,
P.O. Box 355,
N- OSLO 1.
Tel: (02) 41-60-78/41-60-79

Portugal

União De Bancos Portugueses,
Dept. Numismatica,
Rue de Sa da Bandeira 53,
PORTO.
Tel: (029) 20133

South Africa

Kaplan & Son (Pty.) Ltd.,
P.O. Box 132,

GERMISTON 1400,
Transvaal.
Tel: 3377774/3378969

Spain

X. & F. Calico,
Plaza del Angel 2,
E-BARCELONA 2
Tel: (03) 310 27 56/310 55 12/310 55 16

Sweden

B. Ahslström Mynthandel A.B.,
Kungsgatan 28,
P.O. Box 7662,
S-103 94 STOCKHOLM 7.
Tel: (08) 14.02.20-10.10.10

Ulf Nordlinds Mynthandel A.B.,
Nybrogatan 36,
P.O. Box 5132,
S-102 43 STOCKHOLM.
Tel: (08) 62.62.61/61.62.13

Switzerland

Bank Leu A.G.,
Numismatik,
Bahnhofstraße 32,
CH-8001 ZÜRICH.
Tel: (01) 219 24 06

Gallerie des Monnaies S.A.,
6 Rue Adhemar-Fabri,
P.O. Box 294,
CH-1211 GENÈVE 1.
Tel: (022) 31 41 35

A. D. Hess, A.G.,
Haldenstraße 5,
CH-6006 LUZERN.
Tel: (041) 51 43 92 and 51 45 35

Münzen und Medaillen A.G.,
Malzgasse 25,
Postfach 3647,
CH-4002 BASEL.
Tel: (061) 23 75 44

Schweizerischer Bankverein,
Numismatische Abteilung,
Aeschenvorstadt 1,
CH-4002 BASEL.
Tel: (061) 20 27 03

Schweizerische Kreditanstalt (*Credit Suisse*)
Numismatische Abteilung,
Bundesplatz 2,
CH-3001 BERN.
Tel: (031) 66 94 07/66 94 10/66 94 11

Schweizerische Kreditanstalt,
Monetarium,
Bahnhofstraße 89, 4. Stock,
CH-8021 ZÜRICH
Tel: (01) 215 25 26

Spink & Son Numismatics Ltd.,
Löwenstraße 65,
CH-8001 ZÜRICH.
Tel: (01) 221 18 85

Frank Sternberg,
Bahnhofstraße 84,
CH-8001 ZÜRICH
Tel: (01) 211 79 80

Heiner Stuker,
Feilengasse 5,
CH-8034 ZÜRICH.
Tel: (01) 55 06 50

United States of America

Bebee's Inc.,
4514 North 30th Street,
OMAHA. NB. 6811.
Tel: 402-451-4766

Capitol Coin Co. Inc.,
1359 Broadway,
NEW YORK N.Y. 10018
Tel: 212-947-0370

Henry Christensen, Inc.,
P.O. Box 1732,
MADISON, NJ. 07940.
Tel: 201-822-2242

Coin Galleries,
123 West 57 Street,
NEW YORK, N.Y. 10019
Tel: 212-582-5955

Coinhunter,
1616 Walnut Street,
PHILADELPHIA, P.A. 19103.
Tel: 215-735-5517/5518

APPENDIX 2

Scott E. Cordrey,
4655 Cass Street,
Suite 310,
P.O. BOX 9828,
SAN DIEGO, CA. 92109.
Tel: 619-272-9440

William Donner Inc.,
P.O. Box 4409,
Grand Central Station,
NEW YORK, N.Y. 10017.
Tel: 212-840-0650

John J. Ford, Jr.,
P.O. Box 706,
ROCKVILLE CENTRE, N.Y. 11571.
Tel: area 516, RO 4-8988 or RO 4-7871

Frank and Laurese Katen,
13311, New Hampshire Avenue,
P.O. Box 4047,
COLESVILLE,
SILVER SPRING MD 20904.
Tel: 301-384-9444/301-384-9449

James D. King,
41 Highview Terrace,
HAWTHORNE, N.J. 07506.
Tel: 201-427-3912

Kreisberg Corporation,
344 N. Beverley Drive,
BEVERLY HILLS, C.A. 90210.
Tel: 213-271-4281

Joel L. Malter & Co. Inc.,
16661 Ventura Bld,
Suite 518,
P.O. Box 777,
ENCINO, C.A. 91316.
Tel: 213-784-7772 and 784-2181

Manfra, Tordella & Brookes Inc.,
59 West 49th Street,
30 Rockefeller Plaza,
NEW YORK, N.Y. 10112.
Tel: 212-621-9500 or 800 223-5818

Richard Margolis,
P.O. Box 2054,
TEANECK, N.J. 07666.
Tel: 201-224-9581

Lester Merkin,
515 Madison Avenue,
Suite 926.
NEW YORK, N.Y. 10022.
Tel: 212-753-1130.

Numismatic Fine Arts Inc.,
342 North Rodeo Drive,
P.O. Box 3788,
BEVERLY HILLS, C.A. 90212
Tel: 213-278-1535.

Rare Coin Company of America Inc.
31 North Clark Street,
CHICAGO, IL 60602.
Tel: 312-346-3443

John G. Ross,
12 West Madison Street,
CHICAGO, IL 60602.
Tel: 312-236-4088

Stack's
123 West 57 Street,
NEW YORK, N.Y. 10019.
Tel: 212-582-2580

Robert L. & William F. Steinberg,
P.O. Box 1565,
BOCA RATON, FL. 33432.
Tel: 305-781-3455

Karl Stephens Inc.,
P.O. Box 458,
TEMPLE CITY, C.A. 91780.
Tel: 213-44-58-154

Carl Subak & Co.,
22 West Monroe Street,
Room 1506,
CHICAGO, IL. 60603.
Tel: 312-346-0609

Superior Stamp & Coin Co. Inc.,
9301 Wilshire Boulevard,
BEVERLY HILLS, C.A. 90210.
Tel: 213-272-0851 or 213-278-9740

Ted Uhl,
P.O. Box Drawer 1444,
AUBURNDALE, FL 33823.

Appendix 3
Priced Catalogues and Handbooks

Africa

Bowles, P. and G., and Hern, B. *Standard Catalogue of the Coins of South Africa 81/82* (1981).

Keogh, J. *The Coins of Zimbabwe-Rhodesia* (Capetown, 1980).

America

Brunk, G. G. *Countermarked Coins of the United States and Canada* (Rockford, 1985).

Charlton, J. E. *Standard Catalogue of Canadian Coins* (Toronto, 1982).

Dushnick, S. E. *Silver and Nickel Dollars of Canada, 1911 to Date* (Ottawa, 1978).

Grove, F. W. *Coins of Mexico* (Lincoln, Mass. 1981).

Guthrie, H. S. *Mexican Revolutionary Coinage, 1913-17* (n.p. 1976). Valuations sheet.

Haxby, J. A. and Willey, R. C. *Coins of Canada* (Racine, Wisconsin, 1984).

Kessler, *The Fugio Coppers* (Boston, 1976).

Kosoff, A. *United States Pattern, Experimental and Trial Pieces* (Los Angeles, 1982).

Lee, K. W. *California Gold, Dollars, Half Dollars, Quarter Dollars* (Santa Ana, C., 1979).

Yeoman, R. S. A Guide Book of United States Coins (Racine, Wisconsin, 1985).

Ancients: Greek, Roman and Byzantine

Calico, X. and F. *Los Denarios Romanos Anteriores a.J.C.* (Barcelona, 1983).

Seaby Publications

Greek Coins and Their Values by D. R. Sear.
  Volume 1 – Europe.
  Volume 2 – Asia and Africa, including the Hellenistic Monarchies.
Greek Imperial Coins and Their Values – The Local Coinages of the Roman Empire by D. R. Sear.
Roman Coins and Their Values by D. R. Sear (London, 1981).
Roman Silver Coins by H. A. Seaby.
  Volume I – The Republic to Augustus, revised by D. R. Sear and Robert Loosley.
  Volume II – Tiberius to Commodus, revised by Robert Loosley.
  Volume III – Pertinax to Balbinus and Pupienus, revised by D. R. Sear.
  Volume IV – Gordian III to Postumus, revised by D. R. Sear.
  Volume V – Carausius to Romulus Augustus, by C. E. King, with valuations by D. R. Sear.
Byzantine Coins and Their Values by D. R. Sear.

Asian

Bruce, G. R. *The Standard Guide to South*

APPENDIX 3

Asian Coins and Paper Money since 1556 (Iola, Wisconsin, 1981).

Tan, S. *Standard Catalogue of Coins of Malaysia, Singapore, Brunei, Coins and Paper Money 1786-1980* (Kuala Lumpur, 1984).

Australasia

McDonald, G. *How to Buy and Sell Australian Coins and Banknotes* Umina Beach, N.S.W. 1985).

Skinner, D. H. *Renniks's Australian Coin and Banknote Guide* (Malvern, South Australia, 14th Edition).

Britain

De Clermont, A. and Wheeler, J. D. *Standard Catalogue of British Commonwealth Coins, with Valuations* (London, 1986).

Dickinson, M. *Seventeenth Century Tokens of the British Isles and their Values* (London 1986).

Dowle, A. and Finn, P. *The Guide Book to the Coinage of Ireland from 995 A.D. to the present day* (London, 1969).

Finn, P. *Irish Coin Values* (London 1979).

North, J. J. *English Hammered Coinage, Vol. 1. c. A.D. 650–1272* Valuations List (London, 1980).

Schwer, S. E. *Price Guide to 18th Century Tokens* (Woodbridge, 1984).

Seaby's *Standard Catalogue of British Coins Part I – England and the United Kingdom* (London, 22nd Edition).
Part II – Coins of Scotland, Ireland and the Islands (London, 1984).

Seaby's *British Tokens and their Values* (London, 1984).

Continental Europe, Mediterannean Countries and U.S.S.R.

Frey, A. R. *The Dated European Coinage Prior to 1501* (Long Island, 1978).

Belgium

De Mey, J. and Pauwels, G. *De Munten van Belgie 1790–1984* (Brussels, 1984).

France

Gadoury, V. *Monnaies Francaises, 1789–1983* (Monte Carlo, 1983).

Gadoury, V. and Cousinie, G. *Monn Coloniales Francaises* (Monte Carlo, 1979).

Gadoury, V. and Droulers, F. *Les Monnaies Royales Francaises de Louis XIII a Louis XVI, 1610–1792 Cuivre Billon, Argent, Or.* (n.p. 1978).

Germany

Davenport, J. S. *German Church and C Talers 1600–1700* (Galesburg, Illin 1975). 1976 Valuations Sheet.

Davenport, J. S. *German Talers, 1700–1800* (London, 1979). New Revised Price List.

Davenport, J. S. *The Talers of the Austrian Noble Houses* (Galesburg, Illinois, 1972).

Divo, J-P, and Schramm, H-J. *Die Deutschen Goldmunzen von 1800-1872* (Zurich, 1985).

Jaeger, K. *Die Deutschen Munzen seit* (Basel, 1982).

Martin, K. *Die Preussischen Munzpragungen von 1701–1786* (Berl 1976). Valuations in separate pamphlet.

Said, E. *Said Malta Stamp and Coin Catalogue* (Malta, 1980).

Schulmberger, H. *Goldmunzen Katalog* (Munich, 1980).

Italy

Sadow, J., and Sarro, T. *The Coins a Medals of the Vatican* (Long Island City, 1971).

Netherlands

Mevius, J. *De Nederlande Munten van tot Heden* (Amsterdam, 1979).

Portugal

Vaz, J. F. and Salgado, J. *Livro das Moedas de Portugal* (Lisbon, 1984–1985).

Spain

Astan & Cayon. *Las Monedas Espanolas desde los Reyes Visigodos ano 406 a Juan Carlos I* (Madrid, n.d).

Calico, F., Calico, S., and Trigo, J. *Monedas Espanolas desde Juana y Carlos a Isabel II, anos 1504 a 1868* (Barcelona, 1985).

De Guadan, A. M. *La Moneda Iberica, Catalogo de Numismatica Iberica e Ibero-Romana* (Lisbon, n.d.). Separate valuations supplement for 1980.

Scott, M. N. *Guidebook of Spanish Coins (Since the Monetary Reform of 1868 to date)* (Madrid, n.d.).

Switzerland

Divo, J-P., and Tobler, E. *Die Munzen der Schweiz im 18. Jahrundert.* (Zurich, 1974).

Divo, J-P and Tobler, E. *Die Munzen der Schweiz im 19. und 20 Jahrhundert* (Zurich, 1969).

Schon, G. *Kleiner Deutscher Munzkatalog mi Liechtenstein, Osterreich und Schweiz ab 1871* (Munich, 1985).

U.S.S.R.

Brekke, B. F. *The Copper Coinage of Imperial Russia, 1700–1917* (Geneva, 1977).

Harris, R. P. *A Guidebook of Russian Coins, 1725–1982* (Maastricht, 1983).

Scandinavia

Ahlström, B., Almer, Y. and Hemmingsson, B. *Sveriges Mynt 1521–1977. The Coinage of Sweden* (Stockholm, 1980).

Almer, Y. and Jonsson, K. *Severiges Besittningsmynt* (Coins of the Swedish possessions) (Stockholm, 1980).

Almer, Y., Brekke, B. F., and Hemmingsson, B. *Norges Mynter: The Coinage of Norway* (Stockholm, 1976). Valuations supplement (Stockholm, 1978).

Gray, J. F. C., *Tranquebar, a guide to the coins of Danish India circa. 1620 to 1845.* (n.p. 1974).

Sieg, F. *Sieg's Montkatalog 1984, Danmark 1766–1983, Gronland, Faeroerne, Island, Dansk Vestindien 1740–1913* (Skole, 1984)

Sieg, F. *Sieg's Montkatalog 1984, Danmark Argansmonter 1873–1983* (Skole, 1984).

Sieg, F. *Sieg's Montkatalog 1984, Norden, 1766–1808–1983* (Skole, 1984).

Islamic

Mitchener, Dr M. *The World of Islam. Oriental Coins and Their Values.* (London, 1977) (Out of Print).

World

Draskovic, F. & Rubenfeld, S. *Standard Price Guide to World Crowns and Talers, 1484-1968.* (Iola, Wisconsin, 1984).

Friedberg, R. *Gold Coins of the World* (New York, 1976).

Krause, C. L. and Mishler, C. *Standard Catalogue of World Coins* (Iola, Wisconsin, 1985).

Krause, C. L. and Mishler, C. *Standard Catalogue of 20th Century World Coins.* (Iola, Wisconsin, 1981).

Krause, C. L. and Mishler, C. *Standard Catalogue of World Gold Coins. 1601 to date* (Iola, Wisconsin, 1985).

Schon, G. *World Coin Catalogue, Twentieth Century* (Seaby, 1985).

Appendix 4
Coin Magazines

Australia

Australian Coin Review,
G.P.O. Box 994,
SYDNEY 2001
N.S.W.
AUSTRALIA

Continental Europe

Soldi Numismatica,
00182, Roma-Via-Taranto,
ROME
ITALY

Money-Trend
FL 9492,
ESCHEN
Ftm,
LICHTENSTEIN

Münzen Revue,
Blotzheimer Straße 40,
CH-4055 BASEL
SWITZERLAND

Japan

Taisei Monthly,
Ohno Building,
No. 1-19-8 Kyobashi,
Chuo-Ku,
TOKYO 104,
JAPAN

North America

Canadian Coin News
P.O. Box 11000,
BRACEBRIDGE,
Ontario,
POB ICO,
CANADA

Coin World,
P.O. Box 150,
SIDNEY,
Ohio 45367,
U.S.A.

Coinage,
Miller Magazines,
2660 E. Main Street,
VENTURA,
CA 93003,
U.S.A.

World Coin News,
Krause Publications,
IOA,
Wisconsin 54945,
U.S.A.

United Kingdom,

Coin & Medal News,
Crossways Road,
Grayshott,
HINDHEAD,
Surrey GU26 6HF
U.K.

Coin Monthly,
Sovereign House,
BRENTWOOD,
Essex CM14 4SE
U.K.

Appendix 5
Further Reading and Works of Reference

*Denotes out of print

General

Seaby Publications
Jacob, K. *Coins and Christianity* (London, 1985).
Purvey, F. *Collecting Coins* (London, 1985).

Carson, R. A. G. *Coins – Ancient, Medieval and Modern** (London, 1970).
Doty, R. G. *Encyclopedic Dictionary of Numismatics* (London, 1982).
Forrer, L. *Biographical Dictionary of Medallists, BC 500–AD 900* 8 volumes originally published in Spink's *Numismatic Circular* and published in 8 volumes 1904–30 Reprint. (London, n.d.).
Frey, A. R. *Dictionary of Numismatic Names** (n.p. [U.S.A], 1947).
Grierson, P. *Numismatics** (Oxford, 1975).
Hill, Sir George F. *Becker the Counterfeiter** Reprint. (Chicago, 1979).
Hoberman, G. The Art of Coins and Their Photography (London, 1981). This work contains some of the finest colour coin illustrations ever published.
Junge, E. *World Coin Encyclopedia* (London, 1984).
Price, M. J. (Editor) *Coins. An Illustrated Survey 650 BC to the Present Day* (London, 1980).

Quiggin, A. H. *A Survey of Primitive Money – The Beginnings of Currency* (London, 1978).
Sutherland, C. H. V. *Art in Coinage** (London, 1985).

America

Canada

Charlton, J. E. & Willey, R. C. *Standard Grading Guide to Canadian Decimal Coins* (Racine, Wisconsin, 1965).
Courteau, E. G. *The Coins and Tokens of Nova Scotia* (1911, reprinted 1982).
McLachlan, R. W. *A Descriptive Catalogue of Coins, Tokens and Medals, issued in or relating to the Dominion of Canada and Newfoundland* (1886, reprinted 1980).

United States

Ahwash, K. M. *Encyclopedia of United States Seated Liberty Dimes, 1837–1891*.
A.N.A. *Official A.N.A. Grading Standards for United States Coins* (Racine, Wisconsin, 1977).
Bowers, Q. D. *Adventures of United States Coinage as illustrated by the Garrett Collection* (1983).
Breen, W. *California Pioneer Fractional Gold* (1983).
Breen, W. *Encyclopedia of U.S. and Colonial Proof Coins, 1722–1977*.

APPENDIX 5

Breen, W. *Proof Coins Struck at the U.S. Mints* (1981).

Breen, W. *Walter Breen's Encyclopedia of United States Half-Cents 1793–1857* (South Gate, Calif., 1983).

Cohen A. R. & Druley *The Buffalo Nickel* (1979).

Evans, G. G. *History of the U.S. Mint and Coinage* (1978).

Kagin, D. H. *Private Gold Coins and Patterns of the United States* (1981).

Newcomb, H. R. *United States Copper Cents 1816–1857* (1981).

Taxay, D. *The U.S. Mint and Coinage** (New York, 1969).

South America

Adams, E. H. *The Julius Guttag Collection of Latin American Coins* (1929, reprinted, Lawrence, Mass 1974).

Furber, E. A. *The Coinages of Latin America and the Caribbean – An Anthology* (1974).

Grunthal, H. & Sellschopp, E. A. *The Coinage of Peru* (Frankfurt, 1978).

Pradeau, A. F. *Numismatic History of Mexico from Pre-Colombian Epoch to 1823* (1978).

Ancient

Byzantine

Grierson, P. *Byzantine Coins* (London, 1982).

Whitting, P. D. *Byzantine Coins** (London, 1983).

Greek

Anthony, J. *Collecting Greek Coins* (London, 1983).

Head, B. V. *Historia Numorum – A Manual of Greek Numismatics** (1911, reprinted, London, 1977). A new work is planned.

Plant, R. *Greek Coin Types and Their Identification* (London, 1979).

Seltman, C. *Greek Coins – A History of Metallic Currency and Coinage down to the Fall of the Hellenistic Kingdoms* (London, 1977).

Roman

Fox, J. *Roman Coins and How to Collect Them* (London, 1983).

Mattingly, H. *Roman Coins from the Earliest Times to the Fall of the West Empire** (London 1977).

Stevenson, S. W. *A Dictionary of Rom Coins* (1889, reprinted, London 19

Australasia

Andrews, Dr A. *Australasian Tokens a Coins** (Sydney, 1921).

Hyman, C. P. *An Account of the Coins Currency of Australia* (1893, reprinte Colchester, 1973).

Meek, W. F. W. *Currency Tokens of N Zealand** (Dunedin, 1951).

Mira, Dr W. J. D. *Coinage and Curren New South Wales 1788–1829 and An Index of Currency References in The S Gazette 1803–1811* (Sydney, 1981).

Sutherland, A. *Numismatic History of Zealand** (New Plymouth, 1939–19

British

Askew, G. *The Coinage of Roman Brita* (London, 1980).

Brooke, G. C. *English Coins* (London 1966).

*Burns, E. *The Coinage of Scotland*, 3 volumes (Edinburgh, 1887).

Davies, P. J. *British Silver Coins since* (n.p., 1982).

Elias, E. R. D. *The Anglo-Gallic Coins* (London, 1984).

Grueber, H. A. *Handbook of the Coins Great Britain and Ireland in the Britis Museum* with revisions by J. P. C. Kent, I. H. Stewart, P. Finn and W. Linecar (London, 1970).

Hawkins, E. *Silver Coins of England (1841)*. Reprinted London, 1975, from the author's family copy and substantially more complete than ordinary issue.

Keary, C. F., Grueber, H. A. and P R. S. (Editor) *A Catalogue of Englis Coins in the British Museum*, 2 volun (1887, reprinted, London, 1970).

APPENDIX 5

Kent, J. *2000 Years of British Coins and Medals* (London, 1978).
Kenyon, R. L. *Kenyon's Gold Coins of England*, with addendum by Norris D. McWhirter (1884, reprinted, London, 1970).
Mack, Commander R. P. *The Coinage of Ancient Britain* (London, 1975).
Mackay, J. A. *History of Modern English Coinage Henry VII to Elizabeth II* (London, 1984).
Marsh, M. A. *The Gold Sovereign* (Cambridge, 1980).
Marsh, M. A. *The Gold Half Sovereign* (Cambridge, 1982).
Mays J. O'Donald. *The Splendid Shilling – A Social History of an Engaging Coin* (Ringwood, 1982).
McCammon, A. L. T. *Currencies of the Anglo-Norman Isles* (London, 1984).
Nathanson, A. J. *Thomas Simon – His Life and Work, 1618-65* (London, 1975).
North, J. J. *English Hammered Coinage Vol 1. c. AD 1650-1272* (London, 1980).
North, J. J. *English Hammered Coinage Vol. 2. Edward I to Charles II* (London, 1976).
Oman, C. *The Coinage of England* (1931, reprinted London, 1967).
Peck, C. W. *English Copper, Tin and Bronze Coins in the British Museum 1558-1958* (London, 1970).
Robinson, Dr B. *The Royal Maundy* (London, 1977).
Ruding, Rev. R. *Annals of the Coinage of Great Britain*, 3 volumes, (London, 1840).
Seaby, H. A. and Rayner, P. A. *The English Silver Coinage from 1649* (London, 1974).
Seaby, P. *The Story of British Coinage* (London, 1985).
Stewart, I. H. *The Scottish Coinage** (London, 1976).
Sutherland, Dr C. H. V. *English Coinage, 600-1900* (London, 1973).
Sweeny, J. O. *A Numismatic History of The Birmingham Mint* (Birmingham, 1981).

British Commonwealth

For Australia and New Zealand, see under 'Australasia'. For Canada see under 'North America – Canada'.

Chalmers, R. *A History of Currency in the British Colonies* (1893, reprinted, Colchester, 1972).

Pridmore, F. *The Coins of the British Commonwealth of Nations*
Part 1: *European Territories** (London, 1960).
Part 2: *Asian Territories** (London, 1965).
Part 3: *West Indies* (London, 1965).
Part 4: *India*:
    Volume 1: *East India Company Presidency Series c.1642-1835* (London, 1975).
    Volume 2: *Uniform Coinage. East India Company 1835-58. Imperial Period 1858-1947* (London, 1980).

Pridmore, F. *Coins and Coinage of the Straits Settlements and British Malaya 1786 to 1951* (London, 1968).
Vice, D. *The Coinage of British West Africa and St Helena 1684-1958* (Birmingham, 1983).

Continental Europe

General
Sections on Continental European coinages are to be found in R.A.G. Carson's *Coins – Ancient, Medieval and Modern* edited by M. J. Price – see under **General**.
Hazlitt, W. C. *The Coinage of the European Continent** (London, 1893).

APPENDIX 5

Specific

The number of works in the English language is understandably small. Here is a selection:

Broome, M. R. *The 1780 Restrike Talers of Maria Theresia*. Reprinted from the Numismatic Chronicle, 1972, as Doris Stockwell Memorial Paper No. 1.

Chernetsov, A. V. *Types of Russian Coins of the XIV and XV Centuries. An Iconographic Study*.

Davenport, J. S. *German Secular Talers, 1600–1700* (Gelesburg, Illinois, 1976).

Davenport, J. S. *European Crowns, 1484–1600* New Edition in Preparation.

Davenport, J. S. *German Talers 1500–1600* (Galesburg, Illinois, 1979).

De Vos, R. *History of the Monies, Medals and Tokens of Monaco, 1640–1977* (1977).

Divo, J-P. *Modern Greek Coins, 1828–1968* (Zurich, 1969).

Gardiakos, S. *The Coinage of Modern Greece, Crete, the Ionian Islands and Cyprus* (Chicago, n.d.).

Metcalf, D. M. *The Coinage of South Germany in the Thirteenth Century* (London, 1961).

Skaare, K. *Coins and Coinage in Viking-Age Norway* (London, 1976).

Islamic

Broome, M. A Handbook of Islami[c] Coins (London, 1985).

Plant, R. *Arabic Coins and How to R[ead] Them* (London, 1980).

Other Countries

Brown, C. J. *The Coins of India* (19[ ] reprinted Bologna, 1976).

Coole, A. B. *Encyclopedia of Chinese* [ ] 7 volumes (various dates).

Cresswell, O. D. *Chinese Cash* (Lon[don] 1979).

Jacobs, N & Vermule, C. C. *Japan[ese] Coinage* (1972).

Kann, E. *The Currencies of China* (1[ ] reprinted, New York, 1978)

Le May, Ramsden, Guehler & Kneedler, H. *Siamese Coins and T*[okens] (reprint, London 1977).

Robinson, M. & Shaw, L. A. *The C[oins] and Banknotes of Burma* (1984).

Roy, P. C. *The Coinage of Northern* [India] (1980).

Szego, A. *The Coinage of Medieval A*[ ] *1156–1521, A Basic Outline* (West Sayville, 1970).

Takekawa, H. *Gold and Silver Japane[se] Coins from the XVIth to the XIXth Century* (Paris 1981).